Foundations for Pe Training

Foundations for Performance Training: Skills for the Actor-Dancer explores the physical, emotional, theoretical, and practical components of performance training in order to equip readers with the tools needed to successfully advance in their development as artists and entertainers.

Each chapter provides a fresh perspective on subjects that students of acting and dance courses encounter throughout their training as performing artists. Topics include:

- Equity, diversity, and inclusion in performance
- Mind/body conditioning for training, rehearsal, and performance
- Developing stage presence and spatial awareness
- Cultivating motivation and intention in performance
- Expanding repertoire and broadening skillset for performance
- Auditioning for film and stage
- Developing theatrical productions

This book also offers experiential exercises, journal writing prompts, and assignments to engage readers, enrich their learning experience, and deepen their exploration of the material described in each chapter. Readers will grow as performing artists as they analyze the principles of both acting and dance and discover how deeply the two art forms are intertwined.

An excellent resource for students of acting, musical theatre, and dance courses, *Foundations for Performance Training* encourages a strong foundation in creative analysis, technique, artistic expression, and self-care to cultivate excellence in performance.

Cara Harker is a Professor and Associate Chair of the Department of Theatre and Dance at East Tennessee State University (ETSU), where she teaches musical theatre dance, theatre movement, jazz, tap, ballroom, aerial, improvisation, and composition. She also serves as program coordinator for the dance minor program.

Foundations for Performance Training

Skills for the Actor-Dancer

Cara Harker

Routledge
Taylor & Francis Group

NEW YORK AND LONDON

Cover image: © Getty Images

First published 2022
by Routledge
605 Third Avenue, New York, NY 10158

and by Routledge
4 Park Square, Milton Park, Abingdon, Oxon, OX14 4RN

Routledge is an imprint of the Taylor & Francis Group, an informa business

Library of Congress Cataloging-in-Publication Data
Names: Harker, Cara, author.
Title: Foundations for performance training : skills for the actor-dancer / Cara Harker.
Description: New York, NY : Routledge, 2022. | Includes bibliographical references and index.
Identifiers: LCCN 2021050824 (print) | LCCN 2021050825 (ebook) | ISBN 9780367711726 (Hardback) | ISBN 9780367711801 (Paperback) | ISBN 9781003149699 (eBook)
Subjects: LCSH: Movement (Acting)—Study and teaching. | Dance—Study and teaching.
Classification: LCC PN2071.M6 H37 2022 (print) | LCC PN2071.M6 (ebook) | DDC 792.02/8—dc23/eng/20220128
LC record available at https://lccn.loc.gov/2021050824
LC ebook record available at https://lccn.loc.gov/2021050825

ISBN: 978-0-367-71172-6 (hbk)
ISBN: 978-0-367-71180-1 (pbk)
ISBN: 978-1-003-14969-9 (ebk)

DOI: 10.4324/9781003149699

Typeset in Times New Roman
by codeMantra

In loving memory of my parents, who gave me freedom to pursue my dreams and constant support as I navigated my way.

Contents

Acknowledgements

To my husband, David – thank you for listening to me, for believing in me, and for working with me always to create space in our busy lives so that I could complete this project. And thank you for reading and re-reading draft after draft (including these acknowledgements!). To our children, Harry, Isla, and Seymour, I hope to make you proud just as you make me proud every day.

To Jodie Meyn – thank you for reading early drafts, for encouraging me to soldier on with this project, and for being my best friend.

Enormous gratitude to Lucia Accorsi and Stacey Walker at Routledge for their guidance throughout my journey leading to this publication. Your endless patience is truly appreciated! Thank you to copyeditor Tom Bedford, production editor Lauren Ellis, technical editor, reviewers, and everyone on the team at Routledge whose feedback did so much to help me continue and progress.

Thank you to my colleagues in the Department of Theatre and Dance at East Tennessee State University: William Cate, Patrick Cronin, Brad Fugate, Bobby Funk, Delbert Hall, Zachary Olsen, Herb Parker, Melissa Shafer, Beth Skinner, and Jonathon Taylor. Special thanks to my colleague and friend, Jen Kintner – your energy, passion, and dedication to dance always inspires me. And special thanks to my Department Chair Karen Brewster for your advocacy and leadership – your unwavering support is deeply appreciated. Making theatre with these incredible people has taught me so much, and I can't begin to describe all that I have learned from their input and expertise. Thanks to this vibrant group of collaborators for making theatre making so much fun!

Thank you to the College of Arts and Sciences, Presidential Grant-in-Aid, Research Development Committee Grant Program, the Honors College Student-Faculty Collaborative Grant, and the Research Discovery Assistantship Program at East Tennessee State University for their support.

Very many thanks to the incredible photographers who have so generously provided their work for this book – I cherish your artistry! To Larry Smith and the ETSU Photo Lab, thank you for sharing your time and talents with me for the last 14 years. To Jeff Burkle, Josh Levinson, Corrine Louie, Mikki Schaffner, and Suzanne Clemons, thank you so very much for contributing your beautiful images.

Thank you to the many teachers in my life who have done so much to help me grow as an artist and educator. There are just too many people to possibly name, but please know that I am eternally grateful for the gifts you have given me, and this book is my way of honoring your teachings and passing on the lessons you selflessly taught to me. Thank you too to my fellow classmates over the years – you set the example.

This book would not exist without the commitment and dedication of my students, who have been so incredibly brave in their performance training. Students, you were in my mind as I typed every word! A special thank you to Eva Alom who helped me in so many ways and at various stages of this writing odyssey. Thank you to Jessica Vest for your much appreciated assistance early on. Thank you to Hunter Thomas for his writing contribution in Chapter 3; our numerous discussions on performance and performance training really helped me to articulate ideas during the later stages of writing. Additionally, thank you to Savannah Arwood, Hannah Chang, Brock Cooley, Gracie Fulghum, Samuel Floyd, Zoe Hester, Josh Holley, Matthew Huffman, Taylor Hutchison, Chelsea Kinser, Danielle Mumpower, Drake Parrott, Camielle Reed, and Everett Tarlton for our Fringe Festival experiences. They continue to inform and inspire. And thank you to student models, Tatum Gross, Sarah Hill, Tyler Mitchell, and Mason Van Horn!

To my sisters, Colleen, Katie, and Kelly and my amazing nieces and nephews, thank you for cheering me on and loving me. To my family in England, thank you for your constant love and support. And thank you to my extended family and friends – you sat in the audience, spread the word about my productions, and let me crash at your place while I was in town – thank you for that and so much more.

As I write the closing words to these acknowledgements, we are in the midst of a global pandemic. During these uncertain times, I am in awe of the power of performance now more than ever. People are turning to the arts to soothe their weary minds, to connect with their family and friends, to cope, to laugh, to celebrate heroism, to honor humanity. I am ever grateful to be part of the performing arts community and rejoice in the work performers do to enhance quality of life.

When we return to our everyday lives, we and the world will emerge changed; perhaps in some ways that will go unnoticed. But we will remember the solace that performance provided. And we will appreciate the performances sure to come that reflect our current circumstances, helping us to process the shock and confusion we are feeling right now. Performers will portray the brave individuals on the frontlines, the essential workers, the survivors, and those less fortunate, telling their stories of triumph and tragedy. Performers and performances will continue to honor humanity and always endeavor to do the world justice.

Introduction

Foundations for Performance Training: *Skills for the Actor-Dancer* aims to equip acting and dance students with the tools needed to produce compelling performances. One book cannot possibly do it all, but it *can* provide a fresh perspective on a number of topics in acting and dance to assist performers in exploring their range of artistic expression safely and effectively. This book is meant to serve as a companion to live instruction in introductory acting and dance courses in order to ignite thoughtful discussions, unlock creativity, and encourage deeper analysis in the study of performance for the stage and screen.

Intended Audience

In 2007, I was hired by East Tennessee State University (ETSU) to create a Dance minor for the primary purpose of accompanying the Theatre major. Today, the program is home to Dance minors with a wide variety of majors (Nursing, Exercise Science, Anthropology, Literature and Language, and more), in addition to Theatre majors looking to gain more experience in Dance and Theatre Movement. Our Dance minor program offers opportunities for anyone interested in dance – from beginning enthusiast to advanced dancer. This makes for a broad range of students entering the dance studio; some have years of dance training, while others have little to none. Although beginner courses are offered and students with previous dance training can forgo those courses, there still remains a mix of newer and more advanced dancers in the same class. This creates an exciting and dynamic learning environment.

I have noticed a trend amongst these students. There are "theatre" kids and there are "dance" kids. In other words, there are students who spent their youth acting in school plays and taking part in forensics and debate competitions. Then there are students who spent their youth in a dance studio preparing for dance competitions and recitals. Perhaps because there simply aren't enough hours in the day, most theatre kids didn't have the

DOI: 10.4324/9781003149699-1

opportunity to receive much dance training and vice versa. Of course, this is a generalization, but I often observe how much students grow as performing artists once they analyze the principles of both acting and dance and discover how deeply the two art forms can intertwine.

Bridging the theatre and dance worlds by preparing actors to become better movers and dancers, I also regularly encounter wonderfully trained dancers whose dancing would benefit from acting technique. I really love working with actors; I appreciate their ability to be emotionally vulnerable and available. I think this vulnerability and openness is something that dancers can learn from. Equally, I love working with dancers; their discipline and dedication sets the bar for everyone in the room. And it has been fascinating to see these students interact.

I always take a deep breath on the first day of class and hope that students are willing and able to release any competitive urges and work together as an ensemble. I have been incredibly fortunate to watch, time and again, actors and dancers share with each other what they know – they give freely their time, training, and talent. This juxtaposition has also created some interesting collaborations, sparking creative ideas and problem solving. This book is intended for the performer-in-training ready to embrace both acting *and* dance disciplines, like so many of my amazing students have done at ETSU, in order to develop as a performer with range and versatility.

To Performers-in-Training

Actors, intimidated by the choreography in a theatrical production, might be tempted to say, "I can't dance," or "I am *so* uncoordinated." Dancers, upon hearing the emotional state that they need to embody while performing a dance, may respond with shy giggles and looks of trepidation. But what every performing artist realizes at some point is that theatre and dance are inextricably linked, and it is enormously beneficial for a performer to fill any gaps in training as an actor and training as a dancer and to acknowledge and embrace the interconnectedness of the two disciplines. Simply put, an actor must dance, and a dancer must act.

For example, nearly every *play* the ETSU Department of Theatre and Dance has produced during my 14 years as the resident dance and movement specialist has required dancing. From an Irish jig in *Playhouse Creatures* to a waltz in *The Cherry Orchard* to regency dances in *Sense & Sensibility* to ballet in *You Can't Take It With You* to a tribal dance in *Middletown* (to name but a few), dance is consistently an essential component of the production season. Then of course, there are *musicals*, that beloved genre of theatre which almost always requires dancing. And there's not one genre of dance you need to know as a musical theatre performer; the variances in dance styles depending on the musical or even within the same musical is enormous.

Likewise, a performer whose primary emphasis is dance also requires the ability to analyze, develop, and portray characters in order to achieve an authentic performance. Consider the ballets *Giselle* and *Swan Lake* as examples. These classic tales tell stories that keep audiences returning to the ballet year after year. Ironically, it is sometimes the ballet dancer that has the most trouble embodying character because advance technical training in acting may be missing from their education. The intense focus on developing ballet technique can obscure the importance of storytelling, leaving the young dancer ill equipped when attempting character work. A dancer-in-training may hear criticisms that they "lack depth" when performing or that they appear disconnected from the intention of the movement because they are thinking about the steps and not embodying their character's emotional state. We should be quick to sympathize with that dancer-in-training because it's a struggle to emote without the tools to produce a fully realized, multidimensional character.

Now you might have thumbed through this book and thought, "I'm a modern dancer and have no real interest in developing acting technique," or "I'm an actor with two left feet, and there's just no chance I'll ever dance." But think of what you might discover if you try broadening the scope of your interests. Here are three points to consider:

1. **Performing art forms are interrelated.**

    If we take even a fleeting glance at the development of a dance form, we see the impact of other dance genres. For example, much of modern dance developed in response to the rules of ballet. Many modern dance pioneers sought to free themselves from the strictures of ballet, and those training in modern dance today cannot fully appreciate the intricacies of the articulated torso seen in Katherine Dunham's work nor master the contract and release method in Martha Graham's technique without also exploring that which those pioneers were countering. Aerial dance developed from modern dance and circus arts; noting the crowd pleasing "ta-da" moments in circus and the avant-garde components of modern dance leads to a better understanding of the aerial dance aesthetic. Jazz dance developed in part from the partnered social dance, swing. Musical theatre dance is an amalgam of jazz, tap, ballet, and ballroom. Tap dance developed from African dances, British clogging, and Irish step dance. The list goes on and on. So, you can see how an important means of improving your performance in one dance genre involves greater appreciation for what influenced the dance form you are passionate about learning.

    Like dance, acting techniques are influenced by and developed in response to other acting techniques, and it's important to explore these methods to learn what works best for you. The level of exploration

I am describing reminds me of a scene from the film *The Jane Austen Book Club*. One character in the film mentions that while reading *Northanger Abbey* by Jane Austen, he also read *The Mysteries of Udolpho* by Ann Randcliffe, which was the book the characters in *Northanger Abbey* were reading. What a great way to gain insight into Jane Austen's influences and learn more about the interests of her characters. You should strive to research with the same level of curiosity and enthusiasm. It may feel like a digression at times, but believe me, everything influences everything (case in point: who knew that turning on Netflix to watch a light romantic comedy would lead to a mention in this book?!). Ultimately, you will pick and choose from the many acting techniques you study and before you know it, you will have weaved them into your very own personal approach to acting. It takes time to develop a system that works for you, but it is well worth the effort. It will not only take you to a place of truthfulness in your performance, it will also aid you in leaving that character behind and returning to your own "self" without damage to your psyche.

So, it is clear that dancers benefit from learning about other dance genres, and actors benefit from learning about different acting methods. Actors also grow as performers by learning dance, just as dancers grow as performers by learning acting. Actors aren't just talking heads, nor are dancers empty vessels. Great acting involves the use of the entire body. Great dancing involves dramatic expression.

Sometimes an actor lacks a strong connection to their body. It's almost as though they are afraid to explore all that their body can do; like something inside them says that if they really let go and move their body freely, they will look foolish. Perhaps this fear, a feeling that they are "not allowed" to move and dance with abandon, stems from a lack of formal movement and dance training. This fear can be overcome in part by learning more about the moving body through dance. Actors owe it to themselves to study dance; it will make them a better performer all around.

I would also argue that all dancing requires acting. Dancers exude character. Think of the chemistry between contemporary ballet dancers performing a pas de deux, the impassioned and fiery energy of tango dancers, and the cool and crisp aura of the Irish step dancer. These performers must present a persona in order to capture the essence of a dance; their movement requires emotive expression and intention. When a dance is completely abstract, the performers still embody a version of themselves as they interpret the dance; even the most seemingly non-representational dances require stage presence.

Character development is important in performance, and we'll explore the concept more specifically through a variety of acting and dance techniques. The lessons learned are translatable to any genre of theatre and dance and are sure to enliven your performances. We will dive into the critical components that make up a performer in every chapter that follows.

2. **Versatility is paramount for anyone serious about advancing as a performer.**

If your goal is to have performing as your primary source of income, you'd do well to diversify. Some may fear this approach will lead them to becoming a jack of all trades, master of none. And while it is without question that you will need to develop an area or two of specialization, you must be willing to step outside of your comfort zone and try something new as often as possible. This will challenge your mind and body in wonderful ways, and it will better inform how to perform in your area(s) of specialization. It's a win-win if you ask me.

Versatility includes being flexible. I'd like to emphasize this point by sharing a memory of my time as an undergraduate student. I'd hear fellow actors-in-training say they *only* had an interest in performing in film. Given the incredibly competitive nature of the industry, why would they want to be so picky that they cut their options to only auditioning for, let's say, dramatic films, when they really should be attending all sorts of auditions in an attempt to get a foot in the door? They should hold onto their ideals and principles and goals, but the hard, cold reality is that being selective with creative projects happens more readily once a performer is *established* in their career (and even then, it's no guarantee).

I've seen something similar with dance students. Some dancers hold out and only audition for the very top tier dance companies, and then find themselves completely disillusioned when they do not make the cut. Many companies, take *Cirque du Soleil* for example, almost never cast a dancer the first time they audition for them ("Getting into Cirque du Soleil", 2012). These students then need reminding that they can't always start at the top, and it's quite often the case that they'll need to work their way up through smaller companies.

Versatility will also set you apart in a truly cut-throat industry, where more and more companies want you to be able to do it all. So, while it's essential to find an area that ignites your passion, I ask the classical ballerina to be curious enough to take an acting workshop with the same level of enthusiasm as their ballet class; the possibility of that acting workshop improving their work as a performer is great. And the possibility of an actor being more employable if they have some training in dance should make them skip into their next dance class with gusto.

As for the performer still in the early stages of training, I believe the best way to reach your goals is by sampling every theatre and dance class you possibly can. Whatever your long-term aspirations, variety will lead to both versatility and growth in the area you wish to pursue more seriously. It wasn't until I began aerial dance that I finally increased my core strength enough to execute floor work in modern dance with a sense of ease and flow (who would have thought that taking dance to the air would improve dancing on the floor?!). It wasn't until I took Dunham technique that I truly appreciated the body isolations of Fosse's jazz style. It wasn't until I took Pilates that I felt the alignment required of ballet. And it wasn't until I took period acting styles classes that I understood the power of gesture in theatre and dance performance. Finding the key that unlocks your inner performer takes time, so best to keep things interesting with a bit of variety.

3. **Your area of specialization as a performer should be discovered and will evolve.**

I think there is a sense among students that they need to have their future all figured out by the time they enter college. That simply isn't true. The question you've heard your whole life – "What do you want to be when you grow up?" – seems innocent enough, but it can create a feeling of dread and a sense that you cannot change your mind once you've made a decision. Your career path *can* evolve, and you do not need to feel locked into the idea you had of yourself when you were little.

The US Bureau of Labor Statistics reports that baby boomers held an average of 12 jobs in their working life (US Bureau of Labor Statistics, 2019). When you think about the average person changing jobs that much, it takes some of the pressure off feeling you need to find your dream job straight out of college. Someone I know was a pre-K teacher and now she owns a bakery; that's not just a change in job, that's a change in career. I taught ballroom dance at a studio in Chicago, taught high school English, theatre, and speech for a couple of years in my hometown in Northern Kentucky, and now I teach theatre and dance at East Tennessee State University. Yes, I've pretty much always taught, but the subjects and the kinds of people I interact with have changed dramatically. My point is that your journey may not be what you initially imagined, but it might turn out to be even more fulfilling. Acting and dance classes are great places to explore; you never know what opportunities might arise from performance training.

I began as an earnest ballet dancer. Thoughts of the undulating hip action in jazz dance were terrifying to me, but my mother encouraged me to give it a go. Next thing I knew, ballet was something I continued just so I could stay in shape for jazz. Tap dance became an important tool for cardiovascular exercise and increased my rhythmic awareness in jazz. With all that time and training in ballet, tap, and jazz, I was primed and ready for musical theatre. After dancing for the first time in a musical, *West Side Story*, the acting bug bit hard. I fell in love with every aspect of theatre and began seriously pursuing acting.

I then found a strong desire to explore ballroom dance. Ballroom dance tied together my work in acting and my work in dance; both feature partners that collaborate for a common goal. I next explored working with a partner in aerial dance. With the aerial apparatus as my companion, I found a way to express myself on the vertical plane. Through it all, acting and dance was the common thread. So, I began writing, directing, and performing plays that incorporated both acting and dancing equally. When words no longer adequately express what the heart and mind hope to communicate and the dancing body represents that desire most effectively, fusing dance and spoken word to create the fullest storytelling experience felt like the natural next step in my journey. I have found inspiration in composing what I like to call *dance-icals*, plays where the performers break into dance.

My development highlights a series of opportunities that unfolded and led to this moment. I hope it illustrates how important it is to remain open to discovering and pursuing your passions, and that your dreams can and likely will evolve over time. My journey has now filled me with the desire to share the lessons I've learned over the years in the hopes that you, dear performer, will go forth in *your* creative journey bigger, bolder, and braver than you once thought imaginable. To the actor, it's time to dance; and to the dancer, it's time to act!

To Instructors

This book is also intended to be used as a teaching tool for instructors who are laying the groundwork for professional training in acting and dance. As instructors of performance, we are immersed in the discipline, and it is easy to forget how green we were in the early days of our own training and how unseasoned our new crop of students may be. I remember introducing myself as an undergraduate student in my first theatre class. The professor asked us to say something about ourselves, and of course when it was my turn, I mentioned that I dance. The professor said in response, "Oh, are you the next Isadora Duncan?" At 18 years old, and after 15 years of dance training, I had no idea who he was talking about. I stammered some kind of response in an attempt to hide the shame of my ignorance and admitted that I didn't know of Isadora Duncan. The professor was clearly surprised but kindly recommended that I read Duncan's autobiography and explained that she is known as the mother of modern dance. Fast forward 12 years to my very first day teaching an undergraduate dance class, when I mentioned performers Liza Minnelli and Judy Garland, thinking they were household names. I immediately saw the students' faces looking back at me, revealing that they did not know who the mother-daughter Hollywood icons were, and I was reminded of my Duncan faux pas years earlier. While it is certainly to be expected that students will enter our studios with varying degrees of knowledge and experience, it is important to remember our role as instructors in creating common ground, a baseline level of understanding, and a learning environment that empowers students to undauntedly ask questions.

Outstanding early performance education and opportunities in theatre and dance can be scarce depending upon many factors, such as the culture and region in which a student was raised, their socioeconomic status (the expense of theatre and dance classes may prevent many from youth training experiences), and/or the value their family places on the performing arts (some of my undergraduate students pursue performance training despite a lack of support from their family and community, and in rare cases even hide their decision to major in a performing art). Theatre students may enter undergraduate programs with a few theatrical performance experiences from middle and/or high school, but most have likely had more access to athletics programs or even visual art and music education. Theatre and dance as courses of study are not typically standard curricula in elementary, middle, and high school. With limited experience, many young students dreaming of a career in performance enter undergraduate programs naïve to the challenges they are about to encounter.

And although many students enter theatre and dance undergraduate programs with years of training, their previous experiences can range from having learned strong technical skills by well-trained instructors to needing to break from "bad" habits that will not benefit them in the long run (often young performers are taught to mimic without being encouraged to analyze, explore, and develop their unique qualities in theatrical expression). When a new student enters a theatre and dance undergraduate program, their first semester can feel like a baptism by fire. Without much practical experience dealing with the actual demands of a professional training program in performance, these students may long to return to their home dance studio or local community theatre.

By introducing professional training methods in acting and dance, instructors can create a universal lexicon and cultivate a safe space for all who wish to grow as performers-in-training. While some of the material in this book may feel beginner to some students, as instructors, you well know that a strong foundation is absolutely essential for growth. Additionally, students can be afraid to admit when they don't know something (I'm sure the same can be said about a lot of us instructors). Leaning into the work, no matter how familiar it may seem to some, should be the goal of both instructor and student. There is something new to be learned *every* time we work the fundamentals; this book is arranged for those generalist instructors who teach both actors and dancers together to give them common tools for excellence in performance.

Performers benefit from instruction in acting technique and dance technique. My writing journey started out as an exploration of that premise. But the more I thought about it, the more I realized that there's so much more that goes into becoming an effective performer. In my career as a college professor I talk to students about health, fitness, well-being, and responsibility almost as much as I talk about technique. There's little to be gained in giving students instruction in the finer points of acting and dance technique if they lack the life skills to incorporate these alongside everything else that it takes to become a performing artist. And so, the focus in the last part of the book shifts to discuss stress management and emphasizes self-care to prepare students for longevity in this highly demanding discipline.

A Look at the Book

Each chapter explores topics that performers-in-training will encounter throughout their development. Topics include:

- Equity, diversity, and inclusion (Chapter 1);
- Mind/body conditioning (Chapter 2);
- Stage presence and spatial awareness (Chapter 3);
- Motivation and intention (Chapter 4);
- Expanding repertoire and broadening skillset (Chapter 5);
- Auditioning (Chapter 6);
- Developing productions (Chapter 7);
- Life as a performing artist-in-training (Chapter 8).

Chapter Summaries

Chapter 1

In addition to defining acting and dance and discussing the impact performance has on society, Chapter 1, "Embracing Performance & Communing with the Audience: Acting, Dance, & the Performer's Role in Society," explores equity, diversity, and inclusion (EDI) in acting and dance. Discussing EDI increases awareness of the inequities in representation on stage and screen of black, indigenous, and people of color (BIPOC), lesbian, gay, bisexual, transgender, queer, or questioning, plus related communities (LGBTQ+), and people with disabilities. It is the performer's responsibility to represent all characters authentically and to champion stories by and about BIPOC, LGBTQ+, and people with disabilities. Additionally, thinking critically about cultural appropriation, sexual objectification, heteronormativity, and other issues of representation in acting and dance empowers performers to speak up and out when confronted with prejudice and discrimination.

Chapter 2

By exploring theatre movement pre warm-up, warm-up, and cool down exercises, Chapter 2, "Performer Preparation: Practices from Theatre Movement for Mind/Body Connection & Free Expression," encourages a physical and mental environment that is receptive to the possibilities that present themselves during performance training. Meditation-based visualizations (for achieving a sense of calm in audition, rehearsal, and performance situations), cross-training and conditioning exercises (cardio and resistance based movement sequences for stimulating blood flow to the muscles and increasing strength and endurance for the physical demands of performance), stretch and flexibility sequences (to expand range of expressiveness), exercises for developing diaphragm, voice command, and breath control (to safely enunciate and project), and practices in readying for and recovering from performance (for a long-lasting career) are described in this chapter.

Chapter 3

The ballet fundamentals discussed in Chapter 3, "Performance Building Blocks: Key Concepts in Ballet Dance Technique for Presence & Authenticity on Stage & Screen," provide the foundation for many dance forms and period acting styles and builds *stage presence*, the all-important ability to command the attention of an audience. The exercises in this chapter encourage performers to move with purpose and comportment, and through ritual-like repetition of these exercises, performers can achieve a strong connection to the space in which they are performing while also radiating energy far beyond their own physical body. Helping performers to achieve a state of being that draws in their audience, ballet fundamentals speak to every actor-dancer's needs.

Chapter 4

Once an artist commits to performing at fullest expression with body and mind, inspired work abounds. The problem is that finding and maintaining deep physical and emotional connections in performance is exhausting work. Exposing vulnerability is an ongoing challenge. Unearthing intention can be elusive. Cultivating specific associations can feel impossible. These challenges and more are faced in Chapter 4, "Discovering Character Motivation & Intention through Acting Technique & Physical Theatre," by exploring the acting technique of Stanislavski and others. Additionally, physical theatre exercises are introduced to encourage a sense of playfulness in performance training (lest the training become too cumbersome). These comedy exercises motivate performers to fully commit to their character's given circumstances and encourage them to act on their impulses. Inspiring performers to quiet doubt and insecurity and to free themselves from the stronghold of their ego through physical theatre, they learn to trust their instincts and embrace the joy in performance.

Chapter 5

The discussions, assignments, and exercises in Chapter 5, "Jazz Dance & Musical Theatre: The Quintessential Combination of Acting & Dance in Performance," explore the range of performance through the lens of jazz dance and musical theatre. Musical theatre can be anything from opera to hip-hop to farce, and so it serves as a great example to relate all that performance is and can be. Additionally, the development of jazz dance as a genre captures the spirit of collaboration that is essential to performance and exemplifies the amalgam of many performing art forms fusing to create something new and innovative. The expectation is not that performers become a master in every area of performance, but if they are truly committed to exploring their range, they will seek to expand their skillset and become better informed about who they are as a performer; the study of jazz dance and musical theatre can help to do just that.

Chapter 6

For many, acting and dance auditions feel like an insurmountable obstacle preventing them from becoming a successful performer. Chapter 6, "Auditioning: From a Necessary Evil to a Time to Shine," discusses ways to overcome the mental barriers that keep performers from nailing their audition. The practicalities of live auditions, self-tape auditions, and the variances in auditioning for film vs. theatre are also detailed. There's much to learn about auditioning and performing for the stage and auditioning and performing for film, and a performer may find that they move back and forth between the two mediums quite often. While the technical differences between live theatre and film are described, the shared goals of achieving truth in performance and in moving the audience are also acknowledged, concluding that through practice and experience, mastery of both disciplines can be achieved.

Chapter 7

In Chapter 7, "Performer & Theatre Maker: Creating New Works & Breathing New Life into Established Works," performers are encouraged to appreciate the many contributions their colleagues in production and design make and to understand that as a performer, they are a member of a *team*, working toward a common goal. The path of the performer is ever-winding, and as performers, they have a backstage pass to observe how a production comes to life; their keen observations may lead to other opportunities in future productions. The triumphs and pitfalls performers face when creating both new and established works are also explored, and it is determined that acknowledging what inspires the creation of a performance frees the performer to build upon previous interpretations. Performers are also given the opportunity to get on their feet, and with step-by-step instructions guiding them, they can create an original theatrical work in minutes!

Chapter 8

Media and society's influence in shaping perceptions of beauty is keenly felt by aspiring performers. Navigating an ever-evolving relationship with the mind/body is an essential component of growth as a performer. No matter the size or shape, a well-conditioned body is the best vehicle for performance; understanding the body's needs and the constant maintenance it requires are important elements to explore. Self-care and self-love encourage singular performances to shine through to audiences, who in turn see themselves through the performer's unique interpretation. In Chapter 8, "On Health & Wellness: Self-Care for Longevity as a Performer," the goal of committing to support the body, the instrument that creates performances, is the aim. Health and wellness are achieved when the body is nurtured and appreciated throughout the many phases of life as a performer.

How to Use This Book

In addition to a number of topics discussed in the text, the book offers experiential exercises, journal writing prompts, and assignments[1] to engage performers, to enrich the learning experience, and to deepen their exploration of the material described in each chapter.

Assignments & Exercises

Assignments and exercises geared toward cultivating skill and growth as a performer can be found throughout the book. These exercises should be practiced with a sense of child-like curiosity. Performers, allow yourself to engage in the process of exploratory work without fear of judgment as to whether your efforts are "good" or "bad." If you can say, "Given my circumstances on this particular day, I gave it my all," then you can rest easy in the knowledge that the work is happening, and progress will be seen and felt soon.

Journal Writing Prompts

There are many writing prompts throughout the book. As a performer-in-training, everything is a learning opportunity, so performers, take a moment to reflect, and then write down your responses to the prompts in a journal. This will be a tremendous aid in gauging your progress. Journaling in and of itself is a discipline, so think of it as another part of your training; make the time for journaling, just as you make the time for rehearsal.

It can be really meaningful to write in a journal that is special and holds value and significance – a journal that is made by *you* and that is just for *you*. So before starting Chapter 1, create a *one-of-a-kind* journal by following the guidelines below:

Create a Journal with Vision

Close your eyes and see yourself giving the most wonderful performance you can imagine. Dare to dream! Now, gather images that give life and meaning to this vision. These images could include pictures of yourself, other actors, dancers, choreographers, directors, and innovators that you admire. You might also find images that typify the emotions you want to feel and convey, or a visual that expresses the energy you wish to radiate when you are performing with fullest expression. For example, I hope to embody a sense of ease when I perform, and images of nature conjure the feeling of peace I endeavor to personify. As a choreographer and director, I am constantly drawn toward the bright and bold works of visual artists, Mark Rothko, Piet Mondrian, Wassily Kandinsky, Jeff Koons, and other greats. I also find some quotes and memes very inspiring; they become mantras I repeat to myself whenever I need a boost. "She believed she could, so she did," has motivated me for quite some time, and I am energized every time I read it.

It is important to have an actual tangible representation of your dreams, so once you have gathered lots of images that spark and stimulate, print those images or cut them out of magazines. I know it is easiest and quickest to simply arrange images digitally, but it's fun to get creative by using your hands, returning to the kinds of crafting activities you so enjoyed as children. When you're truly pleased with and proud of your collage, paste the images onto the front and back cover of a notebook with lots of blank pages inside for you to write in soon.

Your intentions are set, and you have now made a bedazzling journal to accompany this book! Your journal is the physical representation of your dreams. Let it inspire you. If it does not make you feel happy and motivated, reconsider the images. For example, if the image of the perfectly chiseled dancer you chose makes you feel inadequate, then maybe that's not the right image. You might need a few tries to get to the place where every time you look at your journal, you smile. Your first journal writing prompt is coming soon.

Figure I.1 Savannah Hutson created this inspiring vision journal when she took the course Dance Repertory for Performance, Spring 2020

Make the Pledge to Commit

The work of a performing artist requires a sincere commitment to building a strong foundation in creative analysis, safe practices, proper technique, self-care, and artistic expression. Performers, if you can agree to those commitments, you're ready to start a new chapter in this deeply rewarding journey. *Now is always the perfect time.* Let's explore!

I, _____, commit to building a strong foundation in creative analysis, safe practices, proper technique, self-care, and artistic expression. I am ready to communicate my needs and boundaries, to be receptive to the emotions that present themselves during my performance training, and to challenge myself to grow as a performing artist.

_____

(signature)

_____

(date)

Note

1 Instructors, the Appendix provides a sample timeline for journal writing prompts, assignments, and exercises to assist with scheduling a semester-long course (14 weeks). There, you will also find recommendations for journal writing prompts, assignments, and exercises to explore in-class and journal writing prompts, assignments, and exercises for students to explore independently.

Bibliography

"Getting into Cirque Du Soleil." (2012). [Video]. *YouTube*, uploaded by Crime Beat TV, 11 April. www.youtube.com/watch?v=BLouxprAHtQ&t=7s

US Bureau of Labor Statistics. (2019). *Number of Jobs, Labor Market Experience, andEarnings Growth: Results from a National Longitudinal Study*. 22 August. www.bls.gov/news.release/pdf/nlsoy.pdf

1 Embracing Performance & Communing with the Audience

Acting, Dance, & the Performer's Role in Society

Performers and performances are *everywhere*. We are inundated with performances on our televisions, phones, and computers, at our local movie theatres, community theatres, Broadway and regional theatres, concert venues, town hall meetings, wedding receptions, religious events, birthday parties, festivals, parades, at our local pub or gathering hall *(and more!)*. I doubt a day goes by without us taking in a performance. A heartfelt and compelling performance resonates with its audience and provides a unique perspective on society's shared experiences, conjuring memories, emotions, and awareness.

As an audience member and lover of theatre and dance, you've likely watched many moving performances and can think of lots of performers whose work you admire. You have observed what worked well in a performance (and just as importantly, what *didn't* work well). Identifying the ways in which a performer offered a distinct portrayal of universal truths stimulates your development as a performer. Just as a writer improves by reading and interpreting literature, you cultivate your own artistry when you see and critically analyze a performance. Let's take some time now to reflect on a memorable experience you had as an audience member with your first journal writing prompt.

Journal Writing Prompt: Theatre that Made a Lasting Impression

Recall a live or film performance you watched that elicited a strong emotional response from you. Describe the theatrical moment as best you can recall, analyzing how and why it resonated with you emotionally. Next, describe the circumstances and any other memories surrounding the viewing experience (for example: did you see the performance alone or with family or friends?). Try to use all five senses when describing the memory. What emotions do you feel now in

---

DOI: 10.4324/9781003149699-2

conjuring the memory? What lessons can you unearth from that memory and incorporate into your development as a performer? Note how previous experiences as an audience member influenced your decision to pursue performance training. Then take time to share your journal entry with a peer. It will be a wonderful affirmation of how profoundly moving a performance can be. *A great performance can change someone's life!*

Acting & Dance Defined

To establish how the human experience is communicated through performance, let's discuss acting and dance in broad terms. This analysis will help to increase your awareness of the impact that performance can have on a society, clarify your objectives as a performer, and lead to a greater understanding of some of the challenges surrounding the depiction of complex characters. In addition, we will explore the entertainment industry's standards in representing humanity. It is worthwhile for the performer to identify the ways in which the entertainment industry does justice in representing the human experience and how it falls short. Finally, we will seek a deeper appreciation for the importance of portraying characters with truthfulness, a desire to support your fellow performers, and a drive to advance representation and equality in the performing arts. Let's start our adventure with a closer look at the art and craft of acting.

What Is Acting?

Acting concerns the *art* of performance by an actor. Through the mediums of theatre and film, the actor holds a mirror to society. The audience sees something of themselves in the characters on stage and screen. The actor, embodying the vices and virtues of their character, becomes a catalyst for the audience members' catharsis as they look for meaning in life through the drama unfolding on the stage or screen. Acting at its best not only represents the human experience, it provides a service to society by entertaining and enlightening. This is partly why society values actors and not just acting as a discipline.

Great actors seem to possess the ability to draw the audience into their performance. They have a chameleon-like capability to transform from one character to the next. Actors who are consistently successful in creating powerful performances understand their obligation to play their characters with clarity, insight, and authenticity. They are also acutely aware that it takes an enormous amount of collaboration by many artists to create a lasting impact on the audience. They realize that a great theatrical experience transcends the actual performer. In other words, a performance isn't about the actor; it's about creating an experience for the *audience*. For an actor to become a vehicle for the audience's journey, they must move beyond their own personal insecurities and focus on the action taking place in the world of the theatrical work. Quieting uncertainty and concentrating on action are paramount to a successful performance.

Influences on Acting

In life (as well as in art), we play a variety of roles. On any given day, I play the part of wife, mother, teacher, sister, daughter, colleague, friend, and so on. We all wear a lot of different hats! The accumulation of real-life experiences combined with a strong awareness of the different "masks" people wear depending on their environment influence the actor's choices when developing the characters they play. Arguably the greatest actor of our time, Meryl Streep said, "Acting is not about being someone different. It's finding the similarity in what is apparently different, then finding myself in there" (quoted in Hernández, 2016). An actor finds common ground with their character and embraces their character's differences as their own. When a character is difficult for an actor to relate to on a personal level (e.g., the character is a serial killer), they use imagination to connect with the character's motivation. Even the most eccentric characters can resonate with the actor on some level, and it is the work of the actor to discover those connections. Once strong associations are made, the actor produces a distinct perspective and fills the character with dimension.

Through candid and sincere acting, an actor helps to reveal the story's universal themes, which often exposes the flaws of society. When the actor portrays a character, they do not critique or reveal their opinion of the character, which would risk alienating the audience. Rather, the actor plays the character as truthfully as possible without judgment, empowering the audience to make their own decisions about the character's motivation and actions. Because the actor infuses their character with depth, the audience recognizes something of themselves and their society in the story and learns from the character's choices. When the audience relates to and learns from the character, the actor has done their job well!

Acting is demanding work, and self-doubt can creep up at any time; that is why developing a practical approach to performance is essential. We'll discuss ways to release yourself from insecurities that hinder your expressiveness in performance in the chapters that follow. While we will spend much time discussing the *performer's* journey, the ultimate goal of moving the *audience* will never be far from our thoughts. Let's dig deeper now into audience experiences as theatregoers and highlight the value that representing humanity has for society.

Representation in Acting

We have established that the audience learns and grows when they see themselves reflected on stage and screen. At the 2020 Golden Globe Awards, comedian Kate McKinnon described the effect that fellow comedian, Ellen DeGeneres, had on her life. In her speech, McKinnon said:

> In 1997, when Ellen's sitcom was at the height of its popularity, I was in my mother's basement lifting weights in front of the mirror and thinking, "Am I gay?" And I was, and I still am. But that's a very scary thing to suddenly know about yourself... And the only thing that made it less scary was seeing Ellen on TV. She risked her entire life, and her entire career, in order to tell the truth, and she suffered greatly for it. Of course, attitudes change, but only because brave people like Ellen jump into the fire to make them change. And if I hadn't seen her on TV, I would have thought I could never be on TV. They don't let LGBTQ+ people on TV. And more than that, I would have gone on thinking that I was an alien, and that I maybe didn't even have a right to be here. So, thank you Ellen, for giving me a shot at a good life.
>
> (McKinnon, 2020)

McKinnon beautifully sums up the influence that performance can have. When we see ourselves represented in theatre and film, we feel validated. However, theatre and film lack diversity. This problem is multifaceted and systemic. The vast majority of decisions made about plays, television series, and film are in the hands of the white male demographic, and the works produced overwhelmingly represent that demographic. This restricts opportunities for minorities and homogenizes theatre. Consider the following:

While colorblind casting has garnered more opportunities for people of color to perform, it does not resolve the need for more representation of minority experiences. In his 2018 Golden Globe Award acceptance speech for Best Actor in a Television Drama, Sterling K. Brown said,

> Throughout the majority of my career, I've benefited from colorblind casting which means, you know what, hey, let's throw a brother in this role, right? It's always really cool. Dan Fogelman, you wrote a role for a black man. That could only be played by a black man. And so, what I appreciate so much about this thing is that I've been seen for who I am and being appreciated for who I am. And it makes it that much more difficult to dismiss me, or dismiss anybody who looks like me.
>
> (Brown, 2018)

The distinction Brown makes is an important one. The "canon" of theatre still overwhelmingly typifies the white male experience, and opportunities for people of color to portray characters representative of their experiences is lacking.

A black classmate once spoke to me about the lack of acting opportunities she had. In our first semester of the program where we were studying, she was cast as Tituba in *The Crucible*, the single black character in the play. I remember her wondering aloud over lunch as to whether her only acting opportunities during our training would be slaves mired in stereotypes. Opportunities to portray varied black characters were in short supply for her and the only two other black actors in our course.

Traditionally, theatre has largely condoned and perpetuated the stereotyping of minorities or erased their presence altogether. We do not have to look far to notice white actors portraying characters that were initially written as another race (known as *whitewashing*), because it still occurs with regularity. However, as society enters a "woke" period, many audiences and critics are expressing doubts and at times outrage at such rewrites and casting choices. Scarlett Johansson faced backlash from her decision to play a character originally written as Japanese in 2017's *Ghost in the Shell*. Emma Stone faced scrutiny for her portrayal of a character described as a quarter Chinese in the film *Aloha*. On his website, Cameron Crowe, the writer/director of *Aloha*, offered a "heart-felt apology to all who felt this was an odd or misguided casting choice," and said, "I have learned something very inspiring. So many of us are hungry for stories with more racial diversity, more truth in representation, and I am anxious to help tell those stories in the future" (Crowe, 2015).

Nancy Wang Yuen states, "Whitewashing is a descendant of the original yellowface. It's all part of the same story in American media: the underrepresentation, misrepresentation, and usurping of significance of Asians by white actors" (quoted in Fang, 2018). And while the days of *blackface, brownface, yellowface*, and *redface* are no longer the norm on stage, it hasn't disappeared entirely. Angelina Jolie in *A Mighty Heart,* Jonathon Pryce in *Miss Saigon*, and Billy Crystal portraying Sammie Davis, Jr. while hosting the 2012 Oscars are just a few recent examples of brownface, yellowface, and blackface respectively, despite clear protestations that this is offensive and racist.

A white student once told me they were required to darken their skin through spray tanning to play an American Indian at an outdoor drama. They were conflicted but felt powerless to communicate their concern. Nineteen years old at the time and performing in their first professional production, they felt they had "no right to complain." Flawed and insensitive casting, performances, costume, and make-up designs raise concerns that the arts and entertainment industry must address. Committing to better represent people of color and resolving the vital need for more diversity among those in power are crucial steps to take to address white privilege.

The LGBTQ+ community has also encountered stereotyping and lack of representation in theatre and film, and awareness of this discrimination is increasing. With thoughtful and innovative work featuring performers in the LGBTQ+ community about LGBTQ+ experiences, many audience members are seeing themselves represented with authenticity and sincerity for the very first time. That said, there continues to be confusion and inconsistencies in the industry with regard to LGBTQ+ performers and performances.

Opportunities for transgender performers are limited; the sentiment that every effort should be made to cast transgender characters with transgender performers is being expressed by many. Ryan Murphy, a pioneer in creating work with multidimensional LGBTQ+ characters (*Glee*, *Pose*, *The Politician*, and more) said, "I think the day and age where you put a wig on a straight white man and say he's trans is over" (quoted in Real, 2020). When Scarlett Johansson was cast as a transgender man in the movie *Rub & Tug* in 2018, LGBTQ+ activists spoke out against the casting choice, leading Johansson to withdraw from the role. In an interview with *As If* magazine, Johansson said, "I should be allowed to play any person, or any tree, or any animal because that is my job" (quoted in Salle, 2019), but it appears that her decision not to play a trans man suggests an acknowledgement of the inequities in performance opportunities for trans performers.

As society's awareness of sexual orientation and gender identity increases so too have representations of LGBTQ+ characters in theatre and film. But confusion as to whether these roles should be reserved solely for LGBTQ+ actors has also arisen. Darren Criss, a heterosexual actor known for award winning portrayals of gay men, recently decided that he would no longer play gay characters. Criss said, "There are certain [queer] roles that I'll see that are just wonderful. But I want to make sure I won't be another straight boy taking a gay man's role" (quoted in Carlin, 2018). In an article for *The Guardian*, journalist Ryan Gilbey addressed Criss' decision, saying,

> This dilemma could only have arisen in a climate where there is a plenitude of LGBT roles and an eagerness to see diversity on screen. But it would be unwise to outlaw the function played in performances by interpretation, imagination and skill; it's called acting for a reason, after all. What's more, it seems unworkable to say that when an LGBT part is up for grabs, only the out should have a shout. It could operate as a kind of outing-by-default: closeted actors would now need to enter the audition room via the Something to Declare channel. And it would surely encourage category fraud. How long before Hollywood was hit by a sexuality equivalent of the Rachel Dolezal race scandal, with straight actors passing themselves off as gay? I foresee paparazzi snaps of avowed lesbians caught in clinches with men, prompting previously unimaginable tabloid headlines: "Oscar-Winning Actor in 'Not Gay' Shock!
> (Gilbey, 2019)

Gilbey makes some valid points; LGBTQ+ performers may not be out to the public and have no obligation to declare anything to anyone. Perhaps authentic performances by the actor best suited for the role regardless of sexual orientation or gender identity should be the primary aim. What is important to emphasize is that the upsurge in characters with varying sexual orientations and gender identities should be played by actors who also run the gamut in terms of sexual orientation and gender identity. Heterosexual actors have plenty of opportunities to play LGBTQ+ characters, but we must ask whether the same opportunities are afforded to those of other sexual orientations and gender identities.

Women have been underrepresented, underpaid, mistreated, and abused in the entertainment industry. Complex female characters have been in short supply. So too has the production of work by female playwrights and screenwriters. The rampant sexism and sexual harassment plaguing the theatre and film industry reached a breaking point when a *New York Times* article published on October 5, 2017 revealed numerous accusations of sexual harassment and assault from entertainment industry mogul Harvey Weinstein (Kantor & Twohey, 2017). Reactions on social media ignited the #MeToo movement, which was created by activist Tarana Burke in 2006 to provide a platform for sexual assault victims to share their experiences (Burke, 2018). On January 1, 2018, a group of females in the entertainment industry launched the #TimesUp campaign, which has raised over 20 million dollars and recruited nearly 800 volunteer lawyers to help victims of sexual violence seek legal justice (Time's Up, 2020). This movement has shaken the entertainment industry in unparalleled ways. Over the course of three years, awareness has grown, but the journey toward lasting change is a long one.

As female voices continue to gain empowerment, unfettered portrayals of the female experience grow. Shonda Rhimes, television writer, showrunner, producer, and director (*Grey's Anatomy, How to Get Away with Murder, Scandal, Bridgerton*, and more) says:

> There are stories to be told that are still untold and characters to be portrayed that haven't been portrayed correctly. So, there's work to be done.
>
> (quoted in Wittmer, 2017)

> … the goal is that everyone should get to turn on the TV and see someone who looks like them and loves like them. And just as important, everyone should turn on the TV and see someone who doesn't look like them and love them. Because perhaps then they will learn from them.
>
> (Rhimes, 2016, p.235)

Pioneering voices like Rhimes are creating opportunities for women and, importantly, women of color, and audiences are applauding their efforts.

Opportunities for performers with disabilities are limited and their experiences are most often portrayed by non-disabled performers. While examples of casting performers with disabilities exist in mainstream works, such as R.J. Mitte in the television series *Breaking Bad*, Zack Gottsagen in the film *The Peanut Butter Falcon*, Mickey Rowe in the Indiana Repertory Theatre and Syracuse Stage co-production of *The Curious Incident of the Dog in the Night-Time*, these productions seem to be an exception rather than the rule. When asked about his experiences as the first autistic actor to play the role of autistic character Christopher Boone, Rowe said,

> It's really hard for people with any disability to get a large role in a professional theatre, but for the first time in my life I'm getting to star in a major professional production… I've had to be an actor my whole life to pass as neurotypical. Being an actor comes naturally to me. I use scripting in my daily life.

(quoted in Fierberg, 2017)

In 2015, Ali Stroker became the first person to appear on Broadway in a wheelchair with *Spring Awakening* and again made history in 2019 when she became the first performer in a wheelchair to win a Tony Award for her performance in *Oklahoma!*. While her win marks an enormous achievement, it was also noted by many that there was no access ramp to the stage during the live awards ceremony. Elyse Wanshel in her article "Ali Stroker's Tony win was monumental… and a huge slap in the face" (2019) discussed how producers of the show timed the presentation of Stroker's award category so that it was presented shortly after her performance of "I Cain't Say No" from *Oklahoma!*. Stroker was therefore waiting in the wings when her category was announced and thus able to enter the stage without issue when she won.

But later, when the production won the award for Best Revival, Stroker was not on stage to accept the award with the other cast and crew members of *Oklahoma!* because there was no access ramp from the audience to the stage. This sparked disappointment from viewers and highlighted the lack of accommodation that society makes for those with disabilities. In her acceptance speech, Stroker said, "This award is for every kid who is watching tonight who has a disability, who has a limitation or a challenge, who has been waiting to see themselves represented in this arena – you are" (CBSNewYork, 2019). Stroker's words emphasize the importance of representation, and the circumstances surrounding the awarding of her Tony illustrate the extent of the obstacles people with disabilities face each day, the breadth and scope of what needs to be done in order to achieve equal rights, and the enduring insensitivity of many who are not living with a disability.

A recent *Washington Post* article by Travis M. Andrews described actors with disabilities as the "last civil rights movement" in Hollywood. Andrews says,

> The disabled are, arguably, the largest minority in America, its 56.7 million members constituting nearly 20 percent of the population, according to the 2010 Census. But a study from the University of Southern California Annenberg Inclusion Initiative that combed through 900 popular movies from 2007 to 2016 found that only 2.7 percent of characters with speaking roles were portrayed as disabled.
>
> (Andrews, 2019)

There are two issues: characters with disabilities aren't portrayed enough, and actors with disabilities aren't given enough opportunities to perform. There is major upheaval concerning representation in the theatre industry happening on many fronts in real time, and the hope is that the disabled community can finally get the recognition and opportunities they deserve.

Theatre, television, and film have failed to properly value equity, diversity, and inclusivity in a lot of ways, and there are complicated issues to resolve. But there are encouraging signs that many are committed to rectifying them. It's important for performers to be allies that are aware, sensitive, and open-minded. Additionally, performers must carefully research the qualities and characteristics of their characters, especially those qualities of which they have little knowledge or experience, in order to portray every role with depth and understanding. So often performers have relied on playing stereotypes, and while it may not always be consciously understood by the audience, they do sense something amiss in the performance. By respecting the work that goes into developing your character, you are respecting your audience. They will thank you for it.

What Is Dance?

If I were to look up the word *dance* in a number of dictionaries, they would all say something about how dance involves rhythmic movements of the body and music. Of course, there's a lot more to dance than that. Dance is a *primal mode of expression*. World-renowned dancer, choreographer, and educator Jacques d'Amboise perhaps described humanity's innate connection to dance best when he said our first dance encounter occurs in the womb, as we move in time to the sounds of our mother's heartbeat. He says, "Dance is your pulse, your heartbeat, your breathing. It's the rhythm of your life. It's the expression in time and movement, in happiness, joy, sadness, and envy" (Dunlop, 1989). Our bodies are made for dancing, and to dance is to explore through movement.

Dance has healing properties. Studies have shown dance improves mood, boosts confidence, and may even lessen the risk of dementia (Hampton, 2019). It may not be the answer to every health crisis, but there's no doubt that it can benefit the body and mind in many ways. Some of the physical effects of dance are obvious – it improves balance, flexibility, and cardio-vascular health – but some of the effects, while undeniable, are harder to measure. Dance can be a cathartic release of emotion and energy, establishing a sense of mental well-being. Dance/movement therapy (DMT)[1] is a form of treatment that addresses physical and emotional trauma, and more and more people are exploring DMT as a means of therapy. Dance is also used by many as a method of expressing religious faith and communicating with their higher power. For others, dance connects them with their sense of spirituality. Dance provides that much-needed opportunity to explore our feelings and experiences in a healthy and positive way.

Dancing exists virtually everywhere in and among society. It is a representation of the communities from which it originated. When you see how

Figure 1.1 Ethan Bird choreographed and performed an aerial dance in homage to his beloved dog, Willow. In the picture, you see Willow's favorite blanket on the ground below.

Photo credit: ETSU Photographic Services

Figure 1.2 At the end of the dance, Ethan is holding the blanket in his arms. Chan-
neling the pain and loss he was feeling to create a deeply cathartic artistic
experience is a beautiful example of the healing properties of dance and
the power of performance.
Photo credit: ETSU Photographic Services

a society likes to dance, you get to know a bit about their struggles, accomplishments, and hopes for the future. The dance mirrors the values and aesthetics of the people who dance it (Jonas, 2003). Dance is also *universal*; it is
present in just about every known human society, and even in some animal
groups! Take, for instance, the *Waggle dance* performed by honeybees. Using
a figure-eight movement pattern to communicate the whereabouts of a good
flowerbed, bees use dance to direct each other on where to find nectar, pol-
len, water, and other colony members. How cool is that?!

Dance has played a hand in developing interpersonal romantic relationships in many societies. I always think back to the era of Jane Austen, with
beautiful regency dances in ballrooms – how during that time, to partner
dance with someone was really the only way to get the opportunity to touch
the person you were courting to see whether or not they gave you butterflies.
If you were a good match on the dance floor, maybe you would be a good
match in marriage. Although not of the Austen era (I'm not *that* old!), I do
clearly remember going to dances in middle school when the idea of slow
dancing with the person I liked was the most exciting thing in the world.
Standing ridiculously far apart from one another and swaying back and
forth to the popular slow song of the day was a memorable highlight.

Dance can also be utilized to display power and authority to society. Tribal dances reenacting battle and martial art forms incorporating music exhibit strength and celebrate courage. For example, the Changing of the Guard at Buckingham Palace is an impressive public display with precise and synchronous movement to demonstrate their country's prowess. The India Pakistan Border Ceremony and the US Army Drill team are other great examples of awe-inspiring movement sequences that showcase an unparalleled level of organization and focus. Perhaps the greatest use of dance as a representation of authority can be traced to King Louis XIV of France. He used dance to assert supremacy over his kingdom and is known as *ballet's first star*. These are just a few instances demonstrating how dance can be used to communicate unity, power, and security.

Assignment: Dance as a Display of Power

Dance plays many roles; it is a cultural phenomenon, physical discipline, social activity, and performing art. Its presence is found in a variety of environments – from the Broadway stage to the backyard barbecue to the bird of paradise courtship dance and beyond. Dance represents a myriad of possibilities and often reveals the desires, hardships, and strength of a people (Jonas, 2003). Much like the Ballets of Louis XIV, US presidential inaugural dances are carefully orchestrated as a political platform to reinforce the narrative the president wishes to portray to the public. Inaugural dances display the president's persona and the authority figure they intend to be. While the nation watches, dance is the spectacle that helps to define the president. Watch footage from President Obama's 2009 and President Trump's 2017 inaugural dances (available on YouTube; links located in Bibliography). At first glance, the dances appear trivial, but rest assured that every detail was meticulously crafted. This is just one example of dance as a ritualistic and theatrical event used to express vision and power.

Once you've watched the dances, take note of any similarities and differences between them. Here are some prompts to facilitate your writing: Does the way they move "say" anything to you? (Body language experts weighed in, even speculating on the kind of relationship they have with their spouse based on the way they danced). Note the choice of lighting, singer(s), song choice, costume (e.g., black tie vs. white tie; color and style of dresses, etc.), and audience placement. Did the dance reinforce what you already think/feel about the president and/or his platform? Reflect on how dance can be a powerful form of communication, a tool for emphasizing important themes, and a vehicle for emotive expression.

Influences on Dance

When you think of dance as an art form, you might imagine a theatrical performance you saw on stage or screen – perhaps you are reminded of a school fieldtrip to see *The Nutcracker* or you think of your favorite movie musical that you've seen a hundred times. Dance as a performing art influences and is influenced by other art forms. I would be remiss if I ignored the obvious connection between music and dance. Although the absence of music in dance can occur, it is most often the case that music accompanies dance; the bond between the two art forms is steadfast. We also see dance associated with visual art. Edgar Degas and Henri de Toulouse-Lautrec are just two examples of visual artists who were inspired by the dancing body. Ballet dancers were the subject of over half of Degas' work and the can-can dancers of the Moulin Rouge proved famous muses for Toulouse-Lautrec. Visual art has also stimulated the work of dancers. Modern dance innovator Martha Graham drew inspiration from the shapes in Picasso's work, just as Isadora Duncan, known as the "mother of modern dance," looked to classical Greek art to stimulate her choreography. Dance's presence in art, from music and visual art, to theatre and film, to literature and storytelling, distinguishes it as a powerful source for creativity and expression. So, the next time you watch a theatrical dance, take note of the many artistic components culminating to create the dance – lighting, costumes, music, choreography, and more!

When we analyze dance and our relationship to dance, we recognize the sheer magnitude of the art form. Every dance that made its way to a stage has roots in the community from which it originated. And every time we dance, we pay homage to those who danced before us while nurturing our own need for self-expression. The body moving with energy through space and time is perhaps the most fundamental interpretation of the human experience – *art imitating life*. Dance is a living, thriving event and can never be replicated exactly – you must celebrate the dance in the moment. So, dance is a whole lot more than rhythmic movement of the body to music. But it's hard to fit all that in a definition!

Representation in Dance

Like theatre, dance as a performing art is not beyond reproach and has a very long way to go on the journey of embracing equity, diversity, and inclusivity to better represent society. Misty Copeland, American Ballet Theater's first black principal ballerina, has been tireless in her efforts to spread diversity awareness throughout the dance community and beyond. In an interview with Felice León, Copeland remembers being asked to wear skin lightening make-up to perform in "white ballets," called such because the ballets feature ghosts, and the performers are to appear "otherworldly" under white stage lighting. "It's been something that's just been a part of the history of ballet," Copeland said. "It's not an unusual thing to be asked to make your skin lighter… Ballet insiders have said, 'We don't want your skin to look human – we don't want your skin to look shiny.'" Copeland describes her response, "Ok cool, let me just put on *my* color powder and be a brown ghost" (quoted in León, 2019).

Chloé Lopes Gomes, Staatsballett's (Berlin) first Black ballet dance company member, says:

> My experience with racism is not isolated. I have heard over and over the damaging stereotypes that Black dancers aren't flexible enough or don't have the right feet, or that Asian dancers aren't expressive enough. Ballet is still designed for White dancers, down to the shoes and makeup we wear. Nude-colored ballet shoes for Black dancers didn't exist until 2018. I've always had to buy my own makeup, because the foundation provided has always been for White skin. I've always been the only dancer to do my own hair, because the hair stylists don't know how to work with my texture. At Staatsballett, there are 95 dancers and I was the only one spending my own money on makeup. It makes you feel excluded. And it reminds me that when you are Black, you have to work harder to have the same opportunities.
>
> (Gomes, 2021)

The stories shared by Misty Copeland and Chloé Lopes Gomes are just two examples to highlight racial insensitivity in theatrical dance; countless other examples of racism in dance could fill this book. Dance as a performing art needs more voices and opportunities for BIPOC to invite progress.

The professional dance industry also has its share of misogyny, sexual harassment, and abuse. Co-founder and artistic director of New York City Ballet (NYCB) for over 35 years, George Balanchine is a dance icon whose neo-classical choreographic style transformed ballet dance; it is not an overstatement to say that his work is internationally beloved. Balanchine is so highly revered that his infatuations with dancers and treatment of company members Suzanne Farrell and Paul Mejia in the late 1960s are often overlooked or ignored. Balanchine essentially forced his muse, Farrell (she originated roles in 24 of his ballets) into exile when she did not return his romantic affection. With Balanchine's refusal to continue casting her new husband Mejia, Farrell and Mejia had little choice but to leave the company, performing abroad for five years before returning. More recently, serious allegations of physical and sexual abuse were made against Peter Martins, who followed Balanchine as artistic director of NYCB, as well as against male dancers Chase Finlay, Amar Ramasar, and Zachary Catazaro, and donor, Jared Longhitano for photographing dancers in the nude or filming them during sexual acts without their knowledge. The #MeToo movement is shining a light on these and other allegations of abuse in the professional dance community.

Throughout history, partnered social dancing has most often fostered the heteronormative social constructs of male/female courtship and marriage. It has represented the falsehood that male/female romantic relationships were the "only acceptable" romantic relationships, leaving members of the LGBTQ+ community alienated. While the origins of some dances now categorized as ballroom dance did not initially emphasize a male/female partnership, this expectation became emphatic once the dance entered mainstream consciousness. If ballroom dance as a genre reflects the ideals of courtship, as it does for so many, then it is falling short on accurately representing the full range of human romantic relationships. It reflects archaic ideologies and is exclusionary of the LBGTQ+ community, which needs representation on stages, films, *and* dance floors. Dance forms should be honored and preserved, but they can also grow and progress. The ballroom dance "ideal" of a heterosexual couple dancing in "perfect harmony" is evolving to embrace the reality that sexual orientation and gender identity come in many forms. Same-sex ballroom dance is one example of how ballroom dance is taking a step in a new direction, at long last moving toward a broader and more accurate representation of humanity. Ballroom dance events with a *gender-blind* mode of performance can foster inclusivity.

As a feminist who loves ballroom dance, I have also struggled with the feeling that the ballroom dance terms, *lead* and *follow*, promote the archetypal character of the male as a powerful leader with the female as a passive follower; those words conjured images of traditional gender roles. But as I learned more about the complexities and technical components of ballroom dancing, I began to feel that *leading* and *following* are misnomers that do not accurately describe what is occurring. Before the leader can take a step, the partners must embody a dance frame that is jointly created; through forward poise, they share some of one another's weight, which helps them to non-verbally communicate with each other. The leader expresses the desire to take a step by sending energy forward through the dance frame. Another way to think of this moment is to imagine the leader asking for permission to move. It is only when the follower steps back that the leader is enabled to step forward. Although it happens in an instant, they are in constant communication with one another as though the leader is saying, "May I step?" with the follower responding, "Yes, you may," repeatedly. After all, if the follower does not take the step, the dance ends. They are in an abiding mutual surrender to one another; it is a true partnership.

When teaching ballroom dance, my students learn both the lead and follow steps. I also encourage them to explore all hand and arm positions as opposed to enforcing what has been traditionally identified as *masculine* and *feminine* qualities in the movement. Students can investigate all elements of the dance and come to their own conclusions about how their body wants to move, acknowledging and embracing any fluidity in movement quality.

These measures can make a positive impact on students by placing the emphasis on self-expression.

While recognizing the origins of a dance style, we can also modernize the dance form, reflecting the progress we make as a society. However, cultural appropriation in dance occurs with regularity, and dance makers who borrow extensive material from outside their own culture must answer difficult questions about how and whether using dances from other cultures benefits the communities from which they originated. If dance makers are using elements of foreign dances to portray a vague, exotic feel, stripping the dance of its essence and value, then they are misappropriating the dance. Appreciation is welcome; appropriation is not.

Theatrical dance in particular can feel very alienating to those who do not fit the mold in terms of body type; dance as an art form has a history of eschewing performing artists whose shape and size vary from established dance norms. There's a sense that most performers and especially dancers should possess a particular standard of physical appearance, and the pressure performers face to conform to this standard can be brutal. Many performers who do not embody these expectations are seen as outcasts and if they do achieve success, many view it as an anomaly.

Dancers with disabilities have very limited opportunities to explore dance as an artistic outlet. Adam Benjamin, in his book *Making an Entrance: Theory and Practice for Disabled and Non-Disabled Dancers*, says:

> Teaching in the UK in the early 1990s I realized that, while non-disabled students were progressing on to university or dance school, their disabled contemporaries were too often left at the end of a project asking "When will you be coming back? When is the next workshop?" Although in the intervening years there has been an increasing number of community-based dance projects springing up in the UK, with a few notable exceptions, the doors to further and higher education in dance and the performing arts have remained firmly shut to disabled students.
>
> (Benjamin, 2002, p.xvii)

Benjamin also makes the important distinction (while noting dance's general therapeutic effect), that those who teach dance in inclusive groups are not therapists, nor are those dancing in these groups in therapy (p.63). This is an important distinction for many reasons, most notably perhaps because it sends the message that performing artists with disabilities are not in treatment when they work as a dance performer. They contribute to the development of the artistic work as much as their non-disabled colleagues; as Benjamin states, it is "an exchange of equals."

Like theatre, dance as an art form would benefit enormously from equity, diversity, and inclusivity to more fully represent the human experience.

In Summary

So, what does it all mean for you, the performer? A *performer* is defined as someone who entertains an audience. While entertaining is an important component of performing, we've also established that your job as a performer includes bringing important characters to life with sincerity so that society is represented truthfully. Honest performances provide the opportunity for audiences to see accurate depictions of life, which support their existence.

While theatre and dance does so much for so many, it can do better for more. Performers in the arts and entertainment industry can feel powerless. They audition, and they are considered lucky if they are cast. Performers, especially those new to the profession, often feel like they cannot voice their concern if they sense they are being objectified, degraded, directed to play a stereotype, or cast to play a role outside their race. Through increased awareness, performers can promote EDI in a myriad of ways, and in doing so, they help to further social justice in the performing arts.

So, I'd like to add one more responsibility to your growing list: to recognize inequities amongst performing artists. The performance community relies on one another. You become a positive ambassador to your fellow artists every time you actively embrace equity, diversity, and inclusivity. Simply becoming more aware of the work of choreographers, composers, playwrights, screenwriters, and directors with diverse backgrounds is a step towards progress.

Journal Writing Prompt: Pay It Forward

You have accepted the challenge to represent life through performance; what a gift you're giving and receiving! You will face obstacles as an artist-in-training, and it is helpful to remember that you are not alone on this journey. Recall a time when one of your fellow performers helped you through a challenging moment in class, rehearsal, or performance. What did you learn from that experience and what ways can you pay it forward to other performers? How can you facilitate equity, diversity, and inclusivity in the work you do?

Now that we've reflected on the goals of performance, let's change gears and move on to exercises aimed at preparing for performance and assisting in recovery post-performance. Chapter 2 awaits!

Note

1 DMT is defined as "the psychotherapeutic use of movement to promote emotional, social, cognitive, and physical integration of the individual, for the purpose of improving health and well-being" (American Dance Therapy Association, n.d.).

Bibliography

ABC News (2017). "President Trump, First Lady Melania's First Dance" [Video]. *YouTube*, uploaded by ABC News, 20 January. www.youtube.com/watch?v=_LXQdz6YF3w

Acocella, J. (n.d.). "What went wrong at New York City Ballet?" *New Yorker*, 18 February www.newyorker.com/magazine/2019/02/18/what-went-wrong-at-new-york-cityballetAmerican Dance Therapy Association (n.d.). *What Is Dance/Movement Therapy?* ADTA. https://adta.memberclicks.net/what-is-dancemovement-therapy

Andrews, T. (2019). "Disabled actors say they're the 'last civil rights movement' in Hollywood: Hardly anyone's discussing it." *The Washington Post*, 25 January. www.washingtonpost.com/entertainment/disabled-actors-say-theyre-the-last-civil-rights-movement-in-hollywood-hardly-anyones-discussing-it/2019/01/24/cbde57a2-1817-11e9-9ebf-c5fed1b7a081_story.html

Benjamin, A. (2002). *Making an Entrance: Theory and Practice for Disabled and Non-Disabled Dancers*. Routledge.

"Beyoncé at Last HD Video Live for Barack Michelle Obama." (2013). [Video]. *YouTube*, uploaded by Danielle Costa, 13 June. www.youtube.com/watch?v=81Kpzre_gMQ

Brown, S. K. (2018). "Sterling K. Brown Wins Best Actor in a TV series, drama at the 2018 Golden Globes" [Video]. *YouTube*, uploaded by NBC, 7 January. https://www.youtube.com/watch?v=4kGJTWzPABA

Burke, T. (2018). *The Inception*. Me Too Movement. https://metoomvmt.org/the-inception/

Carlin, S. (2018). "Here's why Darren Criss says he won't play gay characters any longer." *Bustle*, 18 December. www.bustle.com/p/darren-criss-wont-play-gay-characters-any-longer-for-a-truly-great-reason-15525677

CBSNewYork. (2019). "Ali Stroker's Inspiring Tony Award Speech" [Video]. *YouTube*, uploaded by CBSNewYork, 11 January. www.youtube.com/watch?v=ANjFUFdJdWU

Crowe, C. (2015). "A Comment on Allison Ng." *The Uncool – The Official Site for Everything Cameron Crowe*, 2 June. www.theuncool.com/2015/06/02/a-comment-on-allison-ng/

Desta, Y. (2018). "Darren Criss will no longer play gay characters." *Vanity Fair*, 20 December. www.vanityfair.com/hollywood/2018/12/darren-criss-gay-characters

Dunlop, G. (dir.) (1989). *Dancing: The Power of Dance* [Video]. Featuring Jacques D'Amboise, produced by Rhoda Grauer.

Fang, J. (2018). "Yellowface, whitewashing, and the history of white people playing Asian characters." *Teen Vogue*, 8 August. www.teenvogue.com/story/yellowface-whitewashing-history

Fierberg, R. (2017). "Watch the first autistic actor to play *Curious Incident of the Dog in the Night-Time*'s lead role in rehearsal." *Playbill*, 10 October. www.playbill.com/article/watch-the-first-autistic-actor-to-play-curious-incident-of-the-dog-in-the-night-times-lead-role-in-rehearsal

Gilbey, R. (2019). "Playing it straight: Should gay roles be reserved for gay actors?" *The Guardian*, 14 January. www.theguardian.com/stage/2019/jan/14/gay-roles-actors-assassination-gianni-versace-bohemian-rhapsody

Gomes, C. (2021). "Ballerina Chloé Lopes Gomes alleged racism at her company: Now she says it's time for change." *CNN*, 19 February. www.cnn.com/style/article/chloe-lopes-gomes-ballet-racism-personal-essay/index.html

Hernández, P. (2016). "What Meryl Streep says about acting." *Backstage*, Backstage, 13 September. www.backstage.com/magazine/article/meryl-streep-says-acting-5578/.

Jimsteichen, P. (2018a). "George Balanchine, Suzanne farrell, and Ballet's #MeToo Moment." 7 October. https://jimsteichen.com/2018/10/07/george-balanchine-suzanne-farrell-and-ballets-metoo-moment/

Jimsteichen, P. (2018b). "Men controlling women's bodies is nothing new at New York City Ballet. Just ask George Balanchine." 17 September. https://jimsteichen.com/2018/09/17/men-controlling-womens-bodies-is-nothing-new-at-new-york-city-ballet-just-ask-george-balanchine/

Jonas, G. (2003). *Dancing: the Pleasure, Power, and Art of Movement*. Harry N. Abrams.

Kantor, J., & Twohey, M. (2017). "Harvey Weinstein paid off sexual harassment accusers for decades." *New York Times*, 5 October. www.nytimes.com/2017/10/05/us/harvey-weinstein-harassment-allegations.html

Keegan, R. (2019). "The season of Scarlett Johansson: Two hot films, her Marvel future, Woody Allen and a pick for president." *The Hollywood Reporter*, 11 September. www.hollywoodreporter.com/features/scarlett-johansson-talks-woody-allen-elizabeth-warren-black-widow-1235618

León, F. (2019). "In an 'insular, white, calcified world,' Misty Copeland centers black women." *The Glow Up*, 26 February. https://theglowup.theroot.com/in-an-insular-white-calcified-world-misty-copeland-c-1832902564

McCormick, R. (2015). "Cameron Crowe offers apology for casting Emma Stone in his latest movie." *The Verge*, 4 June. www.theverge.com/2015/6/4/8726695/cameron-crowe-emma-stone-cast-aloha-apology

McKinnon, K. (2020). "Kate McKinnon's tribute to Ellen DeGeneres – 2020 Golden Globes" [Video]. *YouTube*, uploaded by NBC, 5 January. www.youtube.com/watch?v=1owY3QPg4Bc&t=53s

NBC (2018). "Sterling K. Brown Wins Best Actor in a TV Series, Drama at the 2018 Golden Globes" [Video]. *YouTube*, uploaded by NBC, 7 January. www.youtube.com/watch?v=4kGJTWzPABA

Time's Up. (2020). "Our story." *Time's Up*, https://timesupnow.org/about/our-story/

Hampton, D. (2019). "How dancing gives your brain and mood a big boost." *The Best Brain Possible*, 26 May. www.thebestbrainpossible.com/dance-exercise-brain-mental-health/

Real, E. (2020). "Ryan Murphy says 'pose' could have never happened without trans talent." *The Hollywood Reporter*, 21 April. www.hollywoodreporter.com/live-feed/ryan-murphy-pose-hiring-transgender-talent-1116572

Rhimes, S. (2016). *Year of Yes: How to Dance It Out, Stand in the Sun and Be Your Own Person*. Simon & Schuster.

Salle, D. (2019). "Exclusive: Artist David Salle interviews Scarlett Johansson for *As If Magazine*." *As If Magazine: The Art of Collaboration*. www.asifmag.com/story/scarlett-johansson-david-salle-collaboration-with-as-if-magazine

"US Army Drill Team Performs – Spirit of America 2014." (2014). [Video]. YouTube, uploaded by Gung Ho Vids, 19 December. www.youtube.com/watch?v=SzgSzerrzYI

Wanshel, E. (2019). "Ali Stroker's Tony win was monumental... and a huge slap in the face." *HuffPost*, 14 June. www.huffpost.com/entry/ali-stroker-tony-disability-community_n_5cfe766be4b0aab91c0966c1

Wittmer, C. (2017). "Shonda Rhimes has no time for people who claim it's hard to find talented women in Hollywood: 'I've never had a problem.'" *Business Insider Australia*, 27 September. www.businessinsider.com.au/shonda-rhimes-talks-diversity-hollywood-and-motherhood-2017-9

Yuen, N.W. (2017). *Reel Inequality: Hollywood Actors and Racism*. Rutgers University Press.

Zentner, M., & Eerola, T. (2010). "Rhythmic engagement with music in infancy." *PNAS*, 30 March. HYPERLINK "http://www.pnas.org/content/107/13/5768" www.pnas.org/content/107/13/5768

2 Performer Preparation

Practices from Theatre Movement for Mind/Body Connection & Free Expression

Jacques Lecoq, a brilliant teacher of physical theatre, movement, and mime, perfectly describes the performer's ideal state of mind for creativity in just three words: *playfulness, togetherness, openness* (Pizzato, 2019, p.264). As a performer, you must shift into a mindset that quiets your *internal editor*, the voice inside your head that quietly judges everything you say and do. That voice can be very loud particularly at times when you feel vulnerable. Every time you train, audition, rehearse, and perform, you open yourself to scrutiny, and even in the most welcoming of environments, you can still feel judged. If you constantly edit yourself or try to perform in ways that you think others want to see, you stifle your creativity. You can combat the internal editor with exercises that clear your mind and awaken your body. *If you build a physical and mental environment that is positive, non-judgmental, cohesive, and receptive to the possibilities that present themselves, convincing work will emerge.*

Taking the time to tune into how you are feeling, to center yourself, and to prepare for the work ahead is time well spent and will lead to productivity. The exercises below, listed under the *pre warm-up* and *warm-up* headings, aim to liberate you from the stronghold of fear, so that you can be fully present and ready to work. The exercises listed under the heading *cool down* aim to shift your headspace from work mode to "normal" self. Your goal is to draw inspiration from this chapter to create a pre warm-up, warm-up, and cool down routine unique to your needs. Ideally, your pre warm-up and warm-up sequences will become a ritual that you look forward to doing independently before the start of a class, rehearsal, audition, or performance knowing that it will calm your nerves, ignite your mind and body, and entice free expression to surface from within. And your cool down sequence will be a way to acknowledge the work you've just completed and prepare you for the next part of your day.

Pre Warm-Up

First, try out the pre warm-up exercises in the sequence listed below and complete the journal writing prompt after to assess your experience with the exercises. Some exercises may prove successful in freeing up a sense of

DOI: 10.4324/9781003149699-3

ease, openness, and playfulness, and some may not. If not all the exercises were winners, that's just fine; sometimes we learn what we do need by identifying what we don't need. If there was something that didn't work for you, ask yourself, "How would I modify this exercise to fit my needs?" Whatever works for you is what works best. *It's time to get performance ready.*

Taking Inventory

Place a yoga mat or towel on the floor and lie on your back. Let your legs naturally relax by allowing the feet to fall away from one another, and place your hands near your sides with palms facing upward. Allow your eyes to gently close. Mentally scan your body from the top of your head all the way down to the tips of your toes, taking note of where you might be holding tension in your body. You do not need to do anything about the tension you're feeling; you are merely scanning and registering where stress physically manifests itself in your body.

Releasing Tension

Common tension areas are the jawline, shoulders, and hip flexor muscles. This may be the case for you, but you may have found other tense areas in addition to or instead of these places. Maybe you furrow your brow, or perhaps despite being asked to relax your legs, you couldn't help but keep your toes facing the ceiling with your quadriceps engaged. Or it could be that you're so accustomed to "sucking in your tummy" that you continued to do so, despite lying down.

Wherever you are holding tension, it's now time to release it. As you continue to lie down, scan the body once more and this time, attempt to "let go" of those constricted areas. This might require you to let your lips part and your jaw to drop open (if you've ever woken from a deep sleep with your mouth open, then you have experienced your sleeping body loosen that tension). If you prefer, you can keep your lips together and still allow the jaw to release. Next, lift your head slightly an inch or two above the floor, and gently place it back down so that the occipital bone is touching the floor as opposed to the parietal bones. In other words, lay your head down in such a way that you've given yourself a double chin. Working your way down the body, rotate your shoulders down and then release them. Next, contract and then release the muscles in your arms and hands. Then lift your knees up, keeping the soles of your feet on the floor. Lift your hips a few inches from the floor and then lower down again, and imagine that you are lowering one vertebra at a time, so that your entire back touches the floor. Slowly slide your feet back down, allowing your legs to fall open once more. Contract and release your quadriceps, hamstrings, and calves; flex your feet and then release. Take a nice deep breath inward and exhale with an audible sigh.

Freeing the Mind

Now that the body is as free of tension as it can be in this moment, let's work on clearing the mind. With eyes closed, imagine that there is a filing cabinet located just outside the door of the room you are in right now. Then, imagine that you have a stack of file folders in hand. Picture yourself placing each and every item on your to-do list into the files. Next, imagine placing your fears, insecurities, concerns, and any distractions into the file folders. Once everything that could prevent you from being present in this exercise has been filed, imagine yourself walking those files out the door and to the filing cabinet. Take a moment to imagine yourself opening the filing cabinet drawer, placing the files into the drawer, closing the drawer, and walking back through the door and into the room you are in now. Know that your thoughts are all nicely organized and filed. Those thoughts will be waiting for you when you've finished this work, but for now, let's leave them be, so that you can be as present as possible for the next exercise.[1]

Feeling the Waves

To continue the pursuit of a body freed from tension, let's try another visualization. Imagine that you are lying on a beach. Feel the sand, the heat, and the gentle breeze on your skin. The scent of coconut from the sunscreen you recently applied is present in the air. The taste of the delicious tropical fruit you had for breakfast still lingers on your taste buds. And the sound of the ocean ebbing and flowing has lulled you into a deep state of relaxation.

Now, imagine the tide starting to come in with the ocean waves gently washing over your feet. As the water recedes, it takes with it any tension in your feet. The waves continue to flow, and the water covers your knees. As the water ebbs, the tension is released from your knees, shins, calves, ankles, the heel of the foot, the ball of the foot, and the tips of the toes.

The waves now flow, and warm water washes over your hips. As the water recedes, it releases the tension from your wrists, hands, fingertips, hip flexors, quadriceps, hamstrings, knees, shins, calves, ankles, the heel of the foot, the ball of the foot, and the tips of the toes.

The tide continues to flow, and the water covers your ribcage. As the water ebbs, the tension is released from your elbow, forearms, wrists, hands, fingertips, abdominals, middle and lower back, hip flexors, quadriceps, hamstrings, knees, shins, calves, ankles, the heel of the foot, the ball of the foot, and the tips of the toes.

The waves continue to flow, and the water covers your chest. As the water ebbs, tension is released from your chest, biceps, triceps, middle back, abdominals, elbow, forearm, wrists, hands, fingertips, lower back, hip flexors, quadriceps, hamstrings, knees, shins, calves, ankles, the heel of the foot, the ball of the foot, and the tips of the toes.

The waves continue to flow, and the water covers your neck. As the water ebbs, tension is released from your shoulders, chest, biceps, triceps, middle back, abdominals, elbow, forearm, wrists, hands, fingertips, lower back, hip flexors, quadriceps, hamstrings, knees, shins, calves, ankles, the heel of the foot, the ball of the foot, and the tips of the toes.

And finally, the waves continue to flow, and the water washes over your entire body. As the water ebbs, tension is released from your forehead, cheeks, jaw, neck, shoulders, chest, biceps, triceps, middle back, abdominals, elbow, forearm, wrists, hands, fingertips, lower back, hip flexors, quadriceps, hamstrings, knees, shins, calves, ankles, the heel of the foot, the ball of the foot, and the tips of the toes. Again, the waves wash over your entire body. And again, the tension is released as the water retreats. Once more, the waves wash over your entire body. And again, the tension is released as the water retreats.

All tension has left your body. The ocean moves into low tide as you relax in the sand.[2]

Becoming Present

Let's continue by visualizing your presence in space and time. You are present in the here and now. Acknowledging what has come before and what may lie ahead is valuable, but your focus in this moment is on the *now*. Think of a phrase, statement, or mantra that sparks gratitude and appreciation for this present moment (I like to say, "I have my health, so I have everything I need."). Say your mantra to yourself. Say it to yourself again. Say it aloud. Now let that mantra go and embrace the contentment that comes with the knowledge that your body and mind are a well of positivity, a conduit for your artistry. This body of yours is wonderfully suited for performance. Your body is tangible. It is present. It is here for you. Your body, your *one and only* body, is everything you need. It's important to make the most of your time with your body, by taking care of it and encouraging it to reach its fullest expression. Performance allows your body to reveal its potential and encourages you to physically communicate your *truth*. When you perform, you are creating a singular experience that encompasses your essence, that which is uniquely *you*. No one can perform exactly as you do. Your body belongs to you, and the fact that you are willing to share its beauty through performance is your contribution to the world.

Valuing Breath

Your breathing is the innate bodily function that is always there sustaining you. It is time now to increase awareness of your breathing patterns. Merely take notice of your natural breathing habits. Note the gentle expansion of your chest and abdomen as you inhale, and the lowering of both towards your spine as you exhale. Note whether the inhalation is the same length, longer, or shorter than the exhalation. There is no need to make a change to your breathing pattern in this moment; you're simply observing.

Diaphragmatic Breathing

Let's now explore focusing and directing the breath. Bend your knees up toward the ceiling, keeping the soles of the feet on the floor. Check that your back is touching the floor (avoid any airspace between the lower back and the floor). Place one hand on your chest and the other on your abdomen. As you inhale, allow the breath to move the abdomen outward. Check in with the hand on the chest to make sure the chest is moving as little as possible. Exhale and feel the abdomen draw inward toward the spine while the chest continues to remain relatively still. Take a few more breaths focusing on diaphragmatic breathing and then return to your "normal" breathing pattern for a few easy breaths.

Lateral Breathing

The lateral breathing technique often used during training in Pilates aims to expand both sides of the ribcage out and away from each other on the inhalation, and then return toward one another on the exhalation. Place your hands on your ribcage (I like to wrap my hands around my ribcage, so that I can feel both the front and back parts of the ribcage, like holding a sandwich). As you inhale, direct your breathing to your ribcage and feel your ribs expanding. Take a few lateral breaths, noting how the breath continues toward the pelvic floor while emphasizing movement of the ribs. And then return to your "normal" breathing pattern for a few easy breaths.

Three-Part Breathing

Usually the first breathing technique introduced in yoga, three-part breathing invites you to inhale and expand your belly, chest, and ribs. Take a few breaths, noting the expansion of your upper chest, ribcage, and diaphragm, which extends all the way to the pelvic floor on the inhalation and the return to your center on the exhalation. On your last exhalation, feel free to make a sound and enjoy an audible sigh. And then return to your "normal" breathing pattern.

Baby Movement

Roll over to your right side and rest in the fetal position. Now place the right arm out with palm facing upward. Be sure to stretch the arm directly out from the shoulder so that it creates a 90-degree angle with your torso. Then place the left arm on top of the right so that your hands are palm to palm.

Shift the left shoulder forward about three inches. You'll see that your left hand slides forward as well. Then return back to the starting position. Repeat this small and gentle movement, forward and back to the starting position, five to seven times. There's no need to rush. Let the body's natural momentum propel the small movement back and forth.

Now shift the left shoulder back about three inches. You'll see that your left hand slides back onto your right inner wrist as well. Then return back to the starting position. Repeat this movement, back and forward to the starting position, five to seven times. Again, there's no need to rush.

Next, shift the left hip forward about three inches. You'll see that your left knee slides forward as well. Then return back to the original starting position. Repeat this movement, forward and back to the original starting position, five to seven times.

Now shift the left hip back about three inches. You'll see that your left knee slides back toward your right inner thigh as well. Then return back to the original starting position. Repeat this movement, back and forward to the original starting position, five to seven times. Remember, there's no need to rush.

Shift both the left shoulder and hip forward about three inches. You'll see that your left hand and knee slide forward as well. Then return back to the original starting position. Repeat this movement, forward and back to the original starting position, five to seven times.

Now shift both the left shoulder and hip back about three inches. You'll see that your left hand slides back onto your right inner wrist and your left knee back towards your right inner thigh. Then return back to the original starting position. Repeat this movement, back and forward to the original starting position, five to seven times.

Finally, shift the left hip forward and the left shoulder back and then return to the original starting position. Next, shift the left hip back and the left shoulder forward and then return to the original starting position. Repeat this alternating movement five to seven times.

Once you have completed all of the repetitions, roll on to your back and take note of how your shoulders and hips feel. You may feel a tingling sensation. You may feel more at ease. You may not notice much of a change at all; if that is the case for you, do not fret. You may not sense a release at all and that's okay. Be sure to repeat the entire exercise on your right by rolling onto your left side. Then roll onto your back once more and observe any changes.[3]

Tree Release

Lie on your back and let your legs naturally relax by allowing the feet to fall away from one another. Extend your arms straight out from your shoulders, palms facing upward, so that your body makes a "T" shape. Then, bend your forearms up towards your head and form a 90 angle with your arms (palms facing upwards). In yoga, this is known as "cactus arms." Once in position, check in that your entire back and shoulders are still touching the floor. Next, lift your right knee towards the ceiling with the sole of the foot remaining on the floor. Then open the knee outward, causing the sole of the foot to rest on the knee. Depending on your flexibility, you may find that the foot rests higher on the inner thigh as opposed to the knee or lower on the inner calf. No need to judge where the foot wants to rest, just allow it to lie where it needs. Once again, check in with your back to be sure it is still entirely in contact with the floor. You may find that the hips lean right; try to adjust so that the hip bones continue facing the ceiling. Stay in this position for a minute or two. Repeat with the left leg.

Abstract Painting

Imagine that your hands and feet are paint brushes, and the space all around you is your canvas (Franklin, 2014, p.72). With your back, head, and neck resting on the floor, move your limbs about in the air as though you are creating a beautiful work of abstract art. Imagine your favorite colors splashing about the room as you freely and easily move your arms and legs, isolating and noting the connection of your fingertips to your hands, your hands to your wrists, your wrists to your forearms, your forearms to your elbows, your elbows to your upper arms and your upper arms to your shoulders. Isolate and note the connection of your toes to your feet, your feet to your ankles, your ankles to your calves, your calves to your knees, your knees to your upper legs, your upper legs to your hips. Wiggle your limbs and embrace the jiggle that results, as though you are expanding your skin, giving your muscles and bones more space to move.

Now let the left side of the body rest, while the right arm and leg continues to move. Note how your right body half likes to move.

Then let the right side of the body rest, while the left arm and leg begins to move again. Note how your left body half likes to move.

Now rest your arms and move both legs about the space. Note how the lower half of your body moves when the arms are not participating in the action.

Now rest your legs and move your arms. Enjoy the lightness and ease that results from only moving your arms.

Now move the right arm and left leg, while the left arm and right leg rests.

Now move the left arm and right leg, while the right arm and left leg rests. Note the core engagement that occurs during the cross-body halves movement.

And finally, move on the floor with your entire body, allowing the head and neck to lift as desired, and roll about the floor as needed so that your imagined canvas is completely covered with paint.

Figure 2.1 (L to R): Sarah Hill in *Baby Movement* starting position, *Tree Release,* and *Abstract Painting* with back, head, and neck resting

Taffy Pull

Again, lie on your back, and place your arms overhead with palms facing upward. Imagine that someone takes hold of your wrists and another your ankles and gently pulls you away from your center. Stretch by lengthening your body; hold the stretch for five seconds and then release it, so that your body is completely limp and relaxed. Imagine that you are a piece of saltwater taffy, stretching longer and longer and then relaxing. Repeat as desired.

Figure 4 Stretch

Lie on your back and draw your knees up, keeping the soles of the feet on the floor. Next bend the right leg, so that the heel of the right foot crosses over and rests just above the knee of the left leg. Now place the right arm through the space in between the legs and the left arm outside the left leg ("threading the needle"). Join hands together and place them on either the left shin or hamstring. You can deepen the intensity of the stretch by adding pressure with the hands to draw the left knee towards the chest while flexing the right foot. Repeat on the other side.

Awaken the Senses

Work your way to a standing position, body in alignment, feet hip width apart in parallel first position, arms resting at your sides. Do not lock your knees; rather, keep your knees softened. Close your eyes and breathe. Take

Figure 2.2 Eva Alom in *Figure 4 Stretch*

a moment to notice the way your clothes feel on your skin. Is the fabric soft or itchy? Tight or loosely fitting? Do you feel warm or a bit cold? Simply observe the touch of your clothes. Next, listen to the sounds in the room. Note any noises your body is making. Can you sense your heart beating? Do you hear your breakfast digesting? Now, what do you hear all around you? Can you hear sounds from outside the room as well? Perhaps your neighbor's dog barking? Or the sound of a train in the distance? Next, remember the taste of your last meal. Was it salty or sweet? Hot or cold? Deliciously savory or a bit bland? What did the meal smell like? What do you smell now? Can you smell your shampoo or deodorant? What about any smells in the room or even outside? How would you describe the smells you're smelling right now? Open your eyes with a soft gaze, looking at nothing in particular. See everything and nothing. Next focus your gaze, by looking at your hands and then feet, and gradually widen your focus to take in everything you can with your eyes. Awaken sight, smell, touch, sound, and taste. Observe with all of your senses.

> ### Journal Writing Prompt: Mindful Maven
>
> Ideally, upon completion of the pre warm-up exercises, you are in a state of mind receptive to your innermost thoughts and feelings. Free write for five to ten minutes, describing any frustrations, physical or mental obstacles you faced, discoveries you made, or wandering thoughts that came to mind during these exercises. Take note of which exercises you'd like to incorporate into your pre warm-up repertoire. Also brainstorm modifications and jot down new ideas you might like to try out.

Warm-Up

You have now laid the groundwork to create your very own pre warm-up routine and are ready to enter the warm-up phase. The exercises below are a suggested sequence geared toward increasing heart rate and stimulating blood flow to muscles, so you'll be firing on all cylinders when your work begins. Start the warm-up slowly and increase energy as you proceed. The following sequence may not prove to be a perfect fit for you, but it will give you a better sense of what you need to do to prepare for performance work. Give the following exercises a try!

Channel Your Inner Jane Fonda

Choose your favorite upbeat song with a four-four rhythm, and press play.

- March in place eight times;
- Widen your stance and march in place eight times;
- Repeat;
- March in place four times;
- Widen your stance and march in place four times;
- Repeat;
- March in place two times;
- Widen your stance and march in place two times;
- Repeat as desired.

Repeat the entire exercise a second and third time, increasing energy each time. By the third repetition, give it everything you've got.

Just Dance

Immediately following, start to dance like no one is watching! Simply get your body in motion for two minutes, and loosen up.

Time to Rise and Shine

Next, complete the following sequence, which will help further warm and stimulate the body. Take your time with it.

For your starting position, stand with hands at your sides (palms facing legs), shoulders rotated down and toward the spine, body aligned, with feet parallel, about shoulder width (or less) apart from one another. With feet planted, note your body's connection to the earth and radiate your energy down through the floor. Feel the top of your head radiating energy up toward the sky. Feel your core radiating energy in all directions. Feel the push pull of the earth and sky, and the energy of the atmosphere forward, behind, and around.

Next, raise your arms overhead. Remember to inhale as you raise your arms out to the sides, then turn palms upward and continue to raise arms up over your head in a seamless flow of movement (ultimately palms face one another); as your arms lift outward and upward, radiate energy through your fingertips and the top of your head, while maintaining your connection to the earth, and avoid raising your shoulders up toward your ears.

Figure 2.3 (Top to Bottom): *Time to Rise and Shine* starting position, arms overhead

Then, forward fold. Remember to exhale and lower arms outward turning palms downward, and bend over (aim for a flat back as you lower your upper body towards your legs for as long as possible); you can keep your legs straight to feel a hamstring stretch right away or bend the knees slightly. Let your arms lower to the floor as you fold over.

Inhale, and lift half way. Remember to lift the body slightly and place hands on shins for support, as you focus on a flat back.

Exhale, forward fold. Remember to slide hands from your shins toward the floor and lower your upper body back down. Your abdominals may or may not touch your quadriceps and your hands may or may not touch the floor, depending on flexibility.

Inhale and lift back up. Remember to lift the upper body back to standing (aim for a flat back as you lift), while you move arms out to the side and up overhead, turning palms to face one another.

Continue to move hands toward one another and make a heart shape with hands and arms above the head (the arms will need to curve and the backs of the fingers will touch).

Figure 2.4 (Top to Bottom): Forward fold, halfway lift, forward fold

Figure 2.5 Heart shape

Next, begin to lower the hands down through the center of the body. As you move your hands downward, drop the head (chin towards the chest), round your back, bend your knees, fold over (imagine rolling down vertebra by vertebra). Bend the knees further and allow hands to touch the floor.

Continue the flow of movement by sliding the hands forward away from the feet and move into plank position (aka push-up position, where the front of the body faces the floor and only the hands and the balls of the feet touch the floor; remember to try your best to keep your torso parallel to the floor; in other words, if your hips are lifting above your shoulders, you are not in a fully engaged plank position; wrists should be directly below the shoulders). Hold this position for a slow five count.

While in the plank position, lift the one leg approximately four inches from the ground (keep the leg straight, radiating energy toward the back wall behind you), hold for three counts and place it back on the floor. Repeat with the other leg.

Figure 2.6 (Top to Bottom): Rounding back and rolling down, hands touching the floor

Figure 2.7 Plank position, lifting one leg. Try your best to shift some weight onto your toes with the heel of both the supporting leg and the lifted leg facing the ceiling. That will shift your weight forward onto the upper body and keep your lower body positioning in parallel to encourage engagement of your core and quads.

While in the plank position, lift and bend the one knee drawing it toward the same side elbow. Repeat with the other leg, then again and again.

Next, bend your knees, shift your gaze forward toward your hands, and walk your feet towards your hands and slowly roll your body up to starting position. Repeat the entire exercise.

Figure 2.8 Knee to elbow

Figure 2.9 Rolling back up to the starting position.

Yoga Standing Balance Sequence

Move into a *Tree Pose* (depending on flexibility, place one foot above or just below the standing knee (a relaxed turnout will occur as a result); place hands in prayer position heart center; once you have achieved a sense of balance, you can lift your hands overhead, arch back, close eyes, etc.

Then move into *Eagle Pose* (wrap your free leg around your standing leg; your hands can return to prayer position, or for an added challenge, you can overlap the arms at the elbows and wrap the forearms around one another with hands meeting palm to palm).

Then, move into *Dancer Pose* (unwrap the leg and take it behind you with the same arm as leg holding the inside of the free leg for added support and lift; to help with balance, push your foot into the hand holding it; for a balance challenge, take the free arm up above the head and slowly move it forward).

Then move into *Hand to Big Toe Pose*, by straightening the leg forward with the same arm as leg holding the big toe.

Then take the leg outward for *Hand to Big Toe Side*. To finish, slowly and methodically lower your leg.

Depending on where you are in your training, you can try all of these poses on one leg and then switch to the other side after you've completed the entire sequence (more challenging). Or you can do one pose on each leg and then move to the next pose (less challenging).

Let's Get Fired Up

Take a moment to warm up the core without overdoing it too much. The idea is to get the body ready for performance, not completely wear it out. So, think of the next sequence of exercises as a low repetition cycle to energize and warm your core:

> *Crunch* – I'm sure we've all done crunches before, but it's important to break down every aspect of executing a crunch with technical accuracy, so that you are getting the maximum benefits from the exercise. While it's tempting to skip or gloss over this section, visualize the professional ballet dancer who spends countless hours at the barre perfecting their tendu, channel that level of perfectionism and take the needed time to read this section carefully and then slowly and methodically perform a crunch, making sure that you are tuned in to every aspect of the movement.
>
> Start by lying on your back, knees raised, with feet on the floor. In this neutral position, you'll note the small of your back is raised slightly from the floor. Now adjust your body, so that your entire back is on the floor. You may have the sensation that you are

Figure 2.10 (Top to Bottom): *Tree Pose, Eagle Pose, Dancer Pose, Hand to Big Toe Forward, Hand to Big Toe Side*

"tucking" the pelvis a bit to reach this position. Place one hand behind your head for support, while keeping the neck aligned with the spine (in other words, avoid tucking your chin to your chest). Place the other hand on your lower abdomen. Inhale. Exhale as you lift your head, neck, and shoulders from the floor for the crunch, making sure your neck remains aligned with the spine. Inhale as you lower your head, neck, and shoulders toward the floor and lengthen your torso, as if being pulled by the crown of your head diagonally back. The key is to lengthen the torso as you lower without completely releasing the flexion of your abdominal muscles. Your head, neck, and the upper part of your shoulders should not touch the floor upon completion of the crunch. Repeat as desired.

Bicycle – Start by lying on your back, knees raised toward your chest, with feet off the floor. Place both hands behind your head for support, while avoiding tucking your chin to your chest. Straighten your right leg keeping the heel four to six inches from the ground, while bending the left knee toward the chest. Simultaneously, lift the right shoulder from the floor and rotate to the left so the right elbow is touching or reaching toward the left knee. Now switch, by straightening your left leg keeping the heel four to six inches from the ground, while bending the right knee toward the chest simultaneously lifting the left shoulder from the floor and rotating to the right so the left elbow is touching or reaching toward the right knee. Repeat as desired.

Reclining Balance – Begin by sitting; then lean back and place forearms on the floor behind your back for added support and balance. Be sure that your back is aligned with shoulders lowered. Lift both legs up to a hover above the floor (the heels should be approximately four to six inches above the floor). Hold.

Beats – Stay in the reclining balance position and cross the right leg over the left and then switch to the left leg over the right and continue with a back and forth "beating" or "pulsing" action. While executing this movement, I imagine that there is a party going on downstairs (with my legs) while everyone upstairs (my upper body) is asleep (well, not asleep really so much as still!).

Against a Wall – Stand with your back against a wall. Bend your knees. Make sure that your knees do not extend past your toes and continue to press your back against the wall. Note the activation in your glutes and abdominals. Hold.

Handstand

Handstands are a fun way to help build strength and balance, if it's something you feel comfortable trying. Here are some tips to get you started:

- Use a wall to assist with balance;
- Engage all of your muscles (point your toes, squeeze your thighs and glutes together); imagine sending energy out through the tips of your toes and up through the ceiling;
- Use your core to help with alignment rather than arching your back;

- Spread your fingers out and place weight in the fingertips as well as hands; imagine radiating energy through your hands and down through the earth;
- Don't strain your neck.

Headstand

Next, you may wish to try handstand's companion balance, the headstand. Some like to place their hands on the floor just in front of their shoulders, but others like to place forearms on the ground, interlace fingers (making a "V" shape with the forearms/hands), and use hands to cradle the head for additional stability and support. The tips for handstands also apply to headstands.

Sits Bones Balance

Place hands around ankles or calf or hamstring area, and then slowly straighten legs to achieve a "V" shape with the body and legs while balancing on your sits bones. Maintain alignment and hold.

Figure 2.11 Sits Bone Balance

At this point, you should feel nice and warm and ready for some light stretch. While there's a myriad of stretching exercises you can do, the sequence below provides a nice foundation, and you can add more stretches as needed depending on the kind of performance work you are about to do.

Gentle Side Stretch

Lift arms overhead and widen your stance. Hold your right wrist with your left hand and side stretch leaning toward the left. Use the left hand to gently pull the right wrist for a deeper stretch. Feel the wonderful opening in your right side. Repeat on the other side.

Center Stretch

Lift arms overhead and with a wide stance legs parallel, bend forward with a flat back. Continue moving forward and when you can no longer maintain a flat back, gently fold and enjoy the hamstring stretch. Shift weight forward a bit, so you are not sinking into your heels too much. Hold. Bend your knees and roll up vertebra by vertebra.

Right & Left Hamstring Stretch

Continuing the wide leg stance, move into a gentle turnout and take both arms out to the sides. Engage the glutes and core and hold. Then, lift the left arm overhead and side stretch to the right. Hold. Next, turn the upper body over so the front of the body runs parallel to the floor with a flat back. Hold. Then, fold over to the right for a hamstring stretch. Hold. Then, lift to return to the flat back. Next, turn the upper body back into the side stretch (front of the body facing forward). And finish by lifting back up into the wide leg beginning stance. Repeat on the other side.

Quad Stretch

Stand with legs parallel. Bend the right leg back toward your right glute. Use your right hand to hold your foot and press the right heel toward your right glute. Make sure your right knee remains next to your left knee. Hold and repeat on the other side.

It's time now to awaken the face and vocal instrument. It is the crucial (but often overlooked) last step in your warm-up.

Face, Neck, Shoulder Massage

Using your fingertips, gently tap on cheekbones (as though you're playing piano on your face). Move fingertips down to your jawline, up to your temples, and all around your hairline. Allow your jaw to drop, so it is free of any tension. Work your way down your neck and shoulders, gently massaging your muscles.

Chin Waggle (Jaw Release)

Allow the jaw to drop and gently massage the jawline with fingertips. Take a breath, open your mouth and stretch the jaw vertically and horizontally (as though yawning). Then, allow the face to fully relax. Next, using the palm of your hand, move down along the jawline to further encourage a release of tension in the jawline. Then, place the outside edge of your index finger on the front of the chin and the thumb of the same hand behind the chin. Begin gently moving the jaw up and down. Your jaw should be relaxed with the hand doing the work of moving the jaw up and down. Finally, interlace your fingers (hold your own hands) and place hands in front of you at chest height. Quickly move your hands forward and back to shake your face with the jaw released. Add sound to this movement. It may feel and sound a bit silly, but after this exercise, your jawline will be released and relaxed!

Shock Horror

Widen your eyes, lift your eyebrows, open your mouth, and turn your whole face into an expression that would look to most like "shock."

Then scrunch your face, closing your eyes and mouth and furrowing your brow to what would look to most like "horror" or "fear." Repeat this exercise a few times to awaken expressivity in your face.

High to Low / Low to High

Using diaphragmatic breathing, make an "ah" sound that changes key from high to low and low to high (make the "ah" sound heard in the word, "father"). Allow the voiced sound to glide up and down the scales as high and as low as you safely can go.

Hey! Ho!

Again, using diaphragmatic breathing, repeat the words, "Hey! Ho!" slowing increasing volume. Once you've reached a booming volume that is still in a safe range vocally (the sound should not move into your throat, turning into a raspy scream), repeat the words slowly decreasing in volume.

Tongue Twister

Create or find a tongue twister and do your best to speak it all the way through without fault. Try my favorite:

> All I want is a proper cup of coffee
> Made in a proper copper coffee pot.
> I may be off my dot but I want a proper coffee
> In a proper copper coffee pot.

Iron coffee pots and tin coffee pots
They are no use to me.
If I can't have a proper cup of coffee
In a proper copper coffee pot, I'll have a cup of tea.
                (Lee & Weston, 1926)

Red Leather Yellow Leather

Repeat the phrase, "Red leather, yellow leather" a dozen or so times, focusing on strong pronunciation, hitting your consonants clearly.

Journal Writing Prompt: Just Breathe

Performers often keep their breath shallow by sucking in the tummy, resulting in less oxygen to muscles. What did you notice about your breathing as you attempted these exercises? Was it shallow? Did you ever feel out of breath? Did you note whether you were using any of the breathing methods described in the pre warm-up section (diaphragmatic breathing, lateral breathing, three-part breathing)? Take note of which exercises you'd like to incorporate into your warm-up repertoire. Also brainstorm modifications and jot down new ideas you might like to try out.

While there is no one pre warm-up / warm-up sequence that covers the needs of every situation, I find these exercises give you a taste of what you should be doing before you begin performance work to maximize the time you have with your teacher, director, choreographer, and peers. Your pre warm-up / warm-up routine will change and evolve and may be slightly different depending on the work you're about to do. For example, preparing for a voice lesson will involve more vocal preparation, while a dance class will require more stretch. Your sequence will also differ when you prepare for an actual performance. You might have a fight call or dance call, and you might also have a company warm-up. Even when you have company warm-ups before a performance, you still may need your own personal warm-up time. Again, let these exercises serve as a guide.

Cool Down

Just as important as the time you give yourself to execute a pre warm-up and warm-up is the time you make for a cool down immediately following your training session or performance. Not only does your body physically need a moment for light stretch, your mind needs to be released from the potentially strong emotional work you just performed. Try these exercises to cool down both physically and mentally.

Vertebra by Vertebra

Stand with feet hip distance apart in parallel position, with your arms comfortably at your sides. Put a small bend in your knees. Beginning at the tip top of your head, slowly curve your head, neck, and torso down toward the floor, imagining that you are "rolling down" vertebra by vertebra. If you start to feel a pull in the hamstrings, feel free to bend the knees further. This exercise is about the back, head, and neck and is not intended as a leg stretch. Once you've completed your roll downward, your abdomen should be able to rest on top of your quadriceps. Your arms should have very little energy throughout the entire exercise and could very well be touching the floor by this point. Ideally, the top of your head is parallel to the floor. Shake your head "yes" and then "no" to be sure you are not holding any unnecessary tension in your head and neck. Gently bounce up and down by bending and straightening your knees and swing the torso and arms side to side, keeping the head and neck dropped. Return to stillness. Then, slowly and methodically roll back upward vertebra by vertebra. Your head should be very last to lift. Then, roll the shoulders down and towards the spine. With ease, shimmy your shoulders for a moment; then gently shake each arm and leg (I imagine shaking or jiggling my muscles off the bone).

Bobble Head

Once standing, gently move your head around like a bobble head doll. In other words, do not strain your neck by tucking the chin completely down to the chest or raising your head up to the point that you are looking at the ceiling. Rather, focus on making small head and cervical vertebrae movements, switching directions whenever desired.

Head Side to Side

Have a seat and bend and cross your legs. Sit up nice and tall with shoulders at ease, body aligned, hands relaxing in your lap. Gently drop your head to the right and feel the stretch in the left side of your neck. Take a few breaths in this position. Move your left hand out to the left away from your body to form a 45-degree angle, and note the deepening of the stretch on the left side of your neck. Repeat on the other side.

Reach Center, Right, & Left

Still seated, fold over reaching your hands forward. Make sure your sits bones stay connected to the floor, while your upper body folds over. Then, walk both arms over toward your right, noticing a wonderful stretch in the left side of your back. Walk both arms over to the left and notice the stretch in the right side of the back. Walk your hands back to center and gently roll up.

Thank You, Next

Close your eyes and breathe three cleansing breaths. Say thank you to your mind and body for the work just completed. Then think of one specific moment that you are grateful for that occurred during your work. Imagine yourself taking positive energy to your next destination. Open your eyes, smile with your whole being and… off you go!

Share the Love

On your way out, take a moment to connect with a peer either giving them a smile or nod, or approach them to say something constructive about their work that you observed. A performer never works alone, and it is good to acknowledge each other's presence in your processes. You never really know what's going on in someone else's mind; a word from you might be exactly what they need.

Figure 2.12 Reaching forward

Assignment: Create Your Pre Warm-Up, Warm-Up, & Cool Down Routine

Upon entering the studio, I often see my students looking down at their phones or speaking with their peers while seated. It's just a natural habit that's easily picked up. Perhaps that time before class could be spent either lying down with eyes closed for some needed relaxation or walking briskly around the room while chatting to increase energy. Either option might prove more beneficial. While I (like most teachers) usually take my students through a warm-up and cool down during class, I cannot stress enough the benefits of personally preparing yourself physically and mentally for the demands of performance training. You alone know how your body and mind are feeling, and I believe you will see and feel results faster if you prepare independently and take a moment after on your own to recover from the training session.

I realize that many are rushing from one class to the next and may not have time for a pre warm-up, warm-up, and cool down immediately before and after training. If that is the case for you, I would ask that you consider adding them to your daily routine. Can you imagine how centered you'd feel if you did a pre warm-up and warm-up before heading out the door in the morning? Or how calming it would be for you at the end of the day to take a few minutes to cool down?

Tony and Emmy award winning choreographer Twyla Tharp has composed well over one hundred groundbreaking dances for the stage and screen. In her book, *The Creative Habit: Learn It and Use It for Life* (Tharp & Reiter, 2006), she discusses rituals of preparation and how having a "routine is as much a part of the creative process as the lightning bolt of inspiration, maybe more" (p.7). She begins each day the same as the one before, and her routine gets her into the creative mindset she needs to choreograph (p.14). Do you have a morning ritual? What could you do differently to create a morning ritual that fosters creativity? Are you willing and able to make the time for a pre warm-up and warm-up to start out your day?

Let's try it! Create a ten-minute pre warm-up and warm-up sequence and a three- to five-minute cool down sequence. Then, commit to doing the sequences every day for the next week (either before and after class or rehearsal or at the beginning and end of each day). Remember, the goal is to create a sequence that prepares you and helps you to recover. At week's end, assess and tweak your routine as needed. Then recommit for another week. And another... and another until it's a habit.

Feel free to involve a classmate or roommate but only if it is mutually beneficial. And don't be afraid to do this work alone. I had a student who was fearless in his pre warm-up, warm-up, and cool down rituals; while he was one of the only students who really committed to warming up and cooling down before and after each class, his peers watched in admiration. And let me tell you, I don't think it was a coincidence that he was always fully engaged in the work.

In Summary

There is great value in creating a routine that helps your body and mind shift gears from "everyday living" and into "performance mode." Pre warm-up and warm-up exercises can have a transformative effect on the body and mind when repeated daily; it can become a ritual that channels and directs energy, encouraging you to open and awaken your senses. It helps you to get in the zone, so you are free to explore. Freeing up a sense of ease, openness, and playfulness will lead to imaginative discoveries. Additionally, the performer needs to shift from work mode and return to "normal" self. Through cool down, you take the time to release yourself from any emotional strain the performance session may have caused, so you can safely return to the present moment.

Now that you have explored ways to create the best possible physical and mental environment for creativity in performance, let's move on to Chapter 3 for key concepts in ballet dance technique that actor-dancers can rely on whenever they perform.

Notes

1 I was first introduced to releasing tension through body scanning, inventory, and filing visualizations in a dance improvisation workshop led by Ann Law. Law, a dance improviser, choreographer, educator, and arts activist, visited ETSU as a guest artist to lead the workshop. She also performed her one woman show, *The Passion Flower Project*, which explored her journey with breast cancer. Her performance, a multimedia production that included film footage of her getting a passion flower tattoo on her chest after a double mastectomy and a live dance improvisation with her wielding a samurai sword was a brilliant event.

2 My first experience with the ocean visualization was as a graduate student at the Chicago College of Performing Arts at Roosevelt University. Kristin Goodman, Period Acting Styles instructor and director, encouraged us to release tension using imagery of ocean waves. The meditation took about an hour (give or take). Some found it incredibly relaxing with a few folks even falling asleep. Others found it upsetting and did not like the idea of water covering their entire bodies. I have continued practicing the general idea of that visualization over a shorter timeframe (with the hope that it would more readily invite a feeling of

refreshment over a feeling of anxiety). If at any point the visualization is too intense, please feel free to stop.

3 I was first introduced to the shoulder/hip release exercise I like to call "Baby Movement" during an aerial dance workshop at ETSU, led by visiting guest artist, Jayne Bernasconi. Bernasconi, a dancer, choreographer, author, and faculty member at Towson University, took us through the exercise which eased our sore hips and shoulders. After a week in the air, this exercise was a much-needed stress reliever. I have used it ever since and am always grateful for this exercise taught to me by a preeminent leader in yoga, aerial yoga, and aerial dance.

Bibliography

Franklin, E.N. (2014). Dance Imagery for Technique and Performance. Human Kinetics.

Lee, B., & Weston, R.P. (1926). What I Want is a Proper Cup o' Coffee. Francis Day &Hunter.

Pizzato, M. (2019). Mapping Global Theatre Histories. Springer International Publishing.

Tharp, T., & Reiter, R. (2006). The Creative Habit: Learn It and Use It for Life – A Practical Guide. Simon & Schuster.

3 Performance Building Blocks

Key Concepts in Ballet Dance Technique for Presence & Authenticity on Stage & Screen

When a new theatre and dance student meets with me for advising, the first suggestion I make is that they register for a ballet class. It doesn't matter whether the student is brand new to ballet or if they have been training in the art form for years. Beginning or returning to ballet fundamentals develops key components – *posture, alignment*, *turnout*, *plié, point*, *balance*, *coordination*, *port de bras*, and *épaulement* – which, with minimal adjustments needed, provides the foundation for many dance forms and period acting styles and builds *stage presence*, that essential ingredient every person who steps in front of an audience needs to possess. Let's take a closer look at ballet fundamentals and unlock the power to command attention:

Posture and Alignment

Perhaps the two most important terms in movement and dance training are *posture* and *alignment*. Posture refers to body positioning, the way a person carries themselves when they sit, stand, and move around. Alignment is arranging the body in correct proportions. When our body is aligned, we have good posture.

I would assert that most of us have a certain posture during "everyday" life and another posture when we perform. Take a moment to check in with your posture right now, as you're reading this book. Are you lying on your tummy, slightly arching your back with weight on your forearms? Perhaps you're in a comfy chair with shoulders gently slouching forward. Or maybe you're sat on the floor, legs crossed, elbows resting on your knees with your chin held up by your hands. Whatever position you're in right now, I would venture to guess that your posture is not aligned (to be fair, I've just noticed my shoulders are rounded as I type this). What would it take to move your posture into alignment? (if you're on your tummy, try placing a pillow under your armpits and another under your hips to take some of the weight off your forearms and lower back). Once you feel more aligned, ask yourself, "How familiar am I with this feeling?" Be honest with yourself as you assess your "everyday" posture.

DOI: 10.4324/9781003149699-4

It can be difficult to identify the way you habitually carry yourself, and there are many factors that influence your posture. The National Council on Strength and Fitness says that "genetic predisposition" plays a hand in postural deviations (or distortions), but usually deviations are developed over time in response to long term habits (n.d.). Personal trainer Natalie McClure says, "Postural distortions happen when we repeat an undesirable movement or static position again and again, that leads to muscle imbalances and postural stress" (2015). All this to say, many can improve their posture over time, so it is well worth exploring.

It is often necessary for an outside eye to pinpoint what you need to do to improve posture, and I'd like to discuss two posture deviations I see most often: *anterior pelvic tilt* and *rounded shoulders*.

Anterior pelvic tilt

Stuart Marsh calls it "Instagram butt" (Marsh, 2016). A prevalent posture in the performance community, you've likely seen it in selfies where the photo is taken from above, highlighting a protruding *derrière*. While we all have a natural curve in our spine and should feel a small arch in our lower back, that arch can be accentuated, resulting in the hips tilting forward towards the floor and the butt sticking out. This positioning, known as *anterior pelvic tilt*, can be seen in performers who miss the mark when seeking alignment. I have seen this posture in actors and dancers who do not fully engage their lower abdominals and instead arch the back and release the pelvis down and away from their core (which can ultimately result in lower back pain). These students can often feel like they are demonstrating great posture, but in reality, they may be sticking the chest out, opening the ribcage away from the spine, and releasing the lower back from the core causing the pelvis to tilt. The abdominals, a crucial component to alignment, are virtually ignored. Then, once aware of the issue, the performer can over-correct, causing *posterior pelvic tilt* (I'll discuss *posterior pelvic tilt* later in the section "Plié").

Rounded shoulders

With this postural deviation, the shoulders and upper back hunch forward. The head can also extend forward from the neck. While in stillness, most performers seem capable of avoiding rounded shoulders, but once locomotor movement begins, the shoulders often round and alignment fades. It is tiring to maintain correct carriage while moving, and when fatigue sets in, the first area to falter is usually the shoulders. Rounded shoulders are also often seen when we are out and about in our everyday lives. It seems "easier" to carry ourselves in this way and perhaps it non-verbally communicates a kind of passivity. I remember throughout my teens when I was dancing daily, my posture was at its best. I strove to maintain alignment and never hunched. But then I started hearing similar comments from new acquaintances who confessed their first impressions of me. On many occasions I was told that before getting to know me, I seemed snobby, standoffish, or overly assertive. I came to find out my posture was off-putting to some. In an effort to appear more approachable or perhaps demure, I started to change my daily posture by rounding my shoulders. It quickly became a habit. Suddenly, I had to actively focus on alignment in performance classes. I so wish I had ignored those comments! (I'll speak more on "shouldering" in the section "*Èpaulement*".)

On or off the stage, good posture should be the aim, and you can start by spending a few minutes a day working on body alignment. I cannot stress enough the importance of alignment in performance training; if body placement is off, no amount of flexibility or strength can fully compensate. Try the following exercises below:

Imaginary String

A helpful visualization to aid in achieving body alignment is to imagine a taut string running vertically from the center of your head through your torso. Feel

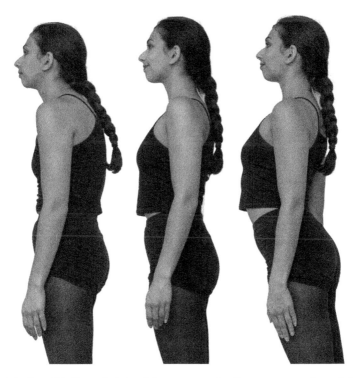

Figure 3.1 (L to R): Rounded shoulders, posture in alignment, anterior pelvic tilt

the string at the top of your head being pulled upward (but do not lift your chin towards the ceiling), then running through the center of your body. As the string continues through the pelvic floor, imagine it being pulled downward. See what minor adjustments you need to make when using this visualization.

Seated

Sit on an exercise ball (or on the edge of a chair) and feel your sits bones connect to the surface on which you are seated. Check that your shoulders aren't creeping up to your ears; they should be down and directed more toward your spine than your chest. Make sure your chin isn't lifting up toward the ceiling or tucking down toward your chest. Imagine that you have a third eye in the center of your forehead, and that eye is looking directly forward. Do not allow the lower lumbar region of your back to tilt out or tuck under. Check that you are not sucking in your tummy unnecessarily and avoid opening your ribcage outward. Imagine that you are wearing a jacket, and as you zip up the jacket, feel each abdominal muscle knit together to protect your back. This is the ideal positioning to have when seated. Try maintaining this posture for a few minutes a day and gradually add time.

Plank Hold

Holding in the plank position (the starting position for a push-up) develops the muscles needed to maintain good posture, and if your form is correct, your body is aligned. First go to your hands and knees. Widen your fingers on the floor (think *jazz hands*) and make sure your shoulders are in line with your wrists, and that they remain pressed away from your ears as you straighten the knees to lift the body into the plank hold. Next, check that the head and neck are aligned and the torso is straight (in other words, make sure your hips are not drooping downward or lifting upward above your shoulders). Feel the power of this position. To take some of the pressure off the wrists, focus on gripping the floor with your fingertips and imagine that you are pushing against the floor. If your wrists continue to be a bother, move onto your forearms. Good form is critical, so as soon as you feel your form slipping, stop and rest.

Assignment: Walk the Walk

One goal with your performance training is to gain a critical eye regarding how the body moves in space. Let's tune into how bodies move naturally. Take notes in your journal on the following:

- Observe someone (who is unaware that you're watching them) walk. How does their body move when they execute a habitual task like walking? Describe their walk with as much detail as you can;

- What does their walk "say" about them? In other words, do you find that their walk conveys any sort of meaning? Does the energy with which they walk express an emotion or attitude?;
- Consider your own walk. What do you hope to project when you walk? How can something as simple as walking be a way of expressing yourself? Are there ways in which you can improve your posture when walking?

Assignment: Walk the Walk Part II – Examples of Characters Walking

There are some amazing examples on screen of characters walking. Watch scenes from *Pride and Prejudice* ("You have bewitched me body and soul."), *Midnight Cowboy* ("I'm walking here."), *Joker* (stairs dance / escape from cops), Beyoncé's music video "Hold Up" from her visual album *Lemonade*, and *Dog Day Afternoon* (robbing the bank) – (caution: viewer discretion advised; videos feature images of violence and adult language). All videos can be viewed on YouTube (see Bibliography for links). Take note of the unique qualities in the characters' movement. Note the energy (force), timing, and space they inhabit as they move. What does their movement non-verbally communicate to you? Then, discuss your observations with your peers in your next performance training class.

Turnout

Let's move on to another dance fundamental by exploring *turnout*. Turnout describes the rotation of the legs outward from the hips. Sounds simple enough, doesn't it? But all too often performers *force* turnout, which may cause physical issues down the road. Dr. William G. Hamilton says, "Turnout has to come from the hip and not from the foot. If it doesn't, then the knee is caught in between. The knee is supposed to work as a hinge joint, meaning it bends, but doesn't rotate" (quoted in Mattingly, 2003). Turnout is a prominent feature in ballet and period acting styles, but it doesn't have to cause undue pain. By understanding the importance of the outward rotation from the hips, effective turnout can be explored safely.

Like just about everything else in performance training, turnout requires a combination of strength, flexibility, and alignment. Tap into your turnout by trying the following exercises:

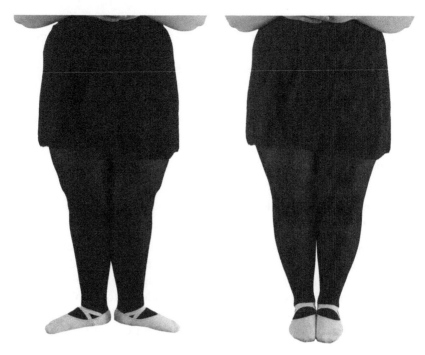

Figure 3.2 (L to R): Turnout body placement (ballet 1st position), parallel body placement

Clam for Rotators

Lie on your side with knees bent. Keep your feet touching while opening and closing your knees. For added resistance, *Dance Magazine* recommends tying a Thera-band above the knees (Grossman, 2019). *Pointe Magazine* offers an extra tip, suggesting the entire exercise be executed with your back and feet pressed against a wall (Larsen, 2020).

Squats for Inner Thighs and Glutes

We all know the standard squat, but this gem from Women's Health aims to fire up the inner thighs and glutes, important muscles in stabilizing your turnout (Thomason, 2019). Stand parallel, then rotate into an easy turnout. Lift heels off the floor for your starting position and keep them up while squatting.

To develop flexibility for turnout, try the following exercises:

Tendu Parallel / Turnout

Stand with your feet parallel, about shoulder width apart. Point one foot forward with a straight leg in parallel (knee faces ceiling), and then rotate

Figure 3.3 Clam for Rotators

Figure 3.4 Mason Van Horn moving into squat position with heels lifted

the pointed foot from the hip to turnout (knee should face outward once in turnout), then return leg to the parallel position (knee faces ceiling again), and finally return leg to the parallel starting position. Repeat to the side by pointing the same foot to the side with a straight leg in the parallel position (knee faces forward), and then rotate the pointed foot from the hip to turnout (knee should face ceiling once in turnout), then return it to the parallel position (knee faces forward again), and finally return leg to the parallel starting position. Next, repeat to the back by pointing the same foot to the back with a straight leg in parallel (knee faces floor), and then rotate the pointed foot from the hip to a turnout (knee should face outward once in turnout), then return it to the parallel position (knee faces floor again), and finally return leg to the parallel starting position. Then move into turnout by placing yourself in ballet first position (heels touching with toes facing out). Point forward (tendu) in turnout, then rotate from the hips to parallel, then return to turnout, and finally close ballet first position. Repeat to the side and to the back. Then, repeat the entire exercise on the other side.

When working through this exercise, imagine that the front of your pelvis has two bright lights (imagine headlights on a car) with rays that need to shine forward throughout every movement.

Butterfly

While lying on your back, draw your knees toward the ceiling, keeping the soles of your feet on the floor. Then, let the knees fall open and out gently,

Figure 3.5 Tatum Gross performing a tendu to the back while in turnout

so that the soles of the feet touch. Imagine your legs as the wings of a butterfly. You may find that your lower back lifts from the floor; if this occurs, adjust so that your entire back is touching the floor. This may cause your knees to lift off the floor, which is not a problem. However, if this is position feels too intense, move the feet further down and away from your pelvic floor. If you want more intensity in the stretch, move the feet closer to your pelvic floor.

Tummy Butterfly

Roll over onto your stomach and repeat the exercise. In this position, you might find your feet lift off the floor. Again, feel free to move and adjust the intensity as needed.

Pigeon

Begin on your hands and knees (also known as *table top position* in yoga). Move your right knee forward and place it on the floor directly in front of your right hip. In this position, the right calf faces inward on the floor toward the center of your body. It is most likely that the placement of your right calf will be diagonal to the pelvis with your right heel in front of your left hip. Straighten the left leg and place it directly behind you with the left heel facing the ceiling. For balance, place hands on the floor on either side of the hips, aim to square the hips as the upper body lengthens, and inhale. As you exhale, walk your hands forward and bend over your right leg, allowing your torso to rest on top of your right leg. You may find yourself wanting to lean to the right or left, but you'll likely feel more of a stretch if you center yourself. Hold this position and then repeat on the left side.

Glute Stretch

Sit on the floor with legs bending and stacking right over left. Check that your body is aligned, noticing your sits bones' connection to the floor. Flex your right foot as the right ankle sits on (or just above) the left knee. There may be space between your right knee and left ankle. If so, you may wish to place a blanket, pillow, or yoga block in this open space. It is important that both knees are bending, not twisting or rotating in any way. Maintaining a flat back, hinge at the waist and bend forward, walking your hands forward on the floor. Breathe into your lower back. Then, release your alignment and allow your upper body to rest over your legs. Repeat the exercise on the left.

Figure 3.6 Pigeon

Straddle

While sat in straddle and maintaining a flat back, hinge at the waist and bend over. Rather than allowing the knees to drop forward, attempt to rotate from the hips, so that the knees stay facing the ceiling. After 30 seconds in this position, release the flat back, allowing your upper body to curve. Hold for an additional 30 seconds.

Psoas Lunge

Kneel on the floor, then draw the right leg forward from the hips and place the sole of the right foot on the floor. You may place a towel under the left knee for support if uncomfortable. Slowly step the right foot out and lunge forward, making sure the right knee does not extend past the right toes. Place hands on hips and maintain alignment. Feel the stretch on the left front of your pelvis (psoas). Repeat on the left side.

At the end of the day, your goal of achieving a 180-degree turnout may not be reached simply because of your body's genetic skeletal makeup. Please do not seek it out. It is completely unnecessary. Instead focus on the words of famed ballet dancer Mikhail Baryshnikov:

> "My jump is not high enough, my twists are not perfect, I can't place my leg behind my ear." Please don't do that. Sometimes there is such an obsession with the technique that this can kill your best impulses. Remember that communicating with a form of art means being vulnerable, being imperfect. And most of the time this is much more interesting. Believe me.
>
> (Baryshnikov, 2019)

The Turnout Aesthetic

Unlike many dance forms that originate among "common people" and work their way up to "high society," ballet originated among the aristocracy and over time, worked its way to the masses. Born in Italy, ballet flourished in France under the reign of King Louis XIV, gained huge momentum in Russia, and today ballet classes are offered around the world. It was King Louis XIV's dance instructor, Pierre Beauchamps, who was instrumental in solidifying turnout as a major component of the ballet aesthetic. Turnout was utilized so that dancers could move side to side with greater ease and speed; it also enabled performers to showcase the dance in a way that gave the audience the best possible view. Most performances were presented on a proscenium stage, and it was essential that the nobles and most importantly, the King (when he wasn't on stage performing himself) could easily see the fancy footwork.

As was the case in Louis XIV's time and still holds true today, the theatrical space makes a difference in the performer's body positioning; there are lots of little adjustments a performer needs to make depending upon where they are performing in relation to their audience. Take a look the theatre configurations in Figure 3.7, and imagine how your body positioning might differ on these stages in order to give the audience the best view.

Turnout & Gesture

Did you know that many Delsarte gestures and poses often studied in acting styles classes also require some degree of turnout? Francois Delsarte (1811–1871), a French singer and orator, developed a system of gestures to represent human emotion.

In his book *Gestures and Attitudes*, Edward B. Warman says, "The Delsarte system is founded on the great principle of the law of correspondence; that is, every expression of the face, every gesture, every posture of the body corresponds to, or is but the outward expression of, an inner emotion

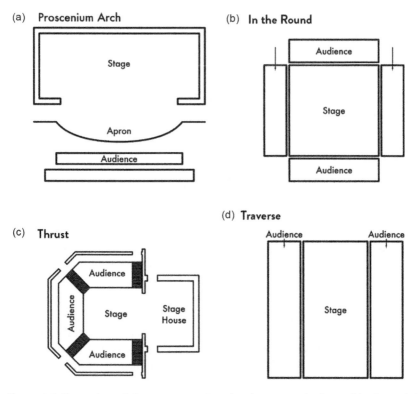

Figure 3.7 Examples of theatre stages Imagine how your body positioning might differ on these stages in order to give the audience the best view.

Images created by Jonathon Taylor

or condition of the mind, be it one of beauty or one of ugliness" (1892, p.23). Delsarte's approach has been utilized in both the acting and dance worlds, and while many now find his work superficial and mechanical, it is actually rooted in the quest for truthfulness through bodily expression. Delsarte said,

> Gesture is more than speech. It is not what we say that persuades, but the manner of saying it. Speech is inferior to gesture because it corresponds to the phenomena of mind. Gesture is the agent of the heart, the persuasive agent. That which demands a volume is uttered by a single gesture.
>
> (quoted in Shawn, 1974, p.25)

Turnout helps to convey gesture, is an effective body position particularly when acting in a period play, and is an essential component of dance. It can enhance stage presence more broadly and enrich a character's physicality.

Figure 3.8 Examples of Delsarte gestures

Plié

Now that you have analyzed alignment with turnout, let's focus our attention on *plié*, a movement that when precisely executed provides the framework for jumps, turns, and intricate footwork and helps the performer to feel

Figure 3.9 Maggie Johnson and I exploring the power of gesture for her performance
Photo credit: ETSU Photographic Services

grounded. Plié describes the motion of bending the knees while in turnout
with the body in alignment.

The value of plié in dance, theatre movement, and physical theatre
cannot be underestimated, and instructors sometimes describe the movement in a way that is often misinterpreted by their students. You may
have heard the advice to "tuck your pelvis" when performing plié in
turnout. This instruction is given to help performers achieve alignment,
avoiding anterior pelvic tilt. But this recommendation can lead students
to *posterior pelvic tilt*, where the tailbone is tucked under in an attempt
to reduce the lower lumbar curvature of the spine. This over-correction
should be avoided.

Dancer/choreographer and movement analyst Rusty Curcio says,

> That's the old school ballet training, tucking the pelvis under, when they
> didn't realize you had the six deep lateral outward rotators, which connect
> to the ischial tuberosities, the femur and the sacrum. So, they were using
> the quadriceps and the gluteus to do the turnout… A lot of it is based off
> the fact that the Russians worked on a raked stage, so not on a level playing
> field… On top of that, they told you to bring the tip of the ribcage as close
> to these bones [pubic symphysis] as possible, but it makes people go down

and so you get this tucking of the pelvis... You've actually got to release the pelvis slightly back, and then go in and up. Then you're totally free. The minute you tuck under, your legs become bound, which then will cause a binding in the hip socket restricting leg mobility and the ability to shift your weight and move through space.

(Curcio, 2009)

Rather than "tucking," instead focus on "lengthening." You are looking to achieve a *neutral spine*, rather than an anterior or posterior pelvic tilt. Again, imagine the string at the top of your head that runs through the center of your body and out through your pelvic floor. The pelvic floor string is being pulled downward, while the head string is being pulled upward.

It takes time and patience to fully grasp the many connections between alignment, turnout, and plié, but once these connections are made, turns, leaps, footwork, stylized theatre movement, and stage combat will improve dramatically. The action of plié also teaches the importance of connecting to the ground below before taking flight. Stability, strength, and a supported foundation are all achieved through the repetition of plié. Stage presence occurs when a performer understands their relationship to the space, particularly to the earth on which they stand; the practice of plié helps to eliminate needless wandering on stage, unnecessary pacing back and forth, and the dreaded sense of rootlessness. Plié is also the set up for power moves and can be developed through the following exercise:

Plié in Parallel, Plié in Turnout[1]

With hands on hips (or lightly touching a barre or chair if additional support is needed), shoulders relaxed downward, body aligned and feet positioned in parallel (shoulder width distance apart), slowly demi-plié (small bend in the knees), then lift heels from the floor with knees still bent, then straighten the knees, and finally lower heels back to the floor. Repeat the sequence an additional three times.

Then reverse the movement (lift the heels from the floor with legs straight, then demi-plié with heels still lifted from the floor, then lower the heels to floor, then straighten legs). Repeat the sequence an additional three times.

Now position the feet into ballet first position and repeat the entire exercise four times each from this turnout position.

In all, you will execute the exercise eight times in parallel, eight times in ballet first, for a grand total of sixteen methodic repetitions. To help maintain balance, think of your connection to the earth below through the feet.

Remember to activate your core, seeking alignment throughout the exercise. Remember too to rotate from the hips when in turnout.

Point

Pointing isn't just for your index finger! Pointing, as it applies to dancing feet, describes the action of arching the foot and activating the toes. So often I see performers overlook how much energy can be radiated from every part of their body. It hurts to see a performance stuck inside the head of the performer. Often, the biggest disconnect I see occurs in the feet. Practice pointing your feet to activate your energy. Try these exercises to awaken and stimulate all the wonderful areas of the foot:

Alphabet Foot

With hands on hips and body aligned, lift your foot four to six inches from the floor. Note how by simply lifting a foot, the core begins to engage and how proper body alignment is needed to maintain balance. Next, "draw" the alphabet with the raised foot on an imagined piece of paper by moving only the foot about in the air. Make these simple movements as precise as possible so that anyone watching would have no doubt as to the letter you were "drawing." Repeat the exercise with the other foot.

Foot Wake-Up Call

With hands on hips, body aligned, and feet positioned in parallel (shoulder width distance apart), lift one heel from the ground, so that only the ball of the foot remains on the floor. Then continue lifting the heel, so that the ball of the foot lifts from the floor and toes roll over with only the front (anterior) part of the toe remaining on the floor. Reverse the process. Now, repeat the exercise with the other foot and continue to alternate feet for a total of four repetitions (heel up, then down is one repetition; two repetitions per foot). Next, position the feet into ballet first position and repeat the exercise for a total of four repetitions (two repetitions per foot). In all, you will execute the exercise four times in parallel, four times in ballet first position, for a grand total of eight slow and methodic repetitions.

Tennis Ball

Place a tennis ball on the floor and roll your foot over it, enjoying the sensations you feel in the arch of your foot. Repeat with the other foot.

Balance & Coordination

Balance refers to physical equilibrium while coordination concerns the body moving in harmony.

It may feel like many people are simply born with balance and coordination, and while there may be a grain of truth to the idea that some folks appear especially gifted in this area, it's also important to know that balance and coordination can be developed over time. Patience is most certainly a virtue and before you know it, movement sequences become easier to memorize, and balancing feels less turbulent when performing.

That said, there are days that despite our best efforts, balance and coordination seem to elude us. The body's equilibrium can shift from one day to the next depending on numerous factors. Or balance can be amazing on one leg, and on the next day, the opposite leg has better balance. Or the connection between mind and body seems to short-circuit, and our ability to coordinate movements does not come as easily as the day before. It's important that we have an "oh well" mentality on these days. Nothing productive can come from berating yourself for an inexplicable blip in your training. I've seen students get really annoyed with themselves when they lose balance and coordination and the tension that results only makes it harder for them to recover. If you can laugh it off, you'll find balance and coordination once again (it may not be in that session, but it will be back tomorrow or the next day). Let's explore balance by trying out the following exercise geared toward steadily increasing the body's stability and harmony:

Ballet Balance Sequence

Throughout this exercise, you will be asked to balance; to do so, slowly remove one hand and then the other from the barre (or the back of a sturdy chair), engage your muscles, and imagine a sense of equilibrium in your balancing body.

To begin, gently place fingertips on the barre (or chair) with feet in ballet first position and check that your body is in alignment.

Next, *Elevé* (from straight legs, shift onto the balls of the feet, raising heels from the floor). See how long you can balance in this position.

Place your hands back onto the barre (or chair), lift one foot and place it behind the standing foot at the ankle in a *coupé* position. Balance. Repeat on the other foot.

Next, lower your heels returning to ballet first position and then straighten one leg behind you in an *arabesque* position. *Relevé* (plié and straighten while shifting onto the ball of the foot of the standing leg) and balance. Repeat the movement on the other leg.

Finally move into a *passé* position (bending one leg and placing it just in front at the knee of the standing leg then rotating the leg outward to achieve turnout). *Relevé* and balance. Repeat the movement on the other leg.

Figure 3.10 (Top to Bottom): *Elevé, Coupé, Arabesque, Passé*

Next, consider the following tips to help develop coordination:

1   **Find the flow.**
    The first step in building coordination is to understand weight shifting (moving from one leg to the other) and its connection to footwork

sequences. Frequently there is a flow to a movement sequence, so over time you can develop a feel for the weight shifts from one movement to the next; it can become almost intuitive. Often, I see students overthinking footwork when it is introduced, even when the weight shifting in the choreography is almost as natural as the weight shifting that occurs when walking. When a student tries to break down every weight shift into the tiniest detail, they overburden themselves at the onset. When steps are first introduced, observe, imitate, and "fake it 'til you make it," as the saying goes. Deep analysis of the movement sequence is most definitely needed at a later stage, but at the earliest stage of learning, try not to overthink it. Instead, focus on the connections of the movements when there is a flow to the weight shifting. And when the weight shifting becomes erratic, note any repetitions or trends in the movement. You'd be surprised at what your body can pick up even before the brain has time to process it all. Trust your body. It knows how to move, and it wants to move.

2   **Know where to look.**
When learning a movement phrase, avoid looking down at your own feet. Be sure to observe the instructor's demonstration by looking at them through the mirror and by looking at the actual person, while you stand at an angle behind them. When introducing new movement, I often see students only looking directly at me, which means they are focusing mostly on the back view. If they can also periodically shift their gaze to the mirror, they will see how the steps look from the front. This helps to take in the movement from every available angle.

When learning movement, students need to use their peripheral vision. Dances will have different facings and when performing those movements, students will not have the convenience of a mirror to see themselves and their fellow dancers, since most dance studios only have one wall of mirrors. It is also often the case that in audition situations, the choreographer curtains off any mirrors when it's time to perform. Peripheral vision will help you to maintain synchrony with your fellow performers.

Working with your peripheral vision is less about sneaking a peak at your peers while you dance and more about developing an awareness of everything happening around you. I mentioned the visualization of a third eye in the center of your forehead a bit earlier when describing posture and alignment. This visualization comes into play in a major way when learning a movement sequence. Not only do you want to have a third eye that looks into the mirror with a non-judgmental focus, you also want to imagine eyes in the back of your head to help with spatial awareness, tuning into the energy of the other dancers and the space around you.

You will need to become less reliant on the mirror once you've learned the material. When students develop a habit of becoming locked into looking at themselves in the mirror, they lose important characteristics of the dance, such as variances in head placement and movement of visual focus. Knowing where to look is of vital importance to understanding a dance or movement phrase, and you'll want to use the mirror less the more you grow in your confidence with the movement.

3   **Think of yourself as ambidextrous.**
Focus less about whether movement is on your "good" side or "bad" side. So maybe your turns are generally better on your right or you have more flexibility on your left. But if you are thinking about your weaknesses while learning the material, you're creating roadblocks that will slow down learning. It will be easier for you to learn the material if you ignore whether movement is on your "good" side or "bad" side and choose to see the movements in relation to one another and the space around you. Note whether the next movement is on the same side of your body as the movement before or whether it is on the opposite side. Or perhaps the next movement crosses your body center. Or perhaps the next movement occurs at the top or bottom half of your body. This helps to process the movement quickly. You can perform movement that has you inverted at interesting diagonals with limbs that are wrapped around one another if you focus less on "right" and "left" or "good" side and "bad" side. You are strong and flexible; you are ambidextrous.

4   **Ask questions.**
You could and should ask questions, *but* take a deep breath and let the instructor demonstrate the sequence before shooting your hand in the air. Often the instructor needs to demonstrate the movement sequence in full as a review for themselves and for you to simply see the flow of the combination and to get a sense of where it begins and ends. Then, they will break down and teach the combination in sections. I have started a movement sequence and two steps in, a student starts shaking their head (with an "I don't get it" air), raising their hand before I've finished the demonstration. That tells me they have given up before we've even begun. They have literally told themselves "No, I can't do it," building a wall of negativity that makes it harder for them to learn. If that sounds familiar to you, please start training yourself now to switch the thought process to, "That looks challenging, and I am up for the challenge." The power of positive thinking really will help you learn the combination. Now, if after the combination has been broken down into smaller parts and you have questions about it, by all means, fire away.

5   **Be patient.**
And finally, be patient with yourself. If coordinated movement is a challenge for you, know that it will come through time and repetition. You must rehearse over and over until it becomes second nature. And if you do it enough, it *will* become second nature. Just keep at it! As the saying goes, "Don't practice until you get it right. Practice until you can't get it wrong."

Journal Writing Prompt: Mirror, Mirror on the Wall

I am keenly aware of how frightening it is for a performer who has little formal dance training to enter a dance studio with students who've had years of dance training. That is a really intimidating room to enter. The added challenge is that you are working in front of a mirror and can see what everyone else is doing. It is difficult not to constantly compare yourself to others in the room, which is exactly what you must avoid. You've got to focus on yourself and the progress that you're making day after day, noting the little successes which will in time lead to big improvements. If you can focus on gauging your own progress, you will see the progress. Again, I know that it is really hard not to compare yourself to others, and it may feel narcissistic to look in the mirror as much as you're being asked, but when learning new movement, that's just doing your job.

Take some time now to honor what your body can do. For the next 60 seconds, look at yourself in the mirror while you improvise any movement that you feel. Then, reflect in your journal on what you noticed about your body as it moved. What is unique about your body? What are you thankful for about your body? Take the time to celebrate what your body can do.

Port de Bras & Épaulement

Port de bras and épaulement are the icing on the cake of creating stage presence. Port de bras describes movement and positioning of the arms. Port de bras solves the "I don't know what to do with my hands" crisis that affects many actors and gives a polished look to the dancer's choreography. The space that is created with port de bras helps to complete the performer's line, and the energy from arm placement radiates far beyond that of the actual performer.

Épaulement is movement of the shoulders by rotating the upper body from the waist. This positioning of the shoulders, neck, and head is critical for presenting the best view of the performer and helps to non-verbally communicate character emotions and motivations. Developing épaulement can be a way of learning how to "cheat out," as they say in the theatre world. Understanding your body placement in relation to the audience is a skill that can be cultivated, and your director (and the audience) will love you for it.

These simple port de bras and épaulement exercises unlock a beautiful energy for performers. There are countless variations for port de bras and épaulement, and I hope you will continue to explore arm placement and shouldering in class and in rehearsal. Give the following a try and observe what it does for you:

Port de Bras: Arm Sequence

Raise both arms over your head, even lifting your shoulders up towards your ears. Then gently lower your shoulders.

Bend at the elbows, lowering the arms until your elbows are parallel to your shoulders with forearms parallel in front of your face.

Then move your elbows out to the sides away from your body (the palms of your hands are now facing your chest area).

Next, take the forearms out and away from your body.

Then, draw the elbows in towards your sides with palms facing upwards. Next, rotate the forearms so the palms face the floor, and begin to lower the arms with wrists in extension.

Isolating each movement as best you can, first release wrists, then hands, and finally fingertips until they rest at your sides.

Épaulement: Shouldering Sequence

Stand facing directly in front of a full-length mirror with parallel feet (shoulder width apart). Take about ten seconds to look at yourself in this position. Next, move your feet so that your entire body is at an angle to the mirror (about a 45-degree angle). Keeping your feet and hips at the 45-degree angle from the mirror, rotate your upper body and shoulders to face the mirror again (your tummy button should still face the diagonal while your shoulders now run parallel to the mirror). You should feel your core engage as you twist your upper body to face the mirror. Next relax your shoulders down. Finally, gently turnout the leg closest to the mirror (to ballet third position and/or closed bevel). Look at yourself in this position for 30 seconds. Then, complete the next writing prompt in your journal.

Figure 3.11 Arm Sequence (Top to Bottom): Tyler Mitchell with arms raised (shoulders lowered), arms parallel, elbows out, forearms out, elbows inward, pressing down, body in alignment. Remember to engage your core throughout the exercise!

Figure 3.12 (L to R): Ballet third position, open bevel, closed bevel

---

Journal Writing Prompt: Observations of Épaulement

Jenifer Ringer, former New York City Ballet principal dancer says, "We're creating art, and it should be beautiful and expressive. So much of that comes from épaulement" (quoted in Foster, 2019). What did you notice about your body's lines and proportions when you tried the épaulement exercise? What energy were you radiating? Give examples of characters or archetypes you could see carrying themselves in this way. Now try a completely different way of holding your shoulders. Look at yourself for 30 seconds in this position. What characters or archetypes could you see posturing in this way?

Needing a bit of inspiration? Check out the following journal writing example from ETSU student Hunter Thomas:

> When starting off in first position parallel, I felt very open. This position typically reminds me of actor's neutral because of the possibility of what can be created from this starting point. When adding

on each step, it felt as if a new section of my body was suddenly saying something. When turning 45 degrees, I went from open to the audience to involved in my own world. When turning my upper body back to the front, it felt more as if I was presenting to them than receiving whatever they would give me. As I rolled my shoulders back, the lines of my arms began sending energy down into the floor and my chest became a strong foundation for a propulsion of energy to stabilize itself. As I took the final step of beveling my foot, I felt something unlock within me, as if energy was finally free to stream out like tendrils in all directions due to the correct mixture of body angularity and mental rootedness to the ground. I noticed that the crisp focus of a bird had overtaken my face, and I felt comparable to an angel about to take flight. It was a powerful pose. I then tried bringing my shoulders in and forward, closing them off in comparison to the previous direction. I noticed that the wing-like motivation of my arms suddenly became something more tired, as if there was nothing I could do, but to let them rest down the length of my body. The purpose of my beveled foot went from preparing for take-off to testing the waters. The turnout of my upper body was less concerned about presenting to the audience and had returned to the self-enveloped world it had discovered way back at the first step. My face recognized this change and shifted into something softer. This pose was less about angled might and more about curved grace. I had transformed from the mighty eagle to an innocent deer... from Jean Val Jean to Cosette. It was an intriguing change, still maintaining so much presence while just changing the color and intensity at which the energy is presented.

In Summary

If you have ever seen a performer enter a space with ease and focus, a strong connection to the earth while also radiating energy far beyond their own physical being and thought, "I want to embody that kind of confidence," then get into a ballet class. Ballet training isn't just about becoming a prima ballerina or a master performer of period acting styles. Ballet speaks to every dancer and actor's needs; it helps performers understand the elements of bearing, comportment, dignity, charisma, authority, and poise on stage. I am sure there are other ways of unlocking physical presence, but in my experience, ballet does the job quickly and effectively. All this ballet stuff works wonders for the performer!

Adding ballet fundamentals to your training will help you achieve a stronger mind/body connection. Through ritual-like repetition of the exercises described in this chapter, you can achieve a sense of ease and focus. When your body is at ease and your mind focused, you are both grounded and transcended, and audiences can't help but be drawn in by that presence.

Next, we explore what is truly needed to perform with presence… *acting*.

Note

1 I practiced this plié sequence under the leadership of *Mountain Movers* artistic director Judy Woodruff, and again later with her successor Jen Kintner.

Bibliography

Accelerated Motion. (n.d.). *"Natural" Movement and the Delsarte System of Bodily Expression*. https://acceleratedmotion.org/dance-history/modern-motion/natural-movement-and-the-delsarte-system-of-bodily-expression/

Baryshnikov, M. (2019). "Commencement Speech." University of Southern California's Glorya Kaufman School of Dance. Los Angeles, CA, 10 May.

Beyoncé (2016). "Beyoncé – Hold Up" [Video]. *YouTube*, uploaded by Beyoncé, 4 September. www.youtube.com/watch?v=PeonBmeFR8o

Curcio, R. (2009). Interview with Joan Melton, "Relating Voice and Dance Techniques." New York City.

"Dog Day Afternoon (1/10) Movie Clip – Robbing the Bank (1975) HD." (2012). [Video]. *YouTube*, uploaded by Movieclips, 7 October. www.youtube.com/watch?v=nvdBfpA8r4o

Foster, H. (2019). "Why épaulement is so important-and how to develop it." *Dance Spirit*, 26 November. www.dancespirit.com/epaulment-in-ballet-2546445578.html

Grossman, G. (2019). "Get more turnout." *Dance Magazine*, 14 November. www.dancemagazine.com/get-more-turnout-2307031810.html

Larsen, G. (2020). "3. Hip abduction with external rotation." *Pointe*, 27 April. www.pointemagazine.com/turnout-exercises-2624948366.html?rebelltitem=5#rebelltitem5

Marsh, S. (2016). "Why 'Instagram butt' is actually a sign of poor posture." *Coach*, 15 November. https://coach.nine.com.au/2016/11/15/16/08/why-instagram-butt-is-actually-anterior-pelvic-tilt

Mattingly, K. (2003). "Baryshnikov goes down." *The Village Voice*, 30 September. www.villagevoice.com/2003/09/30/baryshnikov-goes-down/

McClure, N. (2015). "Exercise and postural distortions." *Nourish Northwest*, 26 August. nourishnorthwest.com/blog/exercise-and-postural-distortions/

Melton, J. (2011). Interview with Rusty Curcio. *Voiceprint 40*. Melbourne: Australian Voice Association.

Melton, J. (n.d.) *Tucking the Pelvis: Actual and Perceived Outcomes*. www.joanmelton.com/tucking-pelvis-actual-and-perceived-outcomes-0

"Midnight Cowboy (2/11) Movie Clip – I'm Walkin' Here (1969) HD." (2014). [Video]. *YouTube*, uploaded by Movie Clips, 6 February. www.youtube.com/watch?v=_Z-tCU-sULA

National Council on Strength and Fitness. (n.d.). *Understanding Common Postural Deviations*. www.ncsf.org/enew/articles/articles-understanding-common-postural-distortions.aspx

Porte, A. (2012). *François Delsarte: Une Anthologie*. Ressouvenances.

Shawn, T. (1974). *Every Little Movement: A Book about François Delsarte; The Man and His Philosophy...* Dance Horizons.

"Stairs Dance | Joker [UltraHD, HDR]." (2019). [Video]. *YouTube*, uploaded by L0ky86, 29 December. www.youtube.com/watch?v=JeyVU4nMWCg

Thomason, K. (2019). "A celebrity fitness trainer shares her secrets for toning your inner thighs." *Women's Health*, 6 March. www.womenshealthmag.com/fitness/g25996674/inner-thigh-exercise/

Warman, E.B. (1892). *Gestures and Attitudes: An Exposition of the Delsarte Philosophy of Expression, Practical and Theoretical*. Lee and Shepard.

"You Have Bewitched Me – Pride & Prejudice (10/10) Movie Clip (2005) HD."(2011). [Video]. *YouTube*, uploaded by Movie Clips, 6 June. www.youtube.com/watch?v=bFsgLhx9dxg

4 Discovering Character Motivation & Intention through Acting Technique & Physical Theatre

When an artist commits to performing at fullest expression with body and mind, inspired work abounds. The problem is that finding and maintaining deep physical and emotional connections in performance is exhausting work. There are many time-tested acting techniques that have proven to be successful aids for the performer seeking to unearth motivation, intention, and specificity. However, the techniques themselves can overburden the performer, leading them to become "in their head"[1] when performing. That's where performance opportunities and training in physical theatre can really come in handy.

Physical theatre is "a type of performance where physical movement is the primary method of storytelling; as opposed to, say, text in a play or music and lyrics in an opera. Also, it may incorporate other techniques such as mime, gesture, and modern dance to create performance pieces" (Sparrow, 2021). Exploring physical theatre encourages a sense of playfulness in performance and provides balance to the performer-in-training's curriculum. Coursework in physical theatre also offers the tools for performers to avoid the trap of becoming encumbered by their technique. And finally, the physical theatre comedy exercises described in this chapter aim to motivate performers-in-training to *fully* commit to their character's given circumstances and to embrace the *joy* inherent in performance. Because lest we forget, *performing is FUN!*

Now, this is not at all to say to that dramatic analysis and the study of acting techniques should be abandoned. In fact, you will receive an introduction to some of the most famous acting approaches in the pages that follow. Developing skill as a performer requires an exploration of the broad spectrum of ways that have proven beneficial aids to achieving truthfulness in performance. Some techniques and exercises in this chapter may work for you, while others may not. Most likely, you will find a combination of these and other approaches helpful; and you can tailor them to suit your own needs. There is no one way of becoming a brilliant performer, so be open to trying a variety of methods, and eventually you'll build your own approach to cultivating emotional depth in your performance.

DOI: 10.4324/9781003149699-5

Acting Techniques

Let's look at some of the most steadfast methodologies and their creators now:

Konstantin Stanislavski

Russian actor, director, producer, and founder of the Moscow Art Theatre Konstantin Stanislavski[2] developed an approach to acting known as the Stanislavski System.[3] In search of greater realism in performance, Stanislavski's technique included:

Emotional Memory

Emotional memory[4] is the practice of unearthing the actor's memory of a personal life experience to ignite emotion that could then be used for their character in a scene experiencing similar emotion. By drawing on real life memories from the *distant past*, the actor had time to come to terms with those emotions and could thereby explore and redirect them to their character to produce a truthful stage performance.

Method of Physical Actions

After observing that drawing from personal experience was causing actors undue emotional pain and suffering, Stanislavski moved away from emotional memory as a viable means of acting technique and pursued the *method of physical actions* to create a more productive ideology. In simplest terms, the idea is that emotion can be stirred through physical actions. This work involved:

TEXT ANALYSIS

In *The Stanislavski System: Growth and Methodology*, Perviz Sawoski describes how Stanislavski developed the system with "points of reference for the actor, which are now generally known as units and objectives. A unit is a portion of a scene that contains one objective for an actor. In that sense, a unit changed every time a shift occurred in a scene. Every unit had an objective" (Sawoski, 2019, p. 6). Once a character's units and objectives in a scene are identified, the actor imagines active verbs that engage with their scene partner (e.g., to caress, to poke, to nudge, to seduce, to destroy) and ignites physical actions to correspond with their character's objectives.

In addition to the numerous *units* and *objectives* within a given scene, a character has a *super-objective*, one overriding desire they carry with them and pursue throughout the entirety of the play. The super-objective creates a *through line of action* lending unity to the character's intention. For example, Hamlet's super-objective is to avenge his father's death. While he has a variety of objectives depending on the scene, his super-objective is singular and unmistakably clear.

Stanislavski devised seven questions to ask during character analysis:

Who am I (the character)?
Where am I (the character)?
What time is it?
What do I (the character) want?
Why do I (the character) want it?
How will I (the character) get what I want?
What must I (the character) overcome to get what I want?

(New York Film Academy, 2015)

Stanislavski also encouraged exploration of *subtext* by analyzing what the characters *want* to say vs. what the characters *actually* say.

IMAGINATION

Stanislavski engaged the use of the actor's imagination through the *Magic "If"* concept. Actors ask themselves:

What would I do if I were in my character's situation?

This simple question helps the actor to place themselves in their character's shoes and explores ways they would genuinely react to the *given circumstances* of their character.

While there is much more of the Stanislavski System to be explored, the primary aim was for the actor to behave truthfully on stage. This goal is still at the heart of contemporary acting today, but the means by which to achieve this objective, while all essentially grounded in the Stanislavski System, have taken on many mutations initiated by a number of acting teachers. Influential teachers include:

Lee Strasberg

Strasberg was introduced to The Stanislavski System in New York City by two of Stanislavski's students, Richard Boleslavsky and Maria Ouspenskaya. While Stanislavski had moved on from the idea of emotional memory in favor of the method of physical actions, Stanislavski's earlier theories of emotional memory resonated with Strasberg and provided the groundwork for his developing The Method.[5] Strasberg coached actors to not only use memories of personal life experiences in their performance (emotional memory), but also encouraged actors to take on the character's experiences described in the play and "live" in them as much as possible so that their character's circumstances become as "real" and "natural" to the actor as their own life.

This ideology has caused controversy when actors completely immerse themselves into the life of the character, so much so that they do not break character. Some film actors dedicated to method acting remain in character all day on set, even between scenes. There are extreme examples of method actors staying in character for the entire duration of filming (even at home!). Method acting blurs the lines between the actor and the character. The actor is the character, and the character is the actor.

Not only does the actor bring their complete self to the role (personal life experiences and emotions), they also "live" in the world of the character, aiming to believe the experiences they are acting are real. While method acting may sound a bit extreme, Strasberg (a controversial individual himself) created a number of exercises worth exploring. Two exercises in particular are often utilized:

Backlife

With *backlife*, the actor creates a narrative for the character before the play begins and after the play ends based on the information provided in the text. The actor constructs what was happening to their character before the start of the play and creates a whole history based on the given circumstances the playwright or screenwriter provided in the script. The actor also creates a narrative for the character as if their "life" (or "death" as the case may be) continues after the story ends. This can help to provide motivation for the character and develop subtext.

Sense Memory

The basic premise is to use all five senses to explore personal experiences, which can then be applied to that of the character facing a similar situation. By focusing on the senses, the actor fully engages both physically and emotionally in the moment.

Stella Adler

Adler strongly disagreed with The Method and instead embraced the use of imagination. She believed the actor could envision the world of the character with "fictional inner justification" creating "specific imaginary circumstances" (Ates, 2018b). Having personally studied with Stanislavski, Adler promoted his later teaching of the method of physical actions and was vocal that Strasberg was outdated in teaching and misinterpreting Stanislavski's earlier work. The use of observation, action, and imagination were paramount to Adler's teachings.

Sanford Meisner

Meisner said, "Acting is living truthfully under imaginary circumstances" (quoted in Ates, 2019a). He believed a powerful way to achieve truthfulness was through repetition. An exercise featured in Meisner's technique is to repeat a single line of text over and over with a scene partner until both actors become attuned to one another. Over time, the line of text organically changes in meaning and emphasis, leading the actors to express authentic natural impulses (Ates, 2019a). The main objective for repetition exercises is for the actor to get "out of their head" and into the moment. By listening and responding to a scene partner, emphasis is moved away from indicating emotion and other acting habits, thereby alleviating many actors' tendency to overthink.

Michael Chekhov

A student of Stanislavski in Russia, Michael Chekhov (not to be confused with his playwright uncle, Anton Chekhov) created the technique psychological gesture (PG), which explores the connection of the body to the mind through physical action. The basic premise of PG is to create a full-bodied movement that expresses the character's inner nature. The act of performing the gesture ignites the physicality and emotional qualities of the character. During the performance of a scene, an actor can imagine their character's PG as and when they need to reconnect to the character.

The key to PG is to fully commit to movement. When finding a PG, an actor generally needs to repeat the gesture a few times before they feel it connecting their mind and body to the character. And they may have to try out a few PGs in order to find the right fit. Chekhov devised a series of "leading questions" to help actors find their PG. Lisa Dalton provides an example of how leading questions can facilitate the generation of a PG:

> For example: if you are playing a villain, you might begin by asking what it is your character desires. Power? Okay, how do you go about getting power? By dominating? Okay, what is a physical movement that dominates? Pressing down. Now, your first practice with PG: Start with your hands as high as possible and press them down against an imaginary resistance. Picture the character's opponents as you press down to the floor. Add to the press a quality: rage, frustration, sinister, conniving, fear, etc.

Try different qualities until you feel the quality and desire to dominate in every cell of your being.

(Dalton, n.d., p.1)

Like the super-objective, an actor can have an overall PG for their character. They can also have PGs to represent each beat or objective in a scene. So again, let's say you are playing Hamlet. Your super-objective is to avenge your father's death. Your "super" PG could be the physical action of stabbing. But throughout the play, you face indecisiveness and fear. So, your PG for the scene where you question life, asking "To be or not to be," could be to tensely pace left and right for a few seconds.

Uta Hagen

Hagen coached actors to investigate their character both internally (thoughts and emotions) and externally (the environment and outside influences). The actor could correlate their own experiences with persons, places, or things to their character to help jumpstart emotional truth, an exercise she termed transference.[6] For example, should the character be falling in love for the first time, the actor could imagine what it was like for them when they spoke to the person that was their first love. This is not to say that the actor should imagine they are speaking to their first love when they speak to their scene partner. Rather, prior to rehearsing, they could imagine that person when analyzing the script to spark memories of that feeling. Hagen espoused that transference should be done on an as-needed basis and should not be the foundation of an actor's process. She also felt strongly that the actor should only mine images of people, places, or things from their life about which they felt comfortable speaking publicly (Ates, 2019b). For Hagen, it was important that the actor not depend on rehashing past personal experiences on stage, but rather on using transference early during text analysis as a way to kick start emotion which would evolve into "being in the moment" with their scene partner and the world of the play (Wood, 2018).

But Wait… There's More!

Viola Spolin developed improvisational games with the aim of achieving a sense of presence and immediacy in the moment so that actors developed the ability to think "on their toes," to listen and respond to what is being presented to them in real time, and to open themselves to their scene partners. Mary Overlie established six viewpoints (time, space, shape, emotion, movement, story), which was expanded by Anne Bogart and Tina Landau to include nine physical viewpoints (spatial relationship, kinesthetic response, shape, gesture, repetition, architecture, tempo, duration, topography) and five vocal viewpoints (pitch, dynamic, acceleration/deceleration, silence, timbre). The viewpoints approach emphasizes voice and movement over internal psychological analysis (Bogart & Landau, 2005, pp. 5–6). William H. Macy and David Mamet created practical aesthetics, a technique strongly based in the teachings of Stanislavski that emphasizes action and "a literal understanding of a scene's driving events" (Wright, 2021).

The work of these and many other actors, teachers, coaches, and directors provides exciting options for the performer to explore. The way you approach a role will likely depend on the character, so it is helpful to have a broad-based knowledge of acting techniques. Unearthing your performance takes both artistry and craft, and discovering new ways to deepen your performance is essential. Just when you think you've got this whole performance thing figured out something happens to shake your confidence; the craft of acting will help keep you on even footing. Your performances will be alive and honest if you commit to the work of being a lifelong student of acting.

While acting techniques vary, the common goal is to achieve truthfulness in performance, so that the audience suspends disbelief and embraces the world of the play. Prior to the great movement toward realism, acting was presentational. Stanislavski brought about a seismic shift in acting, and performance has forever changed as a result. I know that I have at one time or another used all the techniques described above, and I tweak my acting process to suit my personal needs. As a performer, your needs will evolve; prepare in a way that frees you to embrace the world of your character. In both acting and dance, your performance requires you to *fully commit to the action taking place*.

Assignment: Classical Monologue

Now that you have explored some of the physical components of stage presence through ballet in Chapter 3 and read about acting techniques to aid in performing with intention and motivation in this chapter, prepare a one-minute to one-minute-thirty-second monologue from an earlier time period (it can be dramatic or comedic, and the material can be pulled from plays ranging from ancient Greece to the end of the 19th century). Remember to use some or all of the movement components discussed in Chapter 3 to help in creating the physical life of your character – *posture, alignment, turnout, plié, point, balance, coordination, port de bras,* and *épaulement*. Also, remember to try out at least one acting technique from the list described above when you are rehearsing your monologue. The combination of both acting and dance technique will ensure that your classical performance, while demonstrating some of the components of a presentational style physically through the elements of ballet, will also be rooted in truth and authenticity because you've done the important work of adding acting technique which requires you to analyze the motivation and intention of your character.

Dancers, this assignment is in your comfort zone physically because it asks you to focus on placement and ballet technique for your physical characterization. This assignment also stretches you to explore what is sometimes missing for the dancer wanting to perform with *presence*... that missing link comes to you from acting. For the dancer who wants to fully embody character, this exercise will challenge you to use your mind, body, and voice in performance. It will be tempting to disconnect emotionally and simply perform balletic movements that have no real attachment to the text. But the movements should be motivated and embodied; they should relate to the intention behind the text. If your physicality and movement reveal your character's desires, the audience will be drawn in to your performance.

Actors, this assignment asks you to focus on placement and ballet technique for your characterization, which may take you out of your comfort zone physically. Embrace the discomfort and explore how these body positions can inform the development of your character. This assignment also asks you to explore that which is in your wheelhouse: acting. Don't rely solely on the acting technique you've used in the past and stretch yourself to try a new approach from the list above. Challenge yourself to create a fully realized character in mind, body, and voice.

Perform the monologue for your peers.

Assignment: Character Creative Writing

Next, choose a character that you'd really love to perform, and describe the character's life up to the point when the audience meets them in the show, based on the information provided in the text or dance. Give details about who they are and what brought them to the first moment they appear on stage. Then describe what happens to them after the play or dance ends. If they die in the story, describe their final thoughts and whether and where they might be in the afterlife. Or you could write their obituary, and describe their funeral. Write in the first person. Get creative and have fun with it. But remember, the story is your source material; if the work is a period drama or classical ballet, don't suddenly turn it into a sci-fi thriller.

> Be prepared to present an *oral interpretation*[7] of your writing to your classmates.
>
> Dancers, consider how the character creative writing assignment could help you develop an inner monologue when performing, thereby adding depth to your interpretation of a dance.
>
> Actors, consider how the character creative writing assignment could help you to enter your first scene with motivation and intention. It could also help you to interpret subtext, stimulate inner monologues, and uncover the super-objective of your character.

Creating an extraordinary performance requires the performer to inhabit their character in a singular way, which involves drawing themselves out of their physical norms. In addition to the acting techniques described above, you can become empowered to make bold, truthful, and unique choices through training in theatre movement and physical theatre.

Physical Theatre

Theatre movement training explores methodologies that can help to inspire clear and motivated movement when performing. Training includes:

> dance, tai chi, yoga, period styles, combat, physical comedy, acrobatics, mime, mask, clown, or any one of many body use or movement techniques or approaches: Lecoq, Decroux, Bartenieff, Laban, Michael Chekhov, Alexander, Feldenkrais, Meyerhold, Suzuki, Pilates, Williamson, Bioenergetics, Commedia dell'Arte, Improvisation, Martial Arts, Viewpoints, and RasaBoxes.
>
> (Association of Theatre Movement Educators, n.d.)

As you can see, theatre movement covers a broad range of approaches, and to gain a better appreciation for just how expressive the body can be, we are next going to focus our energies on creating and performing works of *physical theatre*.

Performing physical theatre often helps students feel a sense of freedom, which enables the mind and body to play and explore. The wonderful world of physical comedy encourages performers "to get out of their own way." When artists gain the courage and confidence needed to trust their impulses, it fosters their embodiment of singular characterizations on stage and screen. Suddenly, trying out ideas that were once "scary" or "embarrassing" becomes exciting because they are released from the grip of insecurity and judgment.

Figure 4.1 (L to R): Camielle Reed, myself, Hannah Chang, Everett Tarlton, Chelsea
    Kinser, and Josh Holley performing in my physical theatre production,
    bebe, at Know Theatre as part of the Cincinnati Fringe Festival.
Photo credit: Jeff Burkle

So, the aim is to explore the following exercises with courage and a
carefree frame of mind. This liberating course of assignments[8] will inspire you to listen to your instincts and to take action without nagging
doubt. To free yourself from the fear of being laughed at, get in on the
joke and embrace comedy. There's no time to edit yourself; just go for it
and have fun!

If you hit a creative roadblock at any time, remember these tips:

- **Play and explore.** You are working to facilitate a positive and improved
  relationship between mind and body so that you are free to play and
  explore.
- **Find the action.** You can communicate clearly, specifically, and effectively
  using physical (i.e., non-verbal) choices. To do so, focus on the *action* in
  the proposed scenario.
- **Channel your inner child.** Young children's imaginations are just amazing, and they don't seem to feel the need to censor themselves. Channel
  the free expressiveness of a child.

Your journey into physical theatre starts now:

Assignment: Spit-Take, Double-Take on Film

As you are taking a drink, see something wild off-camera... so wild that it makes you spit out your drink! Then see something in the other direction off-camera that is so wild, it makes you do a double-take.[9] You must create the setting in your imagination and be very detailed in what you are seeing in your mind's eye, so that the spit-take and double-take are motivated and believable. Visualizing an honest physical world is key to the success of this physical exercise!

Now, watch your film. Did you believe yourself? Show the film to a peer and encourage them to guess at what you were seeing off screen.

Needing a bit of inspiration? Check out the following videos on YouTube: "Double Take -- TDF's Theatre Dictionary -- Defining Theatre Terms", "The Ultimate Movie Spit-Take Mashup"; "Jeff Garlin Teaches Pete How to do the Perfect Spit Take" (caution: adult language); "James Finlayson – Master of the Comedy Double-Take" (links located in Bibliography).

Assignment: Rule of Three (aka The Comic Triplet)[10]

The rule of three in comedy can be described as:

- Set up, set up, punchline;
- Establish a norm, reinforce the norm, shatter the norm (surprise!);
- Introduce an environment or expectation, further establish the environment or expectation, then overthrow the environment or expectation.

John Kinde describes the following as categories of the comic triplet:

- Same Category/Same Category/Different Category;
- Expected Trait/Expected Trait/Unexpected Trait;
- Something Everyone Loves/Something Everyone Loves/Something Everyone Hates;
- Ordinary/Ordinary/Ridiculous;
- Extreme/Extreme/Ordinary;
- Rhyme/Rhyme/Rhyme.
  (quoted in Alina, 2014))

For example, I might choose to use the "ordinary, ordinary, ridiculous" category to write a simple joke: "I like talking long walks on the beach, horseback riding, and binge-watching serial killer documentaries." Grab your journal and try writing ten simple jokes yourself now. Don't overthink it. If something comes to mind, write it down.

Next, create a physical and vocal life different than your own and become a comedian. Again, don't overthink it; just try on a different way of moving and speaking. Perform your three favorite simple jokes aloud to a peer. Don't worry about being funny. In other words, don't "try" to be funny. Just do it.

Next, remove all language and try to communicate your jokes through sounds and movements only, not unlike a game of charades.

Finally, watch the following YouTube videos that demonstrate the rule of three: "Comedy Tools: The Rule of Three"; "Elements of Comedy Examples"; "How to Use the Rule of Three to Make People Laugh"; "The Trip with Steve Coogan. We Rise at Daybreak" (links located in Bibliography; caution: viewer discretion, adult language). The first three videos demonstrate very clear examples of the rule of three in comedy. The last is a video of comedic actors Steve Coogan and Rob Brydon exploring the concept of the rule of three and repetition through improvisation.

Assignment: Children's Theatre Storyteller

Perform a children's story or fable through movement, dance, and spoken word. The story may be original or known. Create at least three characters distinct from yourself in both body and voice. The story must be told in five minutes. Use the following checklist when developing the work:

- Demonstrate motivated movement;
- Create at least three distinct characters;
- Use movement associated with props, costumes, and set;
- Maintain a sense of ease and focus;
- Exhibit body and spatial awareness;
- Flow from one movement to another;
- Exhibit the emotional state(s) of the story physically;
- Maintain breath control;
- Use artistic expression through engaging movement choices.

Figure 4.2 These performers have certainly found their inner child! In this pre-show to ETSU's production of *Jack & the Beanstalk*, performers entertained audiences by bringing a lucky young volunteer onto the stage to help the performers play out randomly selected fairy tales… the catch was that they had to perform the fairy tale in under a minute. Needless to say, some serious theatre movement was involved!

Photo credit: ETSU Photographic Services

Assignment: Master of Physical Comedy

Watch the YouTube video, "Buster Keaton – The Art of the Gag" (link located in Bibliography). This video highlights the work of one of the greatest physical comedy performers of all time, Buster Keaton. After watching, reflect in your journal how motivated movement can reveal emotion, storyline, and subtext.

Assignment: Movement Only

Voice and sound can no longer aid you in your storytelling. You must completely rely on your movement for communication. Choose a famous novel or play and act out the entirety in 90 seconds (or less). Don't tell the audience the title of the story (let's see if we can figure it out). This may be a solo or group (three performers maximum) performance.

Assignment: Physical Comedy Sketch

Take some time to remember theatrical experiences when you've been entertained by comedy, clowning, and farce – such as pratfalls, spit-takes, and other acts of buffoonery. What performers consistently add dimension to the stock characters of comedy?[11] What "straight man"[12] characters have you enjoyed watching, with spot on deadpan and understated double takes? What performances have you seen where the performers were funny without "trying" to be funny? Take notes in your journal on the successful elements of comedic performances, and think back on what worked in the previous assignments when you had an established story to work with to create your interpretation. With these references as inspiration, create a thirty-second to one-minute-thirty-second original comic sketch of your own utilizing movement and sound (music and/or sound effect). Limit speech and sound (or don't speak at all!). Fully commit to the character's given circumstances and use the "rule of three" to help develop a beginning, middle, and end to your sketch. Your focus and movement should illustrate the physical world for your character. Perform the final version of your sketch for your peers.

I hope you had fun creating your physical theatre masterpieces! After all that work, you should reflect on the experience:

Journal Writing Prompt: A Performance with Distinction

Was there ever a moment when you felt like one or more of your physical theatre performances "clicked" with those watching it? What made the performance distinctive? Explain how you sense the audience's connection to the performance. Things to consider: Did your performance radiate power, vitality, and/or strength? Did you reveal vulnerability? Did your character reflect facets of the audience's cultural identity (e.g., nationality, ethnicity, religion, social class, etc.)? Was the audience quiet or boisterous (e.g., did they laugh, applaud, etc.)? Did you feel a wave of inspiration at any point in your performance? Is it difficult to recall the details of your performance? If you answer "yes," why do you think it is difficult? Share thoughts from your journal writing prompt with a peer.

The Performer's Principles

Before concluding this chapter, I'd like to share a few timeless and universal lessons for the actor-dancer to enhance your experiences in acting training. I often think of these tips as principles that when followed, can lead to very rewarding performance experiences. I hope the following lessons resonate with you throughout your journey in acting and dance training.

1 Be honest. Be vulnerable.

Honesty is the key to unlocking a successful performance. In order to achieve it, you may have to uncover emotions that leave you feeling drained, exposed, and vulnerable, and that takes some serious courage and energy. Release yourself from judgment and surrender physically and mentally to the given circumstances of your character. When you are free from the ties that bind you physically and emotionally, you become an open vessel portraying truthful emotion. Yoga, meditation, and relaxation techniques can help you achieve honesty and vulnerability.

2 But remember, it's a performance.

The whole idea that you must *completely* believe the given circumstances of your character feels a bit dangerous. Yes, you must imagine the circumstances are real, but there's a part of you that knows you are on stage or being filmed. Try pouring yourself a cup of coffee when you're alone and no one is watching. It's easy, right? Now try it on stage with 500 hundred people watching you. Suddenly a task so simple, mundane, habitual to the point that you can do it automatically, becomes something you have to rehearse repeatedly until it *appears* natural to the audience. Make no mistake, you the performer are almost always aware that there is an audience. I say "almost always" because there may be moments when a wave of inspiration overtakes your senses. But if you're *completely* out of control, if you've totally succumbed to the emotion of the scene, you can be a danger to yourself and your scene partner. The craft of performing lies in making this devised moment appear real, not actually be real. You're not a villain, you just play one!

Some of the best acting I've seen was from theatre and dance students performing in *Cat on a Hot Tin Roof.* One scene, where the character Maggie changes clothes while the character Brick pours himself another drink, left me speechless. Maggie had a complete costume change on stage including putting on stockings and clipping them to garters. Brick had his own physical work to do making a drink with a cast on his foot and hobbling back to his chaise. I was gob-smacked by the intimacy they were able to create and the naturalism of their movements. It was a masterclass in acting and theatre movement. They used *action* as the vehicle to realistically portray truthfulness on stage. In that moment, the performer and the character were in communion.

Remember, do not make the work of researching your character a miserable one, rife with personal psychological pain. Rather, strive for the action of the play as your source of exploration. It's all there in the text for you to explore.

3   **Empathy is everything.**
When you can imagine what others are going through, when you sympathize with their experiences, when you withhold judgment about their
decisions and embrace them as they are without trying to change them,
then you will free *yourself* as a performer. This holds true for the characters you play, and it's also true for those people you interact with on a
production. Everyone's path and processes are distinct from your own,
and you may not be aware of what obstacles they are facing; their actions might feel mysterious and misdirected to you. But through empathy, meaningful portrayals of complex characters are formed and
productive collaborations with your fellow artists are achieved.

4   **Your imagination is a gift to be shared.**
Nurture your imagination. Listen to your imagination and allow yourself to explore what you imagine. I don't know how many times I've
heard, "Never mind, it's a stupid question," or "Nah, that wouldn't
work" in rehearsal. I say, let's try it. Even if the idea doesn't meet your
expectations, it could lead to other avenues. Don't be selfish with those
wonderful ideas floating around in your head; share them!

5   **Growth is essential.**
Always, always, always be a student. The moment you stop striving to
learn more is the moment you start falling behind. Growth may lead
to change, and sometimes change can be scary. One of my very favorite
quotes that best sums up how multifaceted we are, how much we can
change and grow and how we can be both one thing and another at the
same time is from the poet Walt Whitman's "Song of Myself". He writes:

Do I contradict myself?
Very well then I contradict myself,
(I am large, I contain multitudes).
                    (Whitman, 1892)

Growth is about expanding, broadening, evolving. Growth will lead you
on the path of *becoming* the fullest performer you can be.

6   **Give it your all... *and* go easy on yourself.**
Here's an example of a contradictory statement of which I think Whitman would approve! Yes, give it your all. Give it everything you've got,
and as they say in the dance world, "Leave it all on the dance floor." But
if the performance doesn't go exactly as you planned, try your best not
to beat yourself up about it. When you continuously berate yourself, you

allow your frustration to linger for too long. Living in regret, replaying past mistakes or missteps over and over and over again will make your days as a performing artist angst ridden.

It is such a nice feeling to leave a rehearsal or performance knowing you've done what you could, given your circumstances on that day. But no doubt, some days are better than others. On those days, love yourself the way others love you and see yourself through the eyes of those who love you.

7   **Performing is *serious* fun.**
Take your preparation and your commitment to giving the best per-formance seriously. But, have fun with it. Maintain a sense of humor. Remember, you are in a room with like-minded individuals who share the goal of creating a wonderful work of art. You are all on the same team. It's very hard work, but I want to enjoy my workday, don't you? So, all this to say, yes take the work seriously but don't cut out the joy. If this work makes you miserable all the time, you should be asking yourself whether you're in the right field. Also, negativity is contagious. That is not a joke. Studies show that negativity can spread much like the common cold (Edward-Elmhurst Health, 2019). Don't be the negative person at rehearsal bringing everybody else down.

8   **It takes a lot of effort to make a performance look effortless.**
There is a perception that performing is easy. In fact, as a performer, you perpetuate that misconception. Performers work to make difficult, even painful things look natural (ballet dancers perform on the tips of their toes; stage combat requires serious training to make the fight appear seam-less and realistic). I'll never forget years ago meeting someone for the first time, and he asked me what I did. I explained that I was an MFA student studying theatre performance. He said, "Why do you have to study that? You just get up there and do it." Needless to say, he didn't make a friend of me that evening, but he is not alone in that sentiment. Audience mem-bers and even performers new to the discipline may think great performers are just "gifted." In truth, performance requires as much discipline as the professional athlete, as much rigor as the chemist experimenting in the lab, and as much an eye for detail as the financial analyst. The perception that performance is reliant on *talent*, and you either have "it" or you don't, is patently false. The reality is that you must work hard, and not only do you have to work hard, you have to make it all seem effortless.

9   **You deserve to be in the room.**
A student once shared what she described as a recurring "stress dream." Every night she'd wake from a dream where she was at rehearsal and the director would say, "You're doing such lousy work that we've decided

to take your scholarship away." She described a feeling that many of us can relate to: that we don't "belong," that we will be exposed for our inadequacies and labeled as the fraud we know we are, that our accomplishments don't mean much.

I remember so clearly my first day of graduate school. Each of us performed a monologue for the class. I watched in wonder at these people who would later become my friends and colleagues and thought, "There's been some kind of mistake. These performers are amazing, and I will never be as good as them. I have no idea how I got into this program." Does any of this sound familiar to you? This pattern of fear that replays in your mind has a name; it's called *imposter syndrome*. Somehow just knowing that we're not alone in this feeling provides solace. While self-doubt will inevitably arise and at times when you least expect it, please know this: *you deserve to be in the room.* You have value. You have much to contribute. You are worthy.

10 Early is on time, on time is late, and late is unacceptable.
That saying has to be a favorite amongst stage managers. If rehearsal starts at 7:00 pm and you arrive at 7:00 pm, consider yourself late. If you arrive at 6:50 pm, ten minutes prior to the rehearsal start time, you are on time. If you arrive 20 minutes early and begin warming up both vocally and physically, changing into rehearsal clothes, setting any props, reviewing notes, then you are fully prepared. Rushing into the theatre, jumping on stage, and diving into the work means the first 20 minutes of rehearsal is you getting warmed-up. Trust me, as a director, it is obvious that you are not fully present in the work until a good 20 minutes into the rehearsal. It's frustrating and feels like a misuse of time. If you want to make the most of rehearsal, get there early whenever possible.

In Summary

Acting training is valuable and important. It is also draining. Honing your craft as an actor can become cumbersome and if so, the joy of performing is lost. Training in theatre movement and performing physical theatre can reignite that passion; it will also help to unlock imagination and playfulness in performance and encourages bold and innovative choices.

The range of acting techniques is vast. Most likely, you will find a combination of approaches best assists you in achieving truthful performances. There is no one way of achieving emotional depth in performance, but accepting the guidelines in what I like to call "The Performer's Principles" can be of help.

You've now read about preparing for performance in Chapter 2, dance technique to unlock stage presence in Chapter 3, and acting technique to perform with motivation and intention in this chapter. It's time to combine acting and dance further by exploring the wonderful world of musical theatre!

Notes

1 A performer "in their head" tends to overthink their every move and second guess their instincts.
2 Alternate spelling of Konstantin Stanislavski: Constantin Stanislavsky
3 The Stanislavski System is also known as the Stanislavski Method.
4 *Emotional memory*, *affective memory*, and *emotional recall* are synonymous with *emotional memory*.
5 *The Method* is also known as *method acting*.
6 Uta Hagen's idea of *transference* was originally termed *substitution*.
7 *Oral interpretation* involves more than merely reading aloud; it requires illuminating the written word with vocal and physical expression.
8 Instructors, it is recommended that the comedy assignments described in the physical theatre section be explored during class over a number of training days. See Appendix for sample timeline.
9 A *double-take* is just as it sounds; you see something that appears so totally amazing or unbelievable that you have to take a second look!
10 I was first introduced to the 'rule of three' in comedy and given the assignment to write ten simple jokes by Comedy and Character instructor, Adrian Danzig, when I was a graduate student at the Chicago College of Performing Arts at Roosevelt University. He encouraged the class to explore the rule of three through movement and sound and introduced us to the wonderful world of physical theatre, clowning, and farce.
11 A *stock character* represents a character type that is immediately recognizable to the audience. In commedia dell'arte, stock characters include *servants* (e.g., Arlecchino), *masters* (e.g., Pantalone), and *lovers* (e.g., Isabella and Flavio).
12 A "straight man" in comedy is the performer who sets up the joke for another performer to deliver the punchline.

Bibliography

Adler, S., & Kissel, H. (2001). *Stella Adler: The Art of Acting*. Applause.Alina. (2014). *Psychology Club with Lena: Sense of Humour. How to Develop*. GreenForest. December 28. https://greenforest.com.ua/journal/read/psychology-club-with-lena-sense-of-humour-how-to-develop

Association of Theatre Movement Educators. (n.d.). *The Mission of ATME*. https://atmeweb.org/our-mission/

Ates, A. (2018a). "The definitive guide to the Stanislavsky acting technique." *Backstage*, 29 October. www.backstage.com/magazine/article/the-definitive-guide-to-the-stanislavsky-acting-technique-65716/

Ates, A. (2018b). "The definitive guide to Stella Adler's acting technique." *Backstage*, 24 December. www.backstage.com/magazine/article/the-definitive-guide-to-the-stella-adler-acting-technique-66369/

Ates, A. (2019a). "The definitive guide to the Meisner technique." *Backstage*, 3 April. www.backstage.com/magazine/article/the-definitive-guide-to-the-meisner-technique-67712/

Ates, A. (2019b). "The definitive guide to Uta Hagen's acting technique." *Backstage*, 6 September. www.backstage.com/magazine/article/the-definitive-guide-to-uta-hagens-acting-technique-68922/

Bogart, A., & Landau, T. (2005). *The Viewpoints Book: A Practical Guide to Viewpoints and Composition*. Theatre Communications Group.

"Buster Keaton – The Art of the Gag." (2017). [Video]. *YouTube*, uploaded by tozlumercek, 26 July. www.youtube.com/watch?v=AXE8xvrlq6M

"Comedy Tools: The Rule of Three." (2016). [Video]. *YouTube*, uploaded by Think Funny, 5 April. www.youtube.com/watch?v=Z4PPO3TVEck

Dalton, L. (n.d.). "Psychological gesture: Hollywood's best kept acting secret!" *Articles about Technique & Teacher*, Reprinted from *Actors Ink*, Issues 35 & 36. https://chekhov.net/articles_secure.html

Edward-Elmhurst Health. (2019). *How Emotions, Like Colds, Are Contagious*. May 2. www.eehealth.org/blog/2019/05/emotions-contagious/

Holmes, P. (2013). "Jeff Garlin Teaches Pete How to Do the Perfect Spit Take" [Video]. *YouTube*, uploaded by Pete Holmes, 19 November. www.youtube.com/watch?v=s-LDjtkVsgc

HuffPostMovieMashups. (2014). "The Ultimate Movie Spit-Take Mashup" [Video]. *YouTube*, uploaded by HuffPost Entertainment, 13 March. www.youtube.com/watch?v=eW5_ZUFaKEw

"James Finlayson – Master of the Comedy Double-Take." (2013). [Video]. *YouTube*, uploaded by Soundbloke1, 30 November. www.youtube.com/watch?v=-dTHaMOz4ws

Roy, J. (2013). "How to Use the Rule of Three to Make People Laugh" [Video]. *YouTube*, uploaded by Jeff Roy, 12 August. www.youtube.com/watch?v=mtyBMit30WQ&t=1s

Sawoski, P. (2019). *The Stanislavski System. Growth and Methodology*. 2nd edn. https://idoc.pub/documents/the-stanislavski-system-growth-and-methodology-perviz-sawoski-2ed-514380pyzglj

Sparrow, P. (2021). *What is Physical Theatre? – Acting Tips: City Academy Guides*. www.city-academy.com/news/what-is-physical-theatre/

New York Film Academy. (2015) *Stanislavski in 7 Steps: Better Understanding Stanisklavski's 7 Questions*. Film School and Acting School of New York Film Academy. December 2. www.nyfa.edu/student-resources/stanislavski-in-7-steps-better-understanding-stanisklavskis-7-questions/

Theatre Dictionary. (2013). "Double Take – TDF's Theatre Dictionary – Defining Theatre Terms." [Video]. *YouTube*, uploaded by Theatre Dictionary, 19 July. www.youtube.com/watch?v=ZbvhKe-smMk

"The Trip with Steve Coogan. We Rise at Daybreak." (2010). [Video]. *YouTube*, uploaded by AKTVUK, 24 December. www.youtube.com/watch?v=K8BPP4ASQWo

Valacosa (dir.). (2014). "Elements of Comedy Examples: Rule of Threes (21 Jump Street)" [Video]. *YouTube*, uploaded by Michael L. Davenport, 8 July. www.youtube.com/watch?v=vnQe2DosQnc

Whitman, W. (n.d.). *Song of Myself (1892 Version) by Walt Whitman*. Poetry Foundation. www.poetryfoundation.org/poems/45477/song-of-myself-1892-version

Wood, A. (2018). *Saving Uta Hagen*. Andrew Wood Acting Studio. February 26. www.andrewwoodla.com/saving-uta-hagen-2/

Wright, K. C. (2021). *8 Important Acting Techniques (in Gifs)*. March 17. www.backstage.com/magazine/article/important-acting-techniques-gifs-10278/

5 Jazz Dance & Musical Theatre

The Quintessential Combination of Acting & Dance in Performance

Of all the theatre and dance styles we could discuss, musical theatre is excellent for further investigation because it combines acting and dancing seamlessly – and the lessons learned in musical theatre training translate to just about any other performance genre out there. Musicals intermingle dance and acting beautifully and regardless of whether you consider yourself a fan of the genre, you can acknowledge that it checks all the boxes for the performer ready to be challenged:

- It incorporates the entire body for expression (acting, voice and movement, song, and dance);
- It offers enormous variety stylistically (consider the hip-hop in *Hamilton*, the movement and puppetry in *The Lion King*, the aerial dance in the recent *Pippin* revival, the dramatic acting in *Les Misérables*, and the rock opera vocals in *Jesus Christ Superstar* as just a few examples of the wonderful variety that musical theatre offers);
- It is a genre in *huge* demand across the US and internationally.

All wonderful reasons to learn more!

Jazz Music & Jazz Dance

Musical Theatre is a prolific area of study, making it a great fit for the student interested in broadening their skillset. When you visualize musical theatre dance, images from a variety of dance styles might spring to mind; ballet, ballroom, and tap have often featured in musicals. But I most often associate *jazz dance* with the dancing seen in musicals because of the impact that jazz dance has made on the development of musical theatre (and vice versa). Jazz dance is a major contributor to musical theatre and has a rich history as a discipline in its own right. Appreciating the origins of jazz dance is an important step toward understanding the technique of the genre; it also provides a shining example of the collaborative nature of performance more generally and reveals the contributions of jazz dance in musical theatre specifically.

DOI: 10.4324/9781003149699-6

When you think of the word *jazz*, what's the first thought that comes to mind? Many of you might conjure the image of "jazz hands," while others might think of jazz music. Jack Cole, known throughout the dance world as the *father of theatrical jazz dance*, described jazz dance as *urban folk dance* (Loney, 1984, p.121). Let's break down those three words. A folk dance is created among the "common people" of an area, typically originating in rural regions. While jazz dance began among the "common people," the dance form truly took shape in highly populated areas, hence Cole dubbing it an *urban* folk dance. Like most things conceived in the US, jazz dance is an amalgam of influences.

The origins of jazz music and dance can be traced to African slaves in the US. Over time, the sounds and movement from a number of African countries were assimilated by African Americans, who experimented with the music and dances of their ancestors and incorporated European elements, such as instruments (e.g., saxophone and trumpet) and harmonies. By the early 20th century, a new sound came to the fore, jazz, and was quickly weaved into the fabric of the US social scene. Likewise, body isolations found in African movement combined with elements of European partner dances to create social jazz dance. In the beginning, jazz music and dance each contributed to the development of the other.

Jazz Music

Jazz music is not an easy sound to describe, but you know it when you hear it! Jazz music icon Louis Armstrong once said, "If you have to ask what jazz is, you'll never know" (quoted in Campbell, 1996, p.53). Perhaps the most defining components of the jazz era are that the musicians themselves were often the composers and, as such, incorporated improvisation into their live performances. While the amount of improvisation varied, the idea of spontaneity in performance was and is a distinguishing characteristic of jazz music. Styles that influenced the early jazz sound include:

Jazz Music Styles

Ragtime

Described as a "propulsively syncopated musical style" (Encyclopaedia Britannica, 2016), ragtime is noted for its fast "off-beat" rhythms. The powerful, bouncy, high energy sounds of ragtime influenced the development of jazz music.

Swing

In *The Swing Era: The Development of Jazz 1930–1945*, Gunter Schuller says:

> In all of jazz there is no element more elusive of definition than swing. Although it is something that almost all good jazz musicians can do and

recognize, and something whose presence or absence almost all jazz audiences can instantly distinguish, it is also something that is extremely hard to define in words.

(1991, p.223)

While difficult to define, distinguishing characters of swing include a big band playing mostly prepared music, leaving less room for lengthy or highly complex improvisation and more opportunity for dance.

Bebop

Generally considered jazz music for listening rather than dancing, bebop features a smaller band playing complex solos and detailed melodies. The bebop sound emerged on the heels of the swing era (Jazz in America, n.d.).

Latin Jazz

A mixture of Cuban and Spanish Caribbean rhythms and instruments with European and African musical stylings, Latin jazz, also known as Afro-Cuban jazz, came to fame in the 1940s, although its rhythms also influenced earlier jazz (Fernandez, 2014).

Jazz Music Pioneers

Scott Joplin

Known as the "king of ragtime," Joplin helped to set the stage for jazz music.

Jelly Roll Morton (Ferdinand Joseph Lamothe)

Self-proclaimed "inventor of jazz," Jelly Roll Morton aided in formalizing the jazz sound. While often criticized for his claim as "inventor," he is an important figure in the development of jazz music and is "believed to be the first jazz musician to put his arrangements to paper" (Biography.com, 2014).

Louis Armstrong

Arguably the greatest innovator in jazz music, Louis Armstrong (lovingly known as "Satchmo") enhanced the artistry of the musician's solo through his mesmerizing performances on trumpet, helped to popularize scat singing, and brought jazz music to the masses through his many film appearances and tours.

Count Basie

A pianist known for his straightforward style, Basie grew to fame as a world class band leader, playing in clubs, theatres, and concert halls, helping to establish jazz as a disciplined art form.

Duke Ellington

Among his many accomplishments, Duke Ellington is remembered for his elegance as a performer and band leader. He was a mainstay throughout the jazz era, and his legacy includes numerous beloved music compositions.

Dizzy Gillespie and Charlie Parker

Known for his upturned trumpet, huge air-filled cheeks when playing, on-stage antics, and innovative compositions, Dizzy Gillespie, along with saxophonist and composer Charlie Parker, are considered co-creators of bebop.

Machito (Francisco Raúl Gutiérrez Grillo) and Mario Bauzá

A charismatic singer and conductor, Machito, along with his brother-in-law Mario Bauzá as musical director, were instrumental in creating Latin jazz.

But wait, there's more...

Benny Goodman, Artie Shaw, and The Dorsey Brothers also helped to create the "big band" swing sound as band leaders. Cab Calloway was a band leader who wowed audiences with his one-of-a-kind scat singing and athletic dance moves. Fats Waller's innovative piano playing laid the groundwork for modern jazz. Billie Holiday and Ella Fitzgerald captured the emotion of jazz music with their voices. Thelonius Monk was another pioneer in creating the bebop sound. Tito Puente was a hugely famous figure in the development of Latin jazz. These are but a few names from such music hubs as New Orleans, Chicago, Kansas City, New York City, and Cuba that were teeming with talent, and the magic of these and many others working together created the musical phenomenon known as *jazz*.

Assignment: Jazz Music Pioneers

Listen to Scott Joplin's "Maple Leaf Rag," Duke Ellington's "Take the 'A' Train," Dizzy Gillespie's "A Night in Tunisia," and Mario Bauza's "Tanga" to hear ragtime, swing, bebop, and Latin jazz respectively (links in the Bibliography). Then, describe your response to each song in your journal. Here are some questions to help facilitate your response: How did the music make you feel when you listened to it? Did you have any kind of emotional response to it? Did it evoke any images, thoughts, or memories while listening to it? Did you visualize yourself dancing to the music? Did you like the music? Why or why not? Which song appealed to you most and why?

Jazz Dance

With new sounds came new ways of dancing; and each new social dance craze provided more material for the development of jazz dance as an art form. Styles that influenced early jazz dance include:

Jazz Dance Styles

Cakewalk

The Cakewalk was originated by African American slaves who were parodying the ballroom dances performed by their white owners. Slave owners missed the satire, and the dance was quickly adopted by professional dancers and performed on stage. It also became a popular dance competition with a cake as the winner's prize. The dance itself involves high knee steps performed by couples to an upbeat tempo. The Cakewalk is an important forerunner to the development of other American and European dance fusions leading to jazz dance.

Charleston

What began as a black folk dance from the American South with African influences, the Charleston (named after Charleston, South Carolina) became a social jazz dance craze known across the US for its "pigeon" toes and twisting legs. The dance's popularity spread throughout the country and was performed on American stages and ballrooms with the young female "flapper" becoming the representation of the lively and carefree dance. What is particularly unique about the Charleston is that it can be performed as a solo, with a partner, or in a group.

Black Bottom

With African dance as its influence – with syncopated rhythms, bent knees, crouched torsos, and pelvic movements – African Americans from the South incorporated shoulder and hip isolations to create the Black Bottom. Once a version of the dance appeared on the Broadway stage, it became a national phenomenon. Like the Charleston, the Black Bottom did not require a partner and was an important influence on the development of jazz dance.

Swing Dance

A catch-all term encompassing a variety of social dances performed to swing music, examples of swing dance styles include: West Coast swing, Jitterbug, Lindy Hop, Shag, and Jive. While the basic steps differed from style to style, most involved couples holding one or both hands and shared a singular energy that captured the spirit of America. As World War II moved American soldiers abroad, swing dance gained prominence on the stage in Broadway musicals.

It is the combination of these and other social dance crazes that sparked the genesis of jazz dance. With roots in African movement and influences from European movement, jazz dance was incorporated into the musical theatre scene with enormous success and remains a mainstay on Broadway and in popular culture.

Jazz Dance Pioneers

Josephine Baker

Combining elements of vaudeville, burlesque, and social jazz dance to create a larger-than-life stage and screen persona, Josephine Baker took the 1920s theatre scene by storm. Her "banana dance," which she performed wearing only a "tutu" of bananas around her waist, caused an international sensation, and audiences in her adopted home of Paris flocked to her performances.

Katherine Dunham

An anthropologist, choreographer, and dancer whose studies in Afro-Caribbean dance forms hugely impacted the development of both jazz and modern dance, Katherine Dunham is known as "the matriarch of black dance."

Jack Cole

Known as the "father of theatrical jazz dance," Jack Cole coached performers such as Marilyn Monroe and Rita Hayworth, and his sleek and sensual technique inspired a generation of jazz dance innovators. He is thought to have taught the first theatrical jazz dance class.

Matt Mattox

Trained in ballet, tap, and ballroom, Mattox found his passion for jazz dance with Cole as his teacher. He later developed a signature style he termed "free style" and formed the dance company JazzArt. Mattox's contributions to jazz dance were many, as a teacher, choreographer, and performer.

Bob Fosse

Influenced by Cole's teachings, Fosse became a superstar choreographer and director, whose unique style revolutionized jazz dance. His work on the musicals *Chicago*, *Cabaret*, *Sweet Charity*, and *All that Jazz* (to name but a few) showcase his signature aesthetic. He eschewed lighter fare in favor of darker themes in his work and preferred broken lines and hunched upper bodies with hands spread over the clean contours seen in other dance styles.

Jerome Robbins

A luminary in both the ballet and jazz dance worlds, Jerome Robbins' noted works include *West Side Story*, *On the Town*, and *Fiddler on the Roof*. A choreographer, director, and performer, Robbins' *jazz ballet* style led him to develop choreography perhaps best described as "explosive containment." This heightened energy mixed with restraint lent itself to mystery and intrigue, leaving audiences on the edge of their seat, eager for more.

Gwen Verdon

An icon of musical theatre, Gwen Verdon brought to life some of Broadway's greatest characters. Verdon is known not only for her exquisite jazz dance technique, but also for the quality of her acting. She was an assistant of Jack Cole's for five years. She was also Fosse's main collaborator (as well as spouse) and originated roles in many of his best works, perhaps most famously as Roxie Hart in *Chicago* and Charity in *Sweet Charity*.

Luigi

With a promising career as a dancer in film taking shape in LA, Eugene Louis Faccuito ("Luigi") suffered from serious injuries from a car accident that left him partially paralyzed. Told he would never dance again, Luigi overcame his prognosis and devised a series of exercises that included isolation, balance, and stretch which enabled him to regain his mobility. He opened a jazz dance school in NYC and taught his technique to a generation of dancers, which included Liza Minelli and John Travolta.

Gus Giordano

A strong dedication to teaching and choreographing jazz dance led Giordano to open the first dance studio in Chicago focused solely on jazz dance. His company was integral in helping to legitimize jazz dance as an art form and genre of dance in its own right.

This is an incomplete list of jazz dance pioneers that professionalized jazz dance, providing a mere glimpse at the innovators who helped to develop the genre. The hope is that this introduction will spark an interest in you to further explore the origins and innovators of jazz dance. But before we move on, take a look at footage of early social dances and the work of jazz dance icons in your next assignment:

Assignment: Early Dance Crazes & Jazz Dance Pioneers

Visit YouTube and watch a few archival clips of the following pioneering dances: Cakewalk, Charleston, Black Bottom, Swing Dance. Then, search clips of Josephine Baker in "La Revue Des Revues", Katherine Dunham in "Ballet Creole", Jack Cole in "Beale Street Blues", Matt Mattox in "1961 Choreography", Gus Giordano's company in "Moves", and Luigi in "Classic Jazz Dance Master" (links located in the Bibliography).

Next, describe your response to the footage you watched. Here are some questions to help facilitate your response: Did you have any kind of emotional response to the dancing you just watched? Did it evoke any images or memories while watching it? Did you visualize yourself dancing as well? Did you like the dancing? Why or why not? Which jazz dance pioneer's style appealed to you most and why?

Jazz Dance Styles of Today

Today's artists and choreographers continue to inspire jazz dance's evolution, and the scope of jazz dance is broadening to include numerous variances within the genre. As you well know, jazz dance is an art, not a science, so there is no one "right" way to jazz dance, nor is there total consensus on the definitive terms to describe jazz styles that have emerged and continue to develop. With that in mind, I will include a description of some of the styles of jazz dance, as well alternative titles that may be used to describe it. You will see these styles and more featured in musical theatre dance:

Theatre Jazz (Broadway Jazz, Classic Jazz, Traditional Jazz)

When Agnes de Mille choreographed *Oklahoma!* (Broadway debut in 1943), she staged a 15-minute ballet as the finale to the first act of the musical. Dubbed the *dream ballet*, the dance explored the character Laurey's romantic feelings toward Curly and her fears about Jud's advances. The dance caused a sensation and *Oklahoma!* was hailed as the first musical to truly integrate dance into the plotline. Jerome Robbins continued to develop dance in musical theatre by utilizing his dance numbers as important devices for telling parts of the story. Robbins' choreography furthered the idea of dance as a means of storytelling with dances that introduced characters and revealed plot. The Broadway program for *West Side Story* did not list a chorus of singers or dancers, but rather identified each cast member by character name. This helped the performers see themselves as fully realized characters. Bob Fosse was instrumental in incorporating dance as an *essential* component of the musical's storyline. His dances emphasized important themes and were vehicles for emotive expression. With the leadership of these and many other choreographers and directors, dance was no longer just an entertaining distraction or "break in the action" in musical theatre. Dance became an indispensable method of communication, and jazz dance was paramount in establishing dance's more meaningful role in musical theatre. Look at the musicals *West Side Story*, *A Chorus Line*, and *Chicago* for examples of theatre jazz in action.

Latin Jazz

Latin jazz integrates the rhythms and style of Latin dance with the rhythms and style of jazz dance. Latin jazz utilizes Cuban Motion and Samba Tic (two movement techniques that feature bending and straightening the knees to accentuate hip movement) combined with the body isolations of jazz dance. You'll also hear Latin and jazz music influencing one another, with the clave rhythm as a key feature. Dances such as rumba, cha-cha, samba, salsa, bachata, and merengue inspire much of Latin jazz choreography, but the primary difference with Latin jazz is that no partner is needed. It is sultry, fiery, passionate, high energy dancing that is eye-popping and entertaining.

Lyrical Jazz (Contemporary)

Lyrical jazz combines elements of contemporary ballet, modern dance, jazz dance, and everyday pedestrian movements to produce an edgy and emotional movement aesthetic. It is often choreographed to popular music of the day and sometimes embodies the lyrics of the music to express the storytelling components of a song. It is a cultural phenomenon the world over, particularly in the US, and appeals to the masses in mainstream television and film. Dance enthusiasts are moved not only by the energy and emotion, but also the Herculean strength and athleticism the performers exhibit throughout the dance.

Hip-Hop

As hip-hop culture spread internationally in the 1980s and 1990s, hip-hop dance gathered enormous momentum, becoming a popular dance genre. Its prevalence continues, and the dance form has solidified its position in the dance canon. Originating predominantly in US African American communities, hip-hop dance draws upon dance elements also found in jazz dance foundations – that of articulated torso and body isolation. Central features of hip-hop are *pop and lock*, both of which require enormous precision, and *breaking*, which includes acrobatic stunts and athletic skills. Hip-hop is known for its origins in urban communities, and as it has developed as an art form, some claim it has lost its authenticity. In a hip-hop masterclass I once took, the instructor said, "As soon as you take hip-hop out of the street and onto the stage, it's no longer hip-hop." As is the case with many dance forms originating among the community, once a dance is theatricalized, it loses some of its connection to the culture from which it originated. That said, hip-hop as a genre of dance is hugely popular, often imitated, appropriated, and admired throughout the world. Derivations of hip-hop include street-jazz, which blends aerobic dance moves with hip-hop and jazz dance, and pop-jazz (commercial jazz), which mixes hip-hop, jazz dance, and popular dance moves of the present day (Dance Spirit, 2019).

Afro-Jazz

Afro-jazz includes elements of African, Afro-Caribbean, Afro-Brazilian, and jazz dance. Features of Afro-jazz dance include a controlled lower body that often moves in a deep plié, with torso and back movements contracting and releasing with seemingly free-flowing arms (although there is method to the arm movements). Afro-jazz requires stamina to execute well, and it emphasizes core and lower body strength. African dance with jazz elements creates a powerful and highly energetic dance style.

Assignment: Jazz Dance Technique Class

Take a jazz class in one of the styles described above. Step out of your comfort zone; if you're a hip-hop fanatic, maybe try lyrical. If you are unable to find a live class in your area, there are a number of virtual classes you could try. Then reflect on your experience participating in a jazz dance class by discussing the following:

- Part I: Give a synopsis of the class. Describe the style you learned in this session;
- Part II: Discuss the discoveries that you made during the session;
- Part III: Discuss the issues or obstacles you faced during the session;
- Part IV: Discuss how you overcame those issues.

Here's some food for thought as you reflect on your experience:

- Did you keep rhythm and timing?;
- Was your footwork technically accurate? Were you able to accurately reproduce selected movement?;
- Did you participate fully in technique building floor exercises, center combinations, and traveling combinations?;
- Did you participate fully in movement that explores the use of rhythm, energy, individual artistic expression, and spatial awareness?;

- Did you recognize the technique terminology presented in the class? If not, list and describe those terms in your journal to further emphasize what you have learned;
- Did you work as a member of an ensemble?;*
- Did you help create and maintain a positive and creative class environment?*

*if you took the class online, you can skip.

Jazz Dance Technique

Now that you have a bit of background on jazz dance and a stronger sense of the depth and breadth of the art form and its influences, let's look at major characteristics that comprise the dance style – *body placement, isolation, musicality, ensemble work*, and *artistic expression*. Every actor-dancer should engage in the study of these characteristics to grow not only as a jazz dancer, but as a performer of musical theatre.

Body Placement & Isolation

Jazz dance uses parallel body positioning, turnout body positioning, as well as inwardly rotated body positioning. Body placement in jazz dance can change from one movement to the next; you may begin a dance sequence with a non-locomotor movement phrase in parallel, then transition to locomotor movement with turnout, and finish with an inwardly rotated pose. It's the blending of techniques from other genres that make the body placement in jazz dance so wonderfully complicated!

Body isolations are also a strong feature in jazz dance. To develop skill in this area, an exhaustive amount of repetition is required, and a positive mindset will help with the frustration that inevitably arises from such precise work. The sequence below is a simple way to warm up for isolation, and most jazz dance classes begin with a sequence much like the following:

BODY ISOLATION: HEAD, SHOULDERS, CHEST, RIBCAGE, TORSO, HIPS

- While standing parallel first in alignment, move your head to the right so that your ear runs parallel to your shoulder. Repeat on the other side. Repeat as desired;
- Lower your head to the right so that your ear runs parallel to your shoulder, then begin circling your head forward and end with your left ear running parallel with your left shoulder. Repeat the exercise a few times, while imagining that your head is drawing a smiley face;
- Lower your head to the right so that your ear runs parallel to your shoulder, then begin circling your head backward and end with your left

ear running parallel with your left shoulder. Repeat the exercise a few times, while imagining that your head is drawing a smiley face behind you. Note: do not allow the weight of your head to completely collapse against the neck;

- Imagine that you have a pencil on top of your head and "draw" circles on the ceiling to the right and then left;
- Using only the head and neck, look to the right, then center, then left, then center. Repeat as desired;
- Roll both shoulders circling back and repeat as desired, then repeat the exercise circling the shoulders forward. Next alternate circling shoulders one after the other back for a time, then forward;
- Lift both your shoulders toward your ears and then let them drop. Repeat as desired. Next, alternate lifting shoulders one after the other;
- Lift your arms to make a "T" shape. Focusing on the chest, reach to the right and left. This movement can be fairly subtle, so remember that you are isolating movement by focusing on the area above the ribcage. Then, place your hands on your hips and move the chest forward and back. Finally, circle the chest area around to the right and then to the left.
- Next focus on the ribcage moving it left and right, forward and back, circling right and left;
- Engage your core and move the entire torso left and right, forward and back, circling right and left;
- Moving down to the hips, shift them right, center, left, center. Then bypass center, and move the hips left and right. Circle your hips to the right and then to the left. Next draw a figure eight with your hips right and left;
- First, arch the back with the crown of the head moving toward the sacrum ("head to tail" positioning). With an arch in the back and stretching the abdominals, bend knees and slowly lower the torso; the shoulders and then head are the last body parts to drop (release downward). Then roll back up starting with a curve in the back. Rise up vertebra by vertebra, slowly straightening the knees with the shoulders and head as the last part of the body to lift.

Body Placement: Bevel, Shouldering, & Arm Movement

This is a wonderful warm-up exercise introduced to me during a Fosse technique workshop that explores both port de bras and épaulement and emphasizes body placement in relation to shoulder and arm movements. Begin with body in alignment and one leg beveled (ball of foot with heel lifted placed in front of the arch of the opposite foot). Lower one arm in front of the beveled leg. Then, bend the elbow, and move the forearm across the torso so that it travels back to its original side.

Extend the arm further out and away from the body; using the wrist and forearm, rotate the hand so that the palm faces the direction of the floor with fingertips "holding an egg" between the middle finger and thumb. Finally, complete the movement by edging the opposite shoulder forward.

Then, lower the arm, with the shoulder rotating, the elbow moving inward toward the ribs, and wrists, hands, and fingertips gently and methodically coming to rest at your sides. Repeat on the other side.

Figure 5.1 (Top to Bottom): Arm low, arm bending, arm extended, opposite shoulder moving forward

Musicality

Musicality as a performer involves the ability to note rhythm, accent, and syncopation in music and to interpret those sounds through dance and movement. When we listen to music, the melody first catches our attention. Over time, as we listen to the music more and more, we begin to note nuances and subtle tones.

A choreographer listens to the piece of music they intend to work with repeatedly, and they might choose to set their choreography within and around the rhythm. One movement phrase might be right on the beat, the next movement might hit an accent of the beat and then the next movements might highlight syncopation. The choreography can feel disconnected from the music at times, but as a performer, you will become more and more acquainted with the piece of choreography and its relationship to the music. You'll eventually feel how the movement compliments the music.

However, at times, the choreography might simply accompany the music and not actually fit neatly with the rhythm. If this choreography is intended to be performed in unison, dancers can find learning it a challenge, as they must find the *rhythm of the movement* together as an ensemble without the help of the rhythm of the music. Dancers work together to find unison through breath and a shared rhythm they create when in motion together.

Assignment: Imagining Jazz Dance

One of the most challenging songs I've choreographed to is Dave Brubeck's jazz classic, "Unsquare Dance". With a 7/4 time-signature, I had my work cut out for me! Give the song a listen (available on YouTube; link located in Bibliography). Close your eyes and imagine the wonderful ways you could express the rhythm through movement.

Then, choose a song that you really enjoy. Some argue that true jazz dance is only performed to jazz music. Not a purist myself, I rather feel that jazz dance can include many other musical genres. So, I encourage you to have fun with your choice. Listen to the song and take note of accent and syncopation and imagine jazz movements that would emphasize the unique sounds you hear. Then, take five minutes and free write in your journal about what you imagined.

Ensemble Work

Working cooperatively with your peers in performing choreographed movement is a requirement in jazz and musical theatre dance. Being a team player is so essential that if you find it difficult to work with others or you've frequently heard that others find it difficult working with you, that's probably the first and most important skill you need to develop... starting right now.

You've heard the Stanislavski quote, "There are no small parts, only small actors." I am telling you, that is the truth. In jazz and musical theatre dance, sometimes you are an individual character, where you get to let your uniqueness shine within the confines of the choreography. I am reminded of *Godspell*, where each performer had the opportunity to fling their hair about in their character's own way. At other times the dance is meant to have a singular look. The final number in *A Chorus Line* and the Rockettes immediately spring to mind when I think of dancing in precise, exact synchrony. But everyone, and I mean *everyone*, is invaluable to the success of a musical theatre dance. While you may not be a principal or soloist, trust me, the audience sees you and your performance. Whatever your role, you are of vital importance to the production.

Building a rapport with your peers creates trust and develops ensemble. Without a strong ensemble, the performance falls flat. It really doesn't matter how good individual performances are; the production feels disjointed without a sense of togetherness. As an audience member, I am rarely more moved emotionally than when I see a large cast working together with a heightened sense of purpose and commitment. The strength I see in those numbers is truly powerful. Be the performer that helps bond the show together; you can help to unite the group when you are a reliable, present, and dedicated performer.

Artistic Expression

Conveying energy and emotion takes dancing with technique to the level of dancing with artistry. Expression in jazz and musical theatre dance is about your entire being dancing the dance – with your mind, body, and energy committed to the present moment. When there is so much going on in your mind about body placement, rhythm, and footwork, it can be a real challenge to dance in character with fullest expression. However, through repetition, you can begin to trust that the body will remember the positions and movements. Then, you must let go and dance freely.

This "letting go" must happen well before opening night. When you dance with fullest expression, your balance shifts; actually, *everything* shifts. Add to it the adrenaline surge that comes with performing before an audience, and you may find yourself out of breath and out of energy if not prepared. So, you must practice performing "full-out." While marking movement (walking through movements as opposed to dancing at 100% energy) is an important tool in rehearsal to remember the choreography and blocking, you should repeatedly build in more full-out runs in order to develop the stamina required of performing before an audience. Barring any injury, dancing with fullest expression should be an important component of your rehearsal regimen.

I personally would cast the performer with great artistic expression and technique that needed developing over the performer with great dance technique and little emotion. I can teach the passionate dancer technique. It is harder to tap into artistic expression in a dancer with an emotional block. Working to free yourself from the weight of insecurities or whatever it is that's keeping you from being the expressive artist you know you are meant to be must be as much a part of your training as developing strength, endurance, and flexibility.

Journal Writing Prompt: Reflections on Expression

Reflect on the ways in which you are *expressive*. How would you describe yourself? Introvert? Extrovert? Sensitive? Assertive? Do you wear your "heart on your sleeve"? Are you an "open book"? Or would you describe yourself as guarded? When something upsets you, do you face the issue immediately? Or do you bottle up your emotional response? Would you describe yourself as non-confrontational?

Do you think the way you are in "real life" echoes the way you artistically express yourself when performing? If so, how so? If not, how not? Do you think directors/choreographers need to coax emotion from you? Or do you dive right into the emotion of the work? Has a director/choreographer ever asked you to "pull back"? Have you been told by a director/choreographer "bigger... more!" in rehearsal? What is one thing that makes the way you perform unique?

I cannot emphasize enough the impact jazz dance has made on many a musical. What's so wonderful about jazz dance in musical theatre is that it blends acting and dance incredibly well; the dancing body interprets the lyrics and music, thereby heightening the theatrical experience. The dance reveals the world of the musical and challenges the performer to utilize their entire instrument to communicate with the audience.

Acting in Musical Theatre

I'd like to change gears now to further explore the acting component of musical theatre. While we discussed acting techniques in the previous chapter, I'd like to build on that information in reference to your performance in a musical. As we have established, the goal for any acting style is truthfulness in performance, and musical theatre is no exception. Musical theatre invites the performer to reveal their character's desires, vulnerabilities, plans, and thoughts through acting, dancing, and singing. While acting in musical theatre can feel more stylized or "over the top" than say, acting in a realistic drama or even musical theatre acting for the screen, the goal of portraying a character with sincerity is universal.

Stage vs. Screen

It's an oversimplification to say that acting in musical theatre is about simply giving it "more" energy. All performing for an audience involves an exchange of energy. Imagine the ways in which the audience's energy can influence a performance. What if a theatre has 1,000 seats but only 50 people are in the audience? What if the theatre has 50 seats but 75 people are crammed into the audience with standing room only? The "buzz" or energy in these scenarios is dramatically different, and the actor is invariably affected by it. An excellent performer can feed off the audience's energy, sense how the audience is responding to the work, and adjust their energy as needed.

Acting for film is very different; there's no live audience for the performer to play to (well, unless it's a sitcom with a live audience), and without the immediate response from an audience, the performer is left to their own devices. The amazing thing about acting in film is that the camera "sees" everything. It seems that everything the actor even thinks can be captured by the camera. This enables the actor to have more subtlety in their performance. So, for example, the actor performing for the camera does not need the same kind of voice projection or movement as the actor performing live for an audience of 1,000 (that actor needs to reach the third balcony). If the actor performs the same way on camera as they do for a live audience of 1,000, I would think we'd find it looks a bit "much" in the film.

That said, the focus and energy needed from the performer are at about the same level regardless of whether they are performing for the camera or a live audience. Often young performers mistakenly think their energy should be less on camera. While yes, your performance on film can have subtleties and complexities in volume and movement that would likely be too understated on stage, that is not to say a film performance should be any less powerful or compelling than a stage performance; it's simply that your energy needs to be directed in different ways.

Musical theatre acting is not just about being "louder, faster, funnier." It requires a strong commitment to character research to portray a multidimensional character vocally, physically, and emotionally. It is not inauthentic acting to break into song and dance or to move broadly and talk with crisp articulation and resounding projection. It is only inauthentic if the actor does not fully embrace the musical theatre convention of song, dance, and spoken word. The audience is perfectly willing to suspend their disbelief and enter a world wherein people break into song and dance. As the performer, it goes without saying that you should too!

Journal Writing Prompt: Making a Connection

There is a simple analogy I learned while training with the Fred Astaire Dance Studios franchise that describes the fundamentals of leading and following in ballroom dance. I think it's safe to assume that you have been grocery shopping, so you know what it's like to push a shopping cart. Well, in this analogy, the shopper is the leader, and the follower is the cart! The shopper must push the cart before stepping. If the shopper steps before pushing the cart, then they step on the cart. In other words, if you do not indicate your desire to move forward through the energy in your dance frame, you will step on the follower's toes. The same concept can be applied any time you work with a partner (e.g., scene work, singing a duet, weight sharing dance improvisations, etc.). Before you speak or sing or begin a movement, you must tune into your partner's energy, so that you are both on the same page. Otherwise, the performance will feel disjointed. And sometimes you must make this connection with your partner, having only met them moments before (did someone say cold audition?!). Take five minutes to free write, brainstorming how to get into the zone and connect with an acting partner to safely create an engaging performance experience. Share your ideas with your peers and try out some of your ideas as you rehearse the next assignment.

Assignment: Making a Connection Part II: Musical Theatre Scene Study

Choose a scene from a musical with two to three characters and develop a performance of the scene. Remember to try out some of your ideas from the "Making a Connection" journal entry with your fellow performers in the scene. When you feel performance ready, film your scene and then watch it. I know it can be tough to watch yourself performing, but in this case, I want you to strive to remain objective and simply observe your work. Next, perform the scene for a live audience of your peers. How was your live performance different from your filmed performance? What adjustments did you make when acting for the camera vs. acting for the stage?

Singing in Musical Theatre

In addition to acting and dancing, musical theatre performers sing, and we simply cannot discuss performing in musical theatre without addressing the importance of song. While the following information stresses the *vital importance of vocal training*, it also emphasizes the power of acting while performing a song. The key ingredient in all of musical theatre performance is acting. Act the dance, act the scene, and act the song.

First and foremost, if you want to be a performer, start taking voice lessons. Even if you don't fancy yourself a singer, voice training will teach you more about your vocal instrument and how to use it safely. You don't want to be the person who misuses their voice by projecting incorrectly nightly in rehearsal, only to suffer laryngitis the day before the show opens. Plus, the ability to read music and safely carry a tune is becoming a baseline expectation for those casting in professional theatre.

But I'm Really Not a Singer

So, you don't fancy yourself a singer. But let's say you've been cast in a role that requires you to sing a little. Or you're a dancer, and you need to sing in the chorus while dancing. In addition to starting or continuing voice lessons, you can alleviate much of the anxiety associated with singing if you *act the song*. Analyze your song as you would a monologue by answering these three questions:

- Who are you speaking to?;
- What do you want?;
- What is the emotional journey of your character in this song? (In other words, how do you feel at the beginning of the song and how do those emotions grow and/or change over the course of the song?)

Let's try an example together with "Were I Thy Bride" from *The Yeoman and the Guard* (see Table 5.A). First, read the lyrics. You'll see that I have added notes with action verbs and imagery. These are simply suggestions that may help to invigorate the performance. When you break the song into beats and imagine an action to underlie the words you are singing, it adds a layer of depth and focuses your character's motivation.

Next, we answer the following:

- Who are you speaking to? *I am speaking to the person I love;*
- What do you want? *I want this person to love and marry me;*
- What is your emotional journey? *I begin hopeful that my love will be returned but realize that my love is unrequited.*

You'll note that these answers are simple, clear and direct. Next, be very detailed and specific about who it is you are singing to in this moment. What

Table 5.A "Were I Thy Bride" from *The Yeoman and the Guard*

Lyrics	Action	Imagery
Were I thy bride, Then all the world beside Were not too wide To hold my wealth of love – Were I thy bride	to envelop	Imagine your energy radiating out to your lover; envelop them with your love.
Upon the breast My loving head would rest, As on her nest The tender turtle dove – Were I thy bride!	to caress	Imagine gently resting your head on your lover's chest and caressing them.
This heart of mine Would be one heart with thine, And in that shrine Our happiness would dwell – Were I thy bride!	to press	Imagine pressing their hands to your heart, so they can feel your love.
And all day long Our lives should be a song: No grief, no wrong Should make my heart rebel – Were I thy bride!	to insist	Imagine your energy pulling them to you.
The silvery flute, The melancholy lute, Were nightowl's hoot To my low whispered coo – Were I thy bride!	to retreat	Begin to doubt your ability to convince them that you are the right person for them.
The skylark's trill Were but discordance shrill To the soft thrill Of wooing as I'd woo – Were I thy bride	to advance	Renew your resolve. Advance to woo them!
The rose's sigh Were as a carrion's cry To lullaby Such as I'd sing to thee, Were I thy bride!	to vow	Vow that your love is the only love they'll ever need.
A feather's press Were leaden heaviness To my caress. But then, of course, you see, I'm not thy bride!	to collapse	After being ignored all this time, realize that there is no hope for your love.

exactly does your lover look like? How long have you felt this way? What is it about this person that you love so much? See this person in your mind's eye as clearly as possible while singing and employ every persuasive tactic you can imagine to achieve your desire, as though your very life depends upon it.

Once you have all of this in mind, you'll be too busy performing "Were I Thy Bride" to feel insecure about the sound of your voice. And the audience will be engrossed in the story. I know this sounds like an oversimplification and yes of course you want to sing on key with lovely tone and technique and so on… but please believe me when I say that you do not need to be the world's greatest vocalist to move an audience. In graduate school, one of my classmates had us all in tears with his rendition of "The Impossible Dream" from *The Man of La Mancha*. He was not a singer in the traditional sense of the word, so he acted the song and spoke the lyrics in time to the accompaniment; and he completely brought the house down with his portrayal. I still tear up when I think about it now. So, while yes, a great voice sure is helpful, don't allow singing to intimidate you. It is another essential method of communication in theatre and dance and developing your vocal instrument is an important addition to your skillset. Start voice training right now so that you can use your instrument safely, and get to the business of acting the song.

The reality is that there's a broad spectrum when it comes to singing ability. Classifying yourself as a singer or a non-singer is not always black and white, and it's quite possible that you fall into the big gray area in-between when it comes to your voice. Maybe you can carry a tune but need help maintaining rhythm. Maybe you've got great rhythm but sometimes sing off key. Maybe you've got the melody on lock, but singing harmonies feels impossible. These "issues" can all be overcome with time, dedication, and training from a qualified voice instructor. Really only about 5% of the population are actually truly tone deaf, so for the vast majority, singing is a teachable thing if you're willing to put in the effort it takes to improve. And as a performer, wouldn't you like to train your *entire* instrument? You may not be the next Bernadette Peters or Ben Platt, but you are YOU and what a joy it would be for audiences to see your unique interpretation of a song.

Should I Be Looking for a Voice Teacher or Vocal Coach?

A *voice teacher's* primary aim is to work with the student to develop healthy singing. They train students in voice technique to improve the sound of their voice safely and effectively. A *vocal coach's* primary aim is to help build a student's song repertoire. They will recommend songs that showcase the singer's voice, help to prepare song cuttings and arrangements, and teach the song to the student. Generally speaking, if you are new to singing, you should seek out a voice teacher first. Over time as you develop good technique, you should add a vocal coach to help you build an amazing repertoire of songs.

Oh, Trust Me, I Can Sing!

So, you've got a great sound and you have years of voice training. That's wonderful! Of course, the same rule applies to you too: *act the song*. It doesn't matter how good your voice is if there's no emotional truth behind it. Remember the ballet dancer with wonderful technique and no expression? The technique is impressive, but without passion, the performance underwhelms. If you really want to move the audience, you must do the homework of telling the story with active emotion.

Assignment: Song Performance

Choose a song from a musical and develop a performance of the song. Remember to create blocking and movement that's motivated and reveals your character's desires. Analyze the lyrics of the song and incorporate action verbs and imagery to help flesh out your portrayal. If you do not have access to live accompaniment, find a karaoke backing track to the song, ideally with piano instrumentation only (there are many audio tracks available on YouTube). Be prepared to perform your song for your peers.

In Summary

More and more performers "do it all." In fact, the goal of achieving the status of triple threat (a performer who can sing, dance, and act), is being replaced by the ambition of becoming a quadruple threat (a performer who can sing, dance, act, and play an instrument!). If you want to expand your skills to include all facets of performance, start training in jazz dance and musical theatre. Performers who pursue opportunities in musical theatre grow as vocalists, dancers, and actors.

The expectation is not that you become a master in every area of performance. But if you are truly committed to reaching your potential as a performer, you should explore every area of performance available to you. This exploration will help you to become better informed about who *you* are as a performer. Musical theatre provides an excellent platform for you to showcase your uniqueness. So, the next time you see a musical theatre audition, see it as a learning opportunity. You will receive instruction in voice (musical director), dance (choreographer), and acting (director) every night in rehearsal.

Don't shy away from jazz dance and musical theatre experiences out of fear that you are lacking skill, and jump at the opportunity to learn more. As and when you can, take classes in voice, movement and dance, and acting. With the help of a voice teacher, you can accumulate the tools to safely use your vocal instrument. Through training in dance and movement, your physical expressiveness in performance can dramatically improve. When combined with acting training, your performance can reach new heights. Through musical theatre, you will gain a new appreciation for the stamina it takes to perform with fullest expression, and you will be gathering the tools necessary to successfully navigate any audition (see the following chapter for more on auditioning!).

Bibliography

American Mutoscope and Biograph Company. (c1903). *Cake Walk*. www.loc.gov/item/96520361/

Berlin, E.A. (1994). *King of Ragtime: Scott Joplin and His Era*. Oxford University Press.

Biography.com. (2014). "Jelly Roll Morton." 2 April. www.biography.com/musician/jelly-roll-morton

British Pathé. (2014a). "Katherine Dunham Performing Ballet Creole (1952) | British Pathé" [Video]. *YouTube*, uploaded by British Pathé, 27 August. www.youtube.com/watch?v=iSTuO5E9_1g&t=37s

British Pathé (2014b). "The Real 'Black Bottom' Dance" [Video]. *YouTube*, uploaded by British Pathé, 13 April. www.youtube.com/watch?v=rQ9qapVmWi4

Brubeck, D. (2014). "Unsquare Dance" [Video]. *YouTube,* uploaded by Dave Brubeck, 7 November. www.youtube.com/watch?v=lbdEzRfbeH4

Campbell, M. (1996). *And the Beat Goes On: An Introduction to Popular Music in America 1840 to Today*. Schirmer Books.

"The 'Charleston' in Charleston – Outtakes." (1926). [Video]. Movie Image Research Collections, Digital Video Repository, University of South Carolina, Fox News Story B2703, Temporal Coverage, Filmed 22 May. https://mirc.sc.edu/islandora/object/usc%3A2747

"Chita Rivera & Jack Cole: 'Beale Street Blues.'" (2018). [Video]. *YouTube*, uploaded by Andrew Choreographer, 31 July. www.youtube.com/watch?v=dWvlFRZejDo

Dance Spirit. (2019). "The Jazz Breakdown." 6 September. www.dancespirit.com/the-jazz-breakdown-2326335865.html

"Dizzy Gillespie feat. Charlie Parker – A Night in Tunisia." (2012). [Video]. *YouTube*, uploaded by Classic Mood Experience, 17 December. www.youtube.com/watch?v=gfLVVHxk4IM/

"Duke Ellington and his Orchestra – Take the 'A' Train (1962) [Official Video]." (2012). [Video]. *YouTube*, uploaded by Storyville Records, 4 December. www.youtube.com/watch?v=D6mFGy4g_n8

Encyclopaedia Britannica. (2016). "Ragtime." *Encyclopædia Britannica*, 5 April. www.britannica.com/art/ragtime

Fernandez, R. (2014). "Latin Jazz." *Encyclopædia Britannica*, 4 October. www.britannica.com/art/Latin-jazz#ref1088972

"Giordano Moves." (2011). [Video]. *YouTube*, uploaded by giordanojazzdance, 18 February. www.youtube.com/watch?v=zAJ4F01kHSE

Gottlieb, W. (n.d.). "Machito & Mario Bauza." *PBS*. www.pbs.org/wgbh/latinmusicusa/legends/machito-mario-bauza/

Hurwitz, N. (2014). *A History of the American Musical Theatre: No Business like It.* Routledge.

Jazz in America (n.d.). *Bebop.* www.jazzinamerica.org/LessonPlan/5/5/230.

"Josephine Baker La Revue des Revues." (2020). [Video]. *YouTube*, Uploaded by American Lindy Hop Championships, 30 May. www.youtube.com/watch?v=R2PCPsXXhm4

Lomax, A., & Gushee, L. (2001). *Mister Jelly Roll: The Fortunes of Jelly Roll Morton, New Orleans Creole and "Inventor of Jazz."* University of California Press.

Loney, G. (1984). *Unsung Genius: The Passion of Dancer-Choreographer Jack Cole.* Watts.

"Luigi – Classic Jazz Dance Master." (2019). [Video]. *YouTube*, uploaded by Bob Boross, 7 January. www.youtube.com/watch?v=KNRsgl671kk

"Maple Leaf Rag Played by Scott Joplin." (2006). [Video]. *YouTube*, uploaded by TJaep, 19 October. www.youtube.com/watch?v=pMAtL7n_-rc

"Matt Mattox 1961 Jazz Dance Choreography – Introduction." (2019). [Video]. *YouTube*, uploaded by Bob Boross, 15 January. www.youtube.com/watch?v=qQeB7mH1FOw

Schuller, G. (1991). *The Swing Era: The Development of Jazz 1930–1945.* Oxford University Press.

"Tanga." (2019). [Video]. *YouTube*, uploaded by Machito and His Orchestra – Topic, 31 May. www.youtube.com/watch?v=fAh5AuQSPoM

"Whiteys Lindy Hoppers… Hellzapoppin." (2010). [Video]. *YouTube*, uploaded by docludi2, 7 September. www.youtube.com/watch?v=ahoJReiCaPk

Count Basie Center for the Arts. (n.d.). *William J. "Count" Basie Biography – Count Basie Theatre.* https://thebasie.org/countbasiebio/

6 Auditioning

From a Necessary Evil to a Time to Shine

For many, auditioning is an anxiety inducing experience. And for good reason: it's difficult to perform when a job is on the line. You feel that you are being judged, and let's face it, you are. Well, not judged in the sense that the casting director is being *judgmental*, but they are certainly looking to see whether you are a good fit for the role. There's a myriad of factors the casting director must take into consideration, and it's all happening while you're up there giving it your all. There's no way around it, auditioning is tough. But it's not impossible! In this chapter, we will explore tips and tricks to hone your skills in auditioning.

Audition Tips

To get started, consider the following five lessons to help redirect your approach from surviving to thriving, from a necessary evil to a time to shine:

1 **It's a performance.**
   If you can train yourself to think of the audition as a performance, one that you rehearse and perform like any other performance, then the focus shifts from "I hope they like me," to playing action.

   All too often I see performers succumbing to the stressful environment of an audition setting. While it's difficult to concentrate and the temptation to become a prisoner to your nerves is great, do not give the audition process the power to throw you off your game. If you do, auditioning will become a monumental obstacle that prevents you from showing your incredible gifts as a performer.

   It's completely natural to have a certain amount of nervous energy, but it is important to channel that energy into a sense of ease and focus (the exercises in Chapter 2 can help). You are able to handle stage fright when you perform, so preparing for an audition in a similar fashion will ensure a strong showing.

DOI: 10.4324/9781003149699-7

2 **Be yourself.**

When I was an undergraduate student, we had a guest artist visit our acting class to coach our monologues. I was thrilled to have the opportunity
to perform for the biggest casting director in our area. I remember so
vividly my performance; I gave it everything I had. Immediately after, she
said, "That was really nice. But this time, do it again and just be yourself."
I had *no idea* what she meant by that. I thought, "But I'm acting." It took
me a long time to understand what that advice really meant.

"Be yourself" means act how *you* act. Use *your* imagination and respond to *your* character's given circumstances and respond using *your*
voice and movement. Perform not how you think your favorite actor
would perform it or how you think the director/producer/casting director wants you to perform it. *You* do it. Just be *you*. The same idea is
true for dancing. Dance how *you* dance. See the movement and use *your*
skills to execute that movement to the best of *your* ability. The choreographer wants to see how *your* body moves to their choreography. And
if you're given the opportunity to improvise, do not back down or shy
away from the opportunity to dance with *your* spirit, showcasing all that
you are as a dancer. Show them *your* light!

3 **Know your type.**

I dread this discussion because you have the ability to portray a variety
of different roles, so try to think of your awareness of character type as
something that can serve as a radar to help you hone in on material that
showcases your strengths as a performer. Your type is not some mold
you must fit yourself into because remember, I just said to be yourself,
and you are wonderfully unique. But the fact remains, general character
types such as leading lady, leading man, quirky sidekick, jock, hero, out-
sider, villain, and lover exist. My type tends to be the "woman scorned"
or more generally the second lead or supporting character.

So, what's your type? I wouldn't be surprised if you don't really know.
It's difficult to distinguish your type if you are in the pre-professional
stage of your training because you are developing your craft by exploring a wide range of characters both in class and in performance. You've
quite possibly performed in productions where your character was 30
years older than you. But in the professional world, if you are 20 years
old, the odds of you being cast as a 50-year-old are nil.

Exploring a variety of characters is important to growing as an artist,
but knowing how to market yourself in this business is also important.
An agent will want to know how you see yourself and will compare
your response to how others see you. Your response will inform them
about your level of self-awareness. They cannot send you out on every

audition, and they want to work with you to discover the roles where you have the best chance of being cast (O'Neil, 2011).

Knowing yourself, sensing how others perceive you, and being honest about your strengths and weaknesses will be great aids in identifying which roles are in your wheelhouse, so you can prepare the right material for an audition. Still unsure how to assess your type? Consider the following:

- Do people ever say you look like a famous performer? If so, look at the roles your doppelganger has played and start analyzing those roles. Notice anything in common about the roles? Make notes on the characters' similarities. And remember, you're not researching how to imitate that famous performer; you are looking for roles that might be right for you, which you will then interpret *your* way;
- Have you ever performed a role that really felt right? What was it about that role that worked so well for you?

Knowing your type can be liberating if you see it as an opportunity to nail your audition. While it may sound limiting, I'd argue that it can be an avenue towards success, opening doors for other varied roles in the future. And your type will evolve as you age. It's not that you are incapable of playing every role out there, it's just that it helps to have a clear sense of which roles casting directors are most likely to consider for you. Help them help you. When you know your strengths, you can find audition material that best showcases them.

The same advice can be applied to those primarily interested in the dance world. Prior to auditioning, do your research and find out what kind of dancer the company is looking for and assess whether you have that skillset. Analyze how your training has shaped you as a dancer, and if you want to break out of that mold, start actively pursuing the training that will expand your dance repertoire. Also be sure to observe whether all company members have a similar body type and assess whether it matches your own. For example, Rockettes must be between 5'6" and 5'10.5" tall and be skilled in ballet, tap, and jazz. If you do not fit that description, move on by looking for companies with less emphasis on a particular body type and check production photos to see whether varied body types are represented in their company.

4   **Don't take it personally.**
Easier said than done, right? There's no two ways about it... rejection is hard. You might feel it in your bones that you are perfect for the part and yet you are not cast. But there are so many factors involved in casting that you have zero control over. There could be something incredibly specific that they are looking for, and you might not know what it is

when you walk into the audition (it could be something as simple as they require certain measurements to fit into the already made costume). All you can do is show your work. When you can walk away from an audition knowing you did what you set out to do with your performance, then managing your response to the outcome whether good or bad is possible and completely necessary for you to continue in this discipline. The rest is simply out of your hands.

5   **It's all about preparation.**
Commit to rehearsing your audition and creating the best possible physical and mental environment in which to perform, so that when the time comes, you are free to perform your interpretation of the piece. Think of auditioning as another very important component of training. You should perform your audition for anyone willing to watch, and you should have an audition coach. You should attend, participate, and even coordinate mock auditions frequently. I hold multiple mock auditions when I teach musical theatre dance, and students often come back to say how much more at ease they felt when they attended the real thing as a result. So, ask your friends, professors, mentors to help you prepare; mock auditions are actually quite fun and can help to shift your mindset from fear to joy. When you create repeated positive experiences with mock auditions, you can transfer that feeling to actual auditions. It just takes time and repetition.

Finding Audition Material

Learn more about yourself by completing the following assignments.[1] These assignments will help you to identify the kind of audition material that best showcases who you are as an artist:

Assignment: You and Your Interests[2]

Answer the following questions. Share your answers with your peers.

1. List at least a dozen adjectives that describe who you are.
2. Who are your favorite playwrights/authors and why?
3. What/who makes you laugh and why?
4. If you could live in any other time or place, where and when would it be and why?
5. With what groups do you identify? (e.g., Irish Catholic; book lover; sci-fi enthusiast)

6. What famous people (not performers) do you most admire and why?
7. What famous performers do you most admire and why?
8. What is something you are passionate about and why?
9. What is something you fear and why?
10. What is something you like about yourself?
11. What is something you would like to change in yourself?
12. What is something you would like to change outside of yourself (family, school, community, country, world)?
13. Outside of performing, what do you most enjoy doing (hobbies, activities, etc.)?
14. What type of animal do you identify with or like most and why?
15. How would your best friend describe you?

Assignment: Object of My Affection

Find an object that is meaningful to you. Discuss with a peer why it is significant. Explore the object with your five senses and rediscover the memories it conjures.

Assignment: Sharing a Memory

Recall a time in your life that is significant. Be as specific as you can in discussing this event with a peer.

Assignment: Common Themes

1. What common themes have you heard from your peers when discussing/performing the assignments listed above?
2. What stands out to you as an important priority in the lives of you and your peers?
3. What plays, musicals, dances can you find that address some or all of these themes, opinions, priorities? Work with your peers and professors to curate a list of audition materials (the next assignment will also help with this task).

Assignment: Did Someone Say Movie Night?!

Even if it feels like auditions are a long way down the road, continuously research possible audition material and add to your audition material list regularly. Make it fun by watching, reading, or researching a new work every week. You don't have to do this alone. You could get together with a group, watch a film adaptation of the work (or have a table-read) and discuss with one another the parts you'd be best suited to play. Then, take notes of the songs/monologues/dance styles that the character(s) performed. Before you know it, your resource of materials from which to pull for auditions will be vast. And, you will need this information soon, if not for an audition then for a class. Better this than spending hours upon hours in the library or online trying to find audition material for an audition the next day. No matter how much you love theatre and dance, those days are exhausting and not very productive. This will also prevent you from making a last-minute dash and googling "audition monologues" or "audition songs" as you know so many others do. Avoiding theatre "lists" strengthens your odds of discovering a hidden gem. So, grab a friend, host a movie night, and take notes of your findings in your journal.

"Non-Singers" Looking for an Audition Song

If you fall into the "non-singer" category but need an audition song, you want to find something that is "talk" heavy. "Pretty Little Picture" from *A Funny Thing Happened on the Way to the Forum*, the title song in *Gigi*, "I've Grown Accustomed to her Face" from *My Fair Lady*, "I'm Just a Girl Who Can't Say No" from *Oklahoma!*, and "A Person Can Develop a Cold" from *Guys and Dolls* are just a few song examples for someone who doesn't fall into the "singer" category but can carry a tune because these songs are really all about personality and acting and not about having the world's most amazing singing voice. To get a better sense of what you're looking for, give these songs a listen and then go out and explore songs that speak to you as a performer. Believe me, there are plenty of songs out there for the actor who does not fancy themselves a singer.

That said, before committing to your choice, do yourself a favor and google "Audition songs on the 'do not sing' list." This will help you to avoid the trap of selecting a song that is overdone. Matthew Edwards, Associate Professor of Voice at Shenandoah Conservatory says, "The problem with an overdone song isn't that we are tired of hearing the song, but rather that so many people sing it that you are going to end up being compared to others" (Edwards & Edwards, 2019). He makes a very good point that it's best not to be compared or confused with another performer who sang the same song if you can.

It's not easy, but selecting your audition song is incredibly important, and it takes a whole lot of time and patience to find something that not only fits your voice and type, but that you feel connected to emotionally because as you well know by now, you must act the song (are you getting tired of me saying that yet?). Research by reading and watching musical after musical.

Once you've found the audition material that showcases your artistry, you're ready to get down to the business of preparing your audition. We'll begin by discussing self-tape auditions and then move on to exploring live auditions.

Self-Tape: The Art of Auditioning at Home

With advances in technology, casting through self-tape auditions (where the performer films their audition and submits the video file electronically) is on the rise. While one might assume that self-tape auditions are primarily for on-camera roles, casting through self-tape auditions for theatre roles is also increasing rapidly; self-tape auditions are being requested now more than ever. So, what does that mean for you, the performer? How can you best showcase your work through a self-tape audition?

Creating an At-Home Studio

Before we discuss practical tips to improve the technical quality of your self-tape audition, remember that the casting director knows it's a self-tape. At the end of the day, your performance is all that matters. If you give a strong performance, the casting director can and will overlook less than ideal video quality. You can have an amazing audition without all of the technical bells and whistles. That said, here are some simple and effective ways to create the best environment for your self-tape audition:

Lighting

The casting director needs to see you clearly. Sometimes natural lighting can do the job more than adequately. The important thing to remember about natural lighting is that filming with a window behind you will likely cause you to appear in silhouette. That is far from ideal lighting, as the casting director can see very little of your face and expression. Fluorescent over-head lighting can make skin appear washed-out. Best to avoid filming under fluorescent lighting whenever possible. While there's lots of amazing (and expensive) lighting equipment out there, most of us are on a budget. If you fall into the budget conscious category, consider purchasing a *ring light*. This piece of lighting equipment is an inexpensive investment that will direct attention to your face. If you have the space and a bit more in your budget, a softbox lighting kit would also make a great addition.

Background

The background in your shot should be free of any visual distractions. Many performers choose to mount a blue, black, grey, or white (be careful with white as it may wash-out skin) backdrop behind them to ensure the viewer's focus remains on them and their performance. However, even these well-intentioned performers can fall into a trap; hanging a *wrinkled* curtain for their backdrop. Honestly, I find a heavily wrinkled curtain more distracting than someone performing in front of a bookshelf filled with interesting titles! Investing in a collapsible (aka pop-up) background will help you avoid the wrinkle trap. Like the ring light, collapsible backgrounds (made of thick muslin) can be found at a good price, and it's a piece of equipment you'll use often in your home studio. Of course, if you have a completely plain wall to use as your background, that's great too.

Camera

With the quality of phone cameras improving at breakneck speed, odds are your phone's camera will work well for your recording. Needless to say, there's a stunning amount of options regarding top of the line cameras you could use for your self-tape, but it's rare these days that I see a camera phone self-tape audition with less than adequate video quality. So, you probably already have what you need. If using your phone's camera, make sure you film with the phone on its side which will produce a landscape orientation. Landscape placement will make it so that your image fills the screen. If you film with the phone upright, the camera produces a portrait orientation, and there will be large black bars on the left and right side of the screen when viewing. Ensure that more of your image is captured by going for landscape composition.

Camera Angle

When filming your audition, the camera should be positioned at the level of your eyeline. You do not want the placement of the camera to be such that you have to look up or down at it. A tripod is a very handy piece of equipment to place the camera exactly where you need it. That said, I've put my camera on a stool and a stack of books, and it worked just fine! But I must say, a tripod makes life so much easier. However you manage to rig your camera, make sure to have the camera at *eye level*.

Camera Shot

There are many camera shots, and while the casting director will likely specify which shot to use for the self-tape audition, you'll most often film your audition as one of the following medium shots:

Medium full shot (aka three-quarter shot): from the knees up
Medium shot: from the waist up
Medium close-up: from the chest up

Take a look at other shot descriptions that you'll need to know:

Full shot: entire body from head to toe
Cowboy shot: from the mid-thigh up
Close-up: full face
Choker: face from just above the eyebrows to just below the mouth
Extreme close-up: small portion of the performer fills the screen (such as the
eyes or mouth)

Sound

Simply put, you need to be heard easily and clearly. If you're filming from your laptop or camera phone, those mics may be adequate. But if you sound distant or as though there is an echo or like you're speaking into a can, then you're going to need an upgrade. While some opt for a lavalier lapel mic, a shotgun mic that can mount to your camera will suit your needs well and give your vocal performance a nice, natural sound to it.

Performer Focus

Probably the most important component of your self-tape audition (besides being truthful) is your visual focus (in other words, where you look when you are performing your monologue, song, or scene). Think of the camera lens as the casting director. Just as you would not use the casting director as your scene partner when performing in a live audition, do not look directly into the camera when performing your on-camera audition. If you were sent a scene to perform for your audition, place your scene partner off camera as near to the camera as possible; your scene partner's eyes should be at the level of the camera. If you are performing a monologue, place your imagined scene partner slightly to the right or left of the camera. This may take some trial and error before you get it right. You want to capture as much of your eyes as possible without looking directly into the camera. Do not, I repeat, *do not* submit an audition with you performing in profile. If one of your eyes is partially obstructed, you're looking too far to the side.

What to Wear

For a general audition, demonstrate your respect for the audition process through your choice in clothing. Professional dress for a general audition is the expectation, however that does not necessarily mean wearing your Sunday best. The most important thing is that you feel comfortable moving and that you are happy with your selection. And be sure to let your clothes compliment you, not overpower you. Also, practice walking in your shoes. Check and recheck that they are comfortable and that you can move about the space with ease. Now is not the time to try out your new 3" wedge heel or to break in your cowboy boots that are one size too small. Even though your self-tape audition will be with you either standing or sitting in one spot, your shoes need to be carefully selected to help ground and balance you, not make you feel wobbly and off-kilter.

Tips: Avoid clothing with writing or graphics on them. Floral prints, plaids, or stripes often work, but if they are distracting, best to go with a solid color (remember it's all about showcasing you, not your clothes). You need to test out your selection by shooting some footage wearing the outfit in front of the backdrop with the lighting you intend to use to be sure your selection works. For example, if you wear a black, long-sleeve turtleneck and black trousers while standing in front of a black backdrop, you might look like a floating head (unless you have professional grade lighting and camera).

If you know the role you are auditioning for, you may wish to wear something *suggestive* of that character, but you should not dress in costume. So, for example, if you are auditioning for a high-power attorney, you may consider wearing a suit. If you're auditioning for a young middle-class housewife from the 1950s, you may consider wearing a tea-length dress. But again, do not run out and buy a superhero costume for your Marvel movie audition!

Next, let's take a look at the variances in performance style when creating a self-tape audition.

Self-Tape Acting Audition: Live Theatre Role vs. Film Role

Whether you are self-taping your audition for an on-camera role (film, television, industrial, web series, commercial) or for a theatre role, you know by now that a truthful and authentic performance is always the aim. If you are self-taping your audition for an acting role in a live theatre production, you can have a fuller physical and vocal life for your character than if you were auditioning for an on-camera role. However, when you are self-taping your audition for an acting role in a live theatre production, you do not need to project your voice as much or move as broadly as you would if you were actually at a live theatre audition. So, while you definitely want to showcase a physical and vocal life for your character, don't let it overpower your performance in the self-tape. If you do, your performance will be jarring to watch on film.

If you are auditioning for an on-camera role, remember that the camera "sees" everything, so finding focus and stillness is important. The camera records even the minutest detail. This is not to say that you cannot move, but know that every movement makes an impact. Habitual movement, such as shifting weight back and forth and unmotivated gesturing do not translate well on film. You simply cannot "phone in" or "fake" your performance because the camera will reveal inauthentic acting instantly. The saying "The eyes are the windows to the soul" certainly applies to on-camera acting. If character emotion and intention are expressed truthfully through the eyes, the camera will capture it, providing the viewer with a glimpse into the soul of your character. But remember, acting for the camera does not mean you radiate less energy. Rather, simply think of your energy as being harnessed and channeled differently than acting for the stage.

Self-Tape Dance Audition

It's quite likely you'll need someone with a steady hand to film your audition if the dance features locomotor movement. If you have the opportunity to film in a dance studio, the videographer should shoot with the mirrors behind them. I find it distracting when they shoot where I can see them holding the camera in the mirror's reflection. If it is a general audition, be sure to put your very best material first on your audition film (aka *demo reel, audition reel*), as the casting director may not have time to watch your entire audition. If you know which style of dance they're looking to cast, make sure to lead your film with that style. They may set a time limit on your audition film, but if they don't, I wouldn't exceed a five-minute dance compilation. And don't forget to act the dance!

Self-Tape Singing Audition

You need accompaniment (live or recorded) during the audition to underscore your vocal performance. That said, you and your voice must be focal points, so be sure the accompaniment isn't louder than you. Ideally the accompaniment is piano only, as additional synthesized instrumentation can be a distraction.

Preparing for a Live Theatrical Audition

There are many possible scenarios when attending an audition for a live theatrical production. At times, you might audition for a single production. Other times, you will audition for a single company that is casting for their entire season. Still other times, you will audition for multiple companies at once (known as a unified audition). The list goes on. Each audition is unique, so your first order of business is to find out as much as you can about the audition, especially what they expect from you and any submission deadlines for applications.

Acting/Singing Auditions

While the exact format of your audition is unknown, there are trusted materials you can begin to assemble to create your performance portfolio now.

At minimum, you need to prepare a contemporary dramatic monologue, a contemporary comic monologue, a period dramatic monologue, a period comedic monologue, and two contrasting songs. This way you'll be ready for just about any audition! Keep the monologues at about one minute, and while you should learn the entire songs, know that you will perform about 16 bars at an audition. Make sure that your sheet music is in the key that you intend to sing it, and if there are cuts in the song, get your voice instructor to assist you in properly indicating the cut in your sheet music.

Dance Auditions

If you are auditioning for a specific musical, then it would be safe to assume that you will be taught a dance combination in the style most heavily featured in the musical. Researching the musical as much as you can prior to the audition will put you at a great advantage, helping you to create a specific physical life in your dancing that reflects the motivation of the characters in the song. While the benefits of play analysis prior to auditioning are massive, that option is not always viable. If you are running to a dance audition without much time to prepare, you have to trust your training and enter the audition with an open mind. I know it's cliché, but seriously, *leave it all on the dance floor*. There's no room for self-doubt. Be open and willing, and your love for dance will be evident to everyone in the room.

If you are auditioning for a specific dance company (as opposed to a musical theatre production), then it is imperative that you do your homework by researching the company's repertoire as much as possible. You may be asked to have a dance prepared, and if so be sure it is in the style of the company (in other words, don't perform a modern dance if the company primarily performs tap!). You will also likely be taught some new material, and be asked to improvise. Focus and give it everything you've got.

Choreographers are looking for potential, not perfection. You need to show them that you can:

- Demonstrate understanding of the dance styles introduced;
- Perform movements and positions introduced demonstrating body alignment, rhythmic ability, spatial awareness, and artistry;
- Work cooperatively with fellow auditionees in performing choreographed ensemble movement.

If you can walk away saying you did your best to achieve those goals, then you nailed it!

Unified Auditions

At a unified audition with multiple theatre companies in attendance, looking to cast perhaps their entire season, you may be given a choice as to whether you wish to audition as an actor only, dancer only, actor and dancer, or actor, dancer, *and* singer. Do not hesitate to contact your instructors to get their opinion on how you should categorize your audition. If you do not consider yourself a singer or dancer, it is more than ok *not* to sing and dance at a unified audition. Better to have a wonderful acting audition than to be terrified of the song you feel certain you will blunder or overly anxious about your lack of training in dance. You can still get a callback with an actor only audition. But if you've been actively training in voice, dance, and acting, I bet you can put together a package that you would be proud to perform.

Get online and pour over every bit of information you can find about the unified audition, and then follow the instructions to the nth degree. Pay close attention to the time limit for the audition, and make sure your audition is *under* that time limit. Note the emphasis on the word *under*. So, for example, if you have 90 seconds total for the audition, your actual audition, which includes your slate (saying your name and audition number), should sit comfortably at 80 seconds (or less). If when you time your audition, you very occasionally go over 90 seconds (even if it's just once or twice), your audition is too long. You need to go back and see where you can make cuts. Trust me, you want ample time so your audition can breathe. You do not want to be rushing just so you can fit everything into 90 seconds. It is unnerving to hear the timekeeper yell out, "Time!" in the middle of your audition. It's awkward for you, and it's an indication to casting directors that you did not take the time to follow their guidelines when preparing your audition. While it's certainly not the end of the world to be over time in an audition, it's not ideal. And you want to create the most ideal environment you can to succeed.

Next, find out who is going to be at the unified audition, and check out what they do! There may be a broad range of companies there, but you may find trends. If so, you can cater your audition package to address their needs and thereby better your chances. So, for example, let's say there are 40 theatre companies attending and looking to cast their summer season. In researching the summer production histories of these companies online (or you may even find that they've already announced their upcoming summer season), you learn that one company produces Shakespeare, over half mainly produce musical theatre, and the rest produce a mix of contemporary comedy and drama. What would you do with your 90 seconds? If it were me, I'd sing a comic 16 bars and perform a dramatic monologue. Shakespeare's out for this unified audition. While it may not be this cut and dry, knowing who you are performing for puts you in a much better position for the audition, and if you are called back, you already know a bit about the company. It shows the casting director that you've taken the initiative to research them. It shows them your level of interest and commitment.

Logistics of a Unified Audition

Next, I'd like to describe two examples of what you may encounter during a unified audition, so that you can visualize what to expect. It may not happen exactly as I am about to describe, but it won't be far off. Are you ready? Here we go!

You enter the facilities and check in, and then you wait (and wait). You're likely to be in a holding area with many other performers. Some of them may be warming up (stretching, vocalizing), some may be chatting with others, some may be listening to their headphones... all will be nervous. Do what feels comfortable to you. Do not feel obliged to make small talk if that will only make your more nervous, but do be courteous and polite to everyone around you. After all, you could be working with someone in that room soon. An audition coach once said to me that the audition starts from the moment you exit your car. In other words, be kind to everyone, treat everyone with respect, and be professional. Be the person you would want to work with the *entire* time you're at the audition.

Unified Audition Scenario 1

Your name and/or number is called. You exit the holding area, and walk to another area just outside the audition space. You wait with a very small group of others in line. It may be a hallway or off stage in the wings if you are auditioning at a theatre. Then, the person auditioning before you exits. Now it's your turn. You walk in alone and audition for the casting directors (usually casting directors from the different theatre companies sit with space in between them, so if you are auditioning in a theatre, they will be dotted about in the audience seats). When you finish, you exit.

Unified Audition Scenario 2

You are put into a group of actors and when it is time, your entire group is called into the audition space. You all sit and watch each person in your group audition. When you finish, return to your seat and wait out any remaining auditions. Then, when everyone in your group is finished, you all depart en masse.

When It's Your Turn to Audition

If you are singing, you have your sheet music in hand and you walk directly to the accompanist, hand them the music, show them where your piece starts and ends, and give them any notes on tempo. Be very, very kind to this person; they are there to help you. Make sure you also tell the accompanist whether you are singing first or performing your monologue first. Then walk center. Remember that the stopwatch starts you as soon as you speak, so make sure you are where you want to be before speaking. Do not start talking while you're still walking to your acting spot. State your name and audition number and begin. When you finish, say thank you, state your name and number again (time permitting), and exit or return to your seat.

If you are disappointed with your audition, do not let it show. If the accompanist moves through the song too quickly or makes a few errors while playing, do not give them a glaring look. Remember they are sight reading the music. Just make it work. Do not apologize in any way through your body language if you are upset or frustrated. Maintain a positive head space, and show them that you can handle the pressures of auditioning. And then, celebrate!

Unified Dance Audition

You've completed your acting/singing audition, and now it's time for the dance audition! At a unified dance audition, you will likely be taught a combination in the theatre jazz style. You might also expect the choreographer to ask intermediate/advanced dancers to learn a more complex dance combination, and it's often quite balletic. They will either select the dancers they wish to see or simply say something along the lines of, "Next we will teach an advanced combination. Advanced dancers, please remain." In this case, the ball is in your court. If you thought the first combination was a real challenge, then this next combination is not for you. If you breezed through the first combination, then stick around for the second.

If at any point, you feel you are so far out of your depth that you might injure yourself, you can always step out. That said, if you just feel a bit overwhelmed or like you know you could do it, but they are teaching it quickly, then stick with it. They are testing you! If you get frustrated and huff off, you have given them a sign that you have a hard time handling stress. If, however, you smile through any missteps, then you've just shown that you are cool under pressure.

What to Wear: Acting/Singing Auditions

Like self-tape auditions, professional dress is the expectation for a live theatrical audition. Most importantly, practice walking in your shoes. Check and recheck that they are comfortable and that you can move about the space with ease.

What to Wear: Dance Auditions

Wear jazz pants, tights, or tights with fitted dance shorts over the top, or a dance skirt with tights on beneath. I advise against only wearing shorts or biker shorts; your legs should be covered to at least the calf for protection should there be any sliding on the floor involved. Wear a leotard or form-fitting shirt. Make sure that if you choose to dance with your midriff showing, you are completely comfortable dancing with this level of skin exposure. All too often I've seen people wearing something that they love the look of when standing still, but they forgot to check in with how they feel in the clothing when dancing. You can see that feeling of discomfort rise as they realize their clothing is showcasing more than they planned; it can be hard for them to continue. Also, for musical theatre auditions, be sure to wear jazz shoes and/or character shoes. Have your dance bag with you, so you can change in and out of shoes as needed.

More on Presentation

Hair: Hair should be out of your face and eyes. They want to see your beautiful and expressive face. If you'd like to have your hair half up, half down, that's fine, just be sure to practice auditioning with it like that. You may find it gets in the way and you'd prefer to pull it all back.

Make-up: Auditions often happen on stage or on film, so you best avoid being washed out by the lights by wearing make-up. Even when auditions are held in a room or studio setting, some make-up to highlight natural features is the norm.

Also note: If you have a monologue, song, *and* dance audition, make sure you bring a bag to change into your dance audition clothes. Include water and towel. And don't forget your dance shoes.

Bottom line: If you feel good about how you're presenting yourself professionally, you'll be comfortable to act, sing, and dance freely and have fun!

Preparing for an In-Person Film Audition

In-person on-camera auditions are much like the self-tape auditions described earlier, except you don't have to worry about the technical issues of filming and submitting the audition yourself. With in-person auditions for on-camera acting, you are usually given the audition material, which will be an excerpt or scene from the script (known as *sides*). Typically, you receive sides in advance of the audition. However, once you're auditioning, the casting director may decide that they'd like for you to read additional scenes or they may want to see you audition for a different role; this is called a *cold reading*, where advanced preparation isn't available to you. When faced with a cold reading, know that your training has prepared you for exactly this moment. The casting director is aware of the advantages of having advanced preparation; there will be many performers capable of memorizing their lines even if they only have an hour with the material. A casting director is also aware of the challenges faced by having no opportunity to prepare. Be kind to yourself, trust your instincts, and just go. It's your job to thrive under pressure, and you want the casting director to see that in you.

For many performers, much of their training is in live theatre technique, and transitioning to on-camera acting can take a moment to adjust. First thing to remember is that you can speak much more quietly for an on-camera audition. If you project in an on-camera audition the way you would for a live theatre audition, you will blow up the microphone (well, not literally, but it will be way too loud).

The second thing to remember is that the individual reading as the other person in the scene you're auditioning for may not give you much to play off. Don't let that make you fumble. And know that they are not meaning to sabotage your audition, they've just been reading the scene over and over for every audition, and it's not about them. It's about *you*. Use all of that acting training and imagine them as the character.

And finally, don't look directly into the camera while you're acting, unless you are specifically told to do so.

But wait, there's more… Lest we forget, the performer must have both a headshot and a resume!

Headshot & Resume

These days, you will most likely submit your headshot and resume electronically, but you should also have hard copies with you on audition days as a backup. It's also handy to have your headshot and resume available electronically, so you can resend if needed; if it's on your mobile device, it will be easier for you should there be technical difficulties on the day. It's no fun being asked for something and not having it available, so hard copies and electronic access ensure you're covered.

Headshot

If you're camera shy, the photo shoot for your headshot can be a nightmare. That said, your headshot is your calling card, so you've got to get photos that speak on your behalf. Think of your photo shoot as another acting job. Have active thoughts in mind as you're being photographed. If you're thinking, "Just smile," or "Don't smile," your eyes in the photo will look a bit vague. Be specific in your thoughts as the camera clicks, and an inner life will be revealed in the photograph.

Figure 6.1 Danielle Mumpower's headshot
Photo credit: Corrine Louie Photo

Figure 6.2 Samuel Floyd's headshot
Photo credit: JKLPhoto, Josh Levinson

Table 6.A Sample resume

Vocal Range	**NAME**	Small Picture
Height	Union Information	
	Phone Number	
	Email	
	Website	
Theatre Experience:		
Jack & the Beanstalk	Mysterious Stranger	Barter Theatre
Oklahoma!	Ado Annie	East Tennessee State
Mr. Burns, A Post-Electric	Marge Simpson	University
Play		East Tennessee State
		University
Training:		
BA Theatre and Dance,		
East Tennessee State		
University		
SAFD Certified: Rapier and		
Dagger & Unarmed Combat		
Special Skills:		
Juggling, Aerial Dance		

Resume

There are lots and lots of way to format your resume, but the most important thing is that it's easily readable with your contact information clearly listed (phone and email). If you don't have many credits at this point, there is no need to pad your resume. If you keep it simple and update it regularly, your resume will always be ready when you need it.

Being a Performer in the Digital Age

Today's performer has a lot more to do than hone their craft. While some hugely famous performers have the luxury of remaining withdrawn from social media (or can afford to hire a team to manage it for them), it's become the norm to network on social media platforms like Facebook, Instagram, Twitter, and LinkedIn. Keeping these platforms professional will serve you well – the last thing you want is for a potential casting director to see last night's indiscretions making the rounds on Facebook. Love it or hate it, social media can be a productive way to promote you and your work.

In addition, it is expected that you have a website that includes a headshot, resume, reel, and links to your social media. Fortunately, constructing a website is easier and more user friendly than ever. And if budget is tight, there are free web builder sites that can help you to create a fantastic webpage; the usual caveats for free webpages are that your domain name will likely include their web builder information, and your site may also have advertising. They still look great, and you can always upgrade at a later time and pay a fee to select your own domain name and remove any advertising. The following websites from ETSU alums Samuel Floyd and Kaleb Stone provide excellent examples: www.samuelfloyd.com, www.kalebmstone.com. Dancers, take a look at ETSU alum Danielle Mumpower's website at: www. daniellemumpower.com.

Demo Reel

Yes, you need one! A reel is an opportunity to show a potential casting director or agent highlights of your work as a performer. As a young artist, you may not yet have professional film credits to use. This is where that at-home studio comes in handy. You can select monologues, dances, songs, and/or scenes (make sure you are the focus in the scene) that you have performed in or worked on in class, record those works, and edit them to create a one- to two-minute demo reel. Put your strongest material first and showcase what you do best. Do not use recordings of performances from live plays or dance concerts where the camera is in the back of the house, and it's difficult to distinguish you from anyone else. It's better to create a clean and clear edit of a selection of your work to demonstrate who you are as an artist at this time. As you land more gigs, you should continue to add in new and edit out older material. Like web builder sites, film editing programs have also never been more user friendly, so there's really no excuse not to create and update your reel regularly.

Make the Internet Work for You

And finally, here's one more note about your life as a performer in this day and age. While there's a myriad of issues that sometimes make me wonder about the cost to benefit ratio of the rapid technological advances occurring seemingly by the minute, there is one undeniable truth to living in the digital age. Access to amazing art is at our fingertips. Our ability to collaborate with artists from around the world is just a click away, and it's never been easier for performing artists to research and explore our medium. Deep and meaningful scholarship can quickly be achieved online with unlimited access to texts, libraries, and archival footage so easily obtainable. New plays can be purchased and downloaded in an instant. You'll find critical theory articles and access to academic journals easily. I recently emailed a well-established musician on the other side of the country, asking him if I could use his music for a new dance film[3] I was choreographing, and he responded with a yes within the hour. All this to say, there's so much more online than social media. Discover the benefits of the internet, and arm yourself with knowledge.

Assignment: Enough Talk. It's Time to Audition!

So, what are you waiting for? It's never too early to start prepping for your next audition. Let's look at a sample action board for preparing for a musical theatre audition:

Table 6.B Example of a musical theatre audition action plan

Musical Theatre Audition Preparation
"He who is best prepared can best serve his moment of inspiration." – Samuel Taylor Coleridge

Day 1	Find and read the musical (read the book, review the score).
Day 2	Watch the musical (if there is a film of a staged version, make that film the one you watch. If there are multiple film versions and you have the time, watch as many versions as you can). Note the differences between the book and the film. If there are multiple film versions, note how the choreography evolved from one film to the next.
Day 3	Research the original choreographer's style. Identify key traits of the choreography.
Day 4	Identify and research the characters you feel you could play.
Day 5	Coaching session with your mentor. Perform any material needed to prepare for the audition.
Day 6	Find an audience and perform your audition (friends, family, anybody who will listen and watch). Do not ask for feedback from them. You just need an opportunity to perform it in front of people.
Day 7	Audition day!

Now, search out an audition, sign up for it, create an action plan to help you prepare, and then actually attend the audition (or submit a self-tape). Seriously, even if you cannot commit to being in a production right now, at least attend an audition. In fact, you might find it easier to audition when you don't desperately *need* the role. We learn by doing, so do it!

In Summary

Don't let a limited budget keep you from making a self-tape audition. While the tools described in this chapter will certainly enhance the technical quality of your work, do the best you can with what you have.

There's a lot more to being a performer than being good at performing. You have to audition. And you have to prepare for an audition like it's your job.

Networking in-person and through social media are also part of the performer's job. A student once shared this saying with me: "You can't be a secret and a success." In other words, get out and audition and create an online presence.

There's no job out there that's all fun all the time. For many, auditioning is the "not so fun" part of the job of being a performer. However, if you can change your perspective on auditioning from fear to confidence, you can and will find joy in every audition.

Notes

1 Instructors, it is recommended that the assignments described in this chapter be explored in class over a number of training days. See Appendix for sample timeline.
2 Acting teacher and performer Belinda Bremner asked many of these questions when I took her acting course as an MFA student at the Chicago College of Performing Arts at Roosevelt University. She demonstrated her interest by taking the time to read everyone's answers and offering suggestions for audition material.
3 You can watch the dance film here: www.youtube.com/watch?v=87A781kjTk0

Bibliography

Edwards, M., & Edwards, M. (2019). "The much-dreaded (maybe over-hyped) do not sing lists." 10 September. https://auditioningforcollege.com/2019/09/10/the-much-dreaded-maybe-over-hyped-do-not-sing-lists/

O'Neil, B. (2011). "Brian O'Neil Talks about 'Type'" [Video]. *YouTube*, uploaded by ActingAsaBusiness, 9 October. www.youtube.com/watch?v=62IKhOJshNU

7 Performer & Theatre Maker

Creating New Works & Breathing New Life into Established Works

Ever watch a performance so moving it brought you to tears? If so, you have felt deeply how truly powerful, transcendent, and cathartic theatre and dance can be. After seeing a performance, have you ever asked yourself, "Exactly, *how* did they go about creating what I just saw?" Producing a theatre and/or dance performance is a varied and unique process; there's simply no one way of doing it. It involves a team of people (writer, producer, director, choreographer, musical director, technical director, stage manager, scenic, lighting, make-up, costume designers, production crew, box office manager, publicity coordinator, and so on) working together for a common goal. As a performer, you are an important member of the theatre-making team.

Your role in the theatre-making process can vary substantially depending on the production. For example, imagine that you are invited to join an amazing theatre company's next production, to find that you will often be collaborating with the director, choreographer, and fellow ensemble members to create a new theatrical work (known as *devised theatre*). A performer who waits to be told what to do by the director and/or choreographer is not as prepared as the performer who enters the rehearsal ready to demonstrate a variety of options and remains open to trying out a myriad of ideas. The latter is a performer who will work time and time again and may find themselves evolving into the position of director, producer, and/or choreographer themselves someday. When a performer lacks the confidence to contribute to the development of a production (whether that production be a new or established work), they are ultimately limiting their opportunities. As we have established, versatility is of vital importance, and the contributions a performer makes to the development of a production are necessary and valued.

Here's a thought (I know it's a bit doom and gloom): a performer could spend more time auditioning than actually performing. So why not *create* performance opportunities for yourself by working with your peers to produce a new or established theatrical work? Ok, so writing, directing, choreographing, and producing may not be for you; they're certainly not for everyone. If that's the case for you, it's still very important to understand everything you can about the process of making a work of theatre because

DOI: 10.4324/9781003149699-8

as a performer, you encounter literally every aspect of a production. When you place yourself in the shoes of other theatre makers, you are more sympathetic to their needs. And remember, you never know what lies ahead. You may find your calling extends beyond that of a performer, so stay open to new opportunities. For the purposes of this chapter, envision yourself not only as a *performer*, but also as a *theatre maker* to explore the conception and development of new and established works for the stage.

Got an Idea? Getting Started

When you have an idea that you want to explore through the medium of performance, turn to the method of *making dances*, also known as *dance choreography* or *dance composition*, to facilitate the creative process. In the simplest terms, choreography requires the manipulation of the three elements of dance, which are:

Energy (force)
Space
Time

Explore the exchange of energy between the dynamic body of the performer and the audience; constantly question how to move the audience through energy, space, and time.

Additionally, turn to theatre by exploring *dramatic structure*. To facilitate the process of creating a new work, first think in terms of identifying the beginning, middle, and end of the story. Although that may seem obvious or childlike in its simplicity, you may often find that you know how you want the piece to end but don't know how to start or vice versa. Then, get specific in developing the framework by exploring Freytag's Pyramid of storytelling: *exposition, inciting incident, rising action, crisis, climax, falling action, resolution, denouement.*

Analyzing these elements in relation to your idea helps to flesh out the work, giving substance and specificity to the themes, characters, and plot. However, do not feel bound to these guidelines; rather, think of them as springboards that you can deviate from at any time. And feel free to shake up your method of delivery. Acting, dance, theatre movement, physical theatre, music, song, sound, spoken word, and film combine in the work I like to make, and I encourage you too to feel free to mix it up; maybe you'll create your own signature genre of performance!

Begin every project by embracing the premise that creativity is innate; we are born with the ability to imagine and create. This can be your mantra throughout the creative process, and you can return to this idea whenever you feel doubtful. *Creativity is innate; we are born with the ability to imagine*

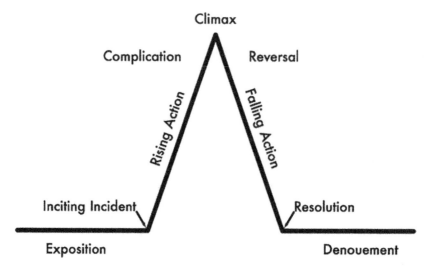

Figure 7.1 Freytag's Pyramid
Image Created by Jonathon Taylor

and create. When you consider creativity as natural as breathing, you may feel the pressure of composing something *new* is eased slightly.

Envisage that the performance is already in your mind and body, and you simply need to let it out. You've heard the saying that you should, "Write what you know." The same notion applies to creating a performance. You can use your personal experiences with visual art, theatre, dance, nature, love, and life to create something new. You can expand, reorder, revive, and reevaluate.

On the other hand, Austin Kleon in his book *Steal Like an Artist* (2012) says, "The best advice is not to write what you know, it's to write what you like. Write the story you like best – write the story you want to read" (p.47). In other words, if you are not feeling particularly stimulated by what you've experienced, then Kleon's viewpoint is a good one to adopt. Find something you feel passionately about and pursue it with zeal. What's important is your level of interest; if your enthusiasm on the subject feels endless, then you owe it to yourself to explore it further.

Sometimes it seems as though an idea for a theatrical work just magically comes to mind. For example, perhaps you've become so captivated and in-spired by the music you're listening to while driving in your car that you start imagining a dance performance unfold (and maybe even miss your exit!). But as the great choreographer Twyla Tharp points out, one cannot *wait* for inspiration to occur (Tharp & Reiter, 2006, p.5). Artists must be proac-tive in their creative pursuits because as with almost any endeavor, there are deadlines to be upheld. In your case, that deadline is *opening night*. There-fore, you must turn to your *craft*, which will ideally help to ignite inspired, purposeful, and thought-provoking theatrical works. One such theatre and dance technique that you can come to rely on when developing a new work is *improvisation*.

Improvisational Structures & Self-Imposed Constraints

Wonderful discoveries are made when working with *guided improvisational structures*. It's amazing how improvisation can unlock material and further build a bond among the ensemble of performers. Improvisation appeals to an ensemble with varying levels of experience and helps to create a com-mon vocabulary between the performers. It evens the playing field for every performer partaking in the spontaneous action because although there are guidelines for the improvisation in place, no one has been given time to pre-pare. Working in the moment creates excitement; none of us *really* knows what's about to happen. Improvisation is an art form in and of itself, but it's also very helpful to try improvisation in rehearsal to help shape what will eventually become a fully realized theatrical work. Improvisation during the rehearsal process fills in the gaps in the production and helps facilitate specificity and depth.

Additionally, *self-imposed constraints* can inspire creativity. When you manufacture an obstacle, restriction, or "problem" that you must solve, your imagination engages. Once your mind starts exploring the variety of ways in which to overcome or navigate the constraint, you begin to see new approaches to the work. The constraint can actually help to accelerate the development of the theatrical work; when the theatre maker fully embraces the constraint, it stimulates their problem-solving capabilities.

I'd like to take a moment now to describe two dances that I choreographed, where *improvisational structures* and *self-imposed constraints* guided much of the process. The hope is that in sharing these experiences, you might identify how you could apply these techniques to whichever theatrical work you're aiming to make; whether it be a one-person show, a contemporary dance, musical, physical theatre, or an innovative interpretation of a character from your favorite play.

The Physics of a Teardrop

The first dance is called *The Physics of a Teardrop*. The inspiration for the dance began with my son. He was three years old when we noticed one eye starting to turn in slightly every now and again. My husband and I took him to the optometrist, where they discovered he needed glasses. That one eye was significantly weaker than the other and so in addition to needing a strong prescription for his glasses, he also needed to patch the stronger eye for a few hours daily. The doctor said it was good that we caught this early as left untreated, it could cause the weaker eye to grow weaker and weaker, leaving the stronger eye to make up for the difference (it can even cause blindness in the weaker eye for some children).

When I tell this story years after the fact, I realize that it's not a particularly unusual tale. Lots of children require glasses, after all. But to me, at the time, I felt terrified... so many questions ran through my brain. Did he always need glasses? Did he spend the first three years of his little life seeing only a blur? Should I have caught this sooner? Or is this something that was only starting? Will the children at his school tease him for needing a patch? He's so young, will he even wear the glasses, let alone a patch? When alone, I'd cover one of my eyes to see what it was like for him. This made me cry a lot. By the way, all my worry was for naught. He loves his glasses, and the kids at his school thought he was super cool for wearing a patch. But at the time, I was a nervous wreck.

So, what to do with all this pent-up emotion? I went to the studio and began working with the movement of a hand covering the eye and with it the idea of tears falling from the eye. Then I asked myself, "How many ways can I physicalize the act of crying?" Once I felt I exhausted every aspect of crying (the shape and quality of a tear; exploring what it would look like if I physicalized weeping with other parts of the body, say my elbow for example; the shuddering shoulders when sobbing; the breath as it holds back the tears, and so on) and through extension, expansion, and connection of these movements together, the beginnings of a dance started to take shape.[1] I then put to use the choreographic device of *canon* (dancers performing the same movement one after the other) to represent the falling of tears one after another.

I then narrowed my perspective. I wanted to study a specific moment in time when we feel a lump in the throat and a tear rising to the surface and we ask ourselves, "Should I really let go and allow the emotion to flow or do I hold back and only permit myself to let a single tear fall?" By thinking of the physical properties of the teardrop, rather than the emotion leading to the teardrop, I found the tears themselves created cold and mysterious shapes. The dancers became the embodiment of a teardrop. And it wasn't until the climax of the dance that the dancers became the person crying. It surprised me that what began as a need to release myself from the fear I was experiencing with my son evolved into a crisp, chilling sort of dance. When I think of my son, I feel such warmth. But by narrowing the focus of the dance and imposing the choreographic device of canon, which was a self-imposed constraint that I strictly adhered to, the dance became its *own thing*. I took myself out of it at some point in the choreographic process, which was good for this dance.

Figure 7.2 Maggi Hines, Eva Alom, and Kelsea Nickels performing *The Physics of a Teardrop* at Northern Kentucky University
Photo credit: Mikki Schaffner

A Line in the Sand

The second dance I'd like to tell you about is called *A Line in the Sand*. I really wanted to challenge the choreographic process by confining myself in terms of space and time. I decided the dancers would move within a square shape and imagined that the dancers were standing outside a square that was outlined with sand. They then step over the sand (crossing over the metaphorical line drawn by the sand) to begin the dance (at one point, I thought we would use sand, but of course, practicality won over). After creating a constraint with space, I also wanted to play around with timing, specifically with stillness and slow motion; I wanted to explore the challenge of engaging through continuous controlled movement (only once in the dance did the performers move quickly).

Thematically I was thinking in terms of questioning, "Do the dancers cross the line in the sand in their relationships, which often requires a good deal of compromise, or do they retreat to their own island, their own way of doing things?" So, it was this back and forth of making and breaking bonds that we were exploring. I had the basic outline of the dance, which was quite simple, but I wanted to reach out to visual art to help in creating the moments of stillness. I chose a handful of abstract sculptures and brought pictures of the sculptures to the dancers, and together we embodied the sculpture pictured as best we could. Now probably no one would look at the dancers in situ and see any resemblance to the sculptures, but it was a really invigorating way to get the creative process going... again, looking to the *craft* of choreography for inspiration. I can easily say that had I not constrained myself in terms of space and time, the dance would be completely different.

It feels a bit strange to discuss what I was thinking about when making a new work because once it's finished, all of that research, all the background information was just to get the work to a point where the audience could watch it and respond to it in whatever way they feel. For example, I don't mind at all if an audience watches a piece and thinks, "Oh they were lovers and they broke up," and they have this whole narrative about what the movement was about that I hadn't considered when choreographing it. And maybe that is what it was about; maybe somewhere in my subconscious that is what it was about for me too.

At the end of the day, it doesn't really matter what my intentions were. Ultimately, it's for the audience to interpret. And it's great for the performers if they can have an exciting or transcendent experience while in rehearsal and performance, but once they're on stage performing, they're there for the audience. If a performer comes offstage and says, "I wasn't really feeling it tonight," the important thing to consider is whether it felt good to the audience. If so, then the performer has done their job well. It's difficult

Figure 7.3 Jenna Middlebrooks, Casey Finkle, Hannah Chang, and Brock Cooley performing *A Line in the Sand* at Northern Kentucky University. Two of the performers in this picture were trained dancers; the other two were actors who began their dance and movement training at ETSU.
Photo credit: Mikki Schaffner

when a performer doesn't get to enjoy that elusive moment of inspiration while performing onstage, but the audience did, so it's all good. As a theatre maker, you must let go because at some point, the production is no longer yours to possess. But I digress… let's get back to creating a new work!

Got a Team? Developing Your Idea

Creating a new work can be lonely. When you think of the countless hours spent alone in front of a computer trying to find the right words or on your own in the dance studio working out the next movement phrase, you are reminded of just how alienating it can be. But once you feel ready to test out what you've been working on, to hear the words performed aloud and see the movement on another person, you get to be in a room filled with generous performers. These artists are critical in the development of the piece. And that is why you always want to be on the lookout for performers willing to test out, to improvise, and to repeat, repeat, repeat. You also need to find performers who are willing to work on something one day, only to throw it all out the next without becoming completely exasperated by the process. When you realize that time wasn't wasted, that it was just part of the journey toward making something greater, you feel grateful and forever indebted to one another. It really does bond the group together, and no matter how far apart you are or how long you go without seeing one another, that process of devising theatre keeps you connected.

I generally cast performers with significantly varying levels of training; some are dancers, and some are actors who can move. The dancers have years of technical training, and so moving within a codified construct feels good to them. The technique is their comfort zone; they have a built-in safety net when performing. The actors have little to no technical training in dance, and so do not have the same movement vocabulary as those with extensive dance training. They have not "tamed" their instrument, so to speak. Both have certain advantages when approaching the work of bringing a newly devised production to life. The trained dancer has intimate knowledge of what works on their instrument, while the actor is open to new and exciting discoveries.

Both also have obstacles to overcome. How does the trained dancer experiment without relying so heavily on what they know already works? And how does the actor develop movement that appeals to a certain established aesthetic (should that be desired)? This is a "problem" I invite and enjoy exploring over the course of the rehearsal period. Once the performers are cast, we get to the job at hand. The performers jump right in and embrace the process, hopeful that whatever we come up with will engage the audience.

So, who challenges you to produce your best work? Look out for those folks who lift you up and let them know you are ready to work! Collaboration is essential to a successful production, and every performance is the result of the efforts of many. Without collaboration, you'll find the making of a theatrical work nigh on impossible. If a person thinks they can do it all on their own, they need to imagine every work as a solo which they not only perform every night, but where they are also the lighting designer, costume designer, sound designer, stage manager, running crew member, house manager, box office manager, and so on – this gives great insight into just how many folks bring a theatrical work to life. Checking ego and insecurities at the door is the surest way to surrender to the experience of making the work, and ultimately it's surrendering that enables *collaboration* to occur. It certainly takes a village!

Got an Audience? Finding Your Platform

I enjoy creating new works that incorporate all the areas of performance I like to explore with themes that I hope will resonate with both the performers and the audience, and when I write a script, I have a *Fringe Festival* audience in mind. This means I can be more experimental in the delivery and format of the show because Fringe audiences know to expect the unexpected. This is an incredibly freeing feeling.

But performing at Fringe Festivals also means that there are a lot of practicalities to consider when creating the work. First, the performance venue is not a place I have worked in before. So not only are we getting to know a new space, we typically have about two hours to tech the show. We have about 15 minutes to set up prior to each show and after every performance, we must make sure we can get everything out of the space fast. Set and prop pieces are required to be struck within 15 minutes of the show ending, so the next performers can set up. Given these parameters, the production must speak for itself without much technical assistance.

What I relish about these kinds of practicalities is that it really puts the focus on the performers to paint the picture. Every facet of the body is required to tell stories in this way. When the body is the primary source of communication, the performer's energy is everything. It's a thrilling experience. Efficiency, the ability to improvise and make changes at a moment's notice, and an understanding of the organized but chaotic performance environment are absolute musts.

Producing new work for Fringe Festivals has opened my imagination in ways that a big budget with ample space and time hasn't always. I find the more obstacles, the more creative the production ultimately becomes. Don't get me wrong, money, time, and space are awesome, but all too often young artists give up because they lack those commodities. Remember, there is never one way of doing things. We are all guilty of getting so locked into our original vision of what we want that we don't allow ourselves to consider the creative alternatives that could solve the problems. Face obstacles head on, and they may unlock creativity. Your work could become even more imaginative than the first iteration.

When creating a new work, you must ask yourself: who do I imagine as the audience? Is it friends and/or colleagues? Do I want to create a family-friendly experience, with children gleefully seated in the front row? Or would I like to create something more edgy? Would my parents and/or family members be uncomfortable seeing it? Does that matter to me? And where do I want to see this work performed? At my high school? A coffee shop? A found space? As part of a theatre or film festival? My local community theatre? Outside my community? A regional theatre? Off-Broadway? Broadway?!

The idea of creating a new work can be daunting. There's just so many things to consider! To take some of the mystery out of it, let's create a new work right now.

Assignment: Create a New Work... NOW!

Imagine an action that you do on a regular basis. *Need some ideas?* Try some or all of these examples:

> playing an instrument; brushing your teeth; petting your dog; washing your hair; turning the page of a book; embracing a loved one; putting on shoes; scrolling through social media on your phone.

Once you've imagined the action, mime exactly how you execute that movement.

Next, start to abstract the action by:

> varying the speed with which you do it; expanding the movement, thereby making it larger than life; minimizing the movement, thereby making it incredibly subtle.[2]

Resist the temptation to revert to dance technique you already know and play with the movement that is evolving when you vary the time and space of the everyday action. And don't worry about whether you are doing the exercise the "right" or "wrong" way.

Once you've found an abstract movement phrase that interests you, repeat the movements over and over until it's fully in your body and you have it memorized. Your movement phrase, which started as an improvisation inspired by an everyday action, is the foundation of your new composition.

1: ***The first goal is to abstract an everyday action by varying the timing and the spacing of the action.***

The next step is to add intention to the movement phrase by performing it with varying energies. Try out any of the infinitives below one at a time as you execute the movement phrase:

> to caress; to stab; to seduce; to press; to gorge; to suffocate; to soothe; to rejoice; to flutter.

If at any time you feel emotionally overwhelmed by the direction the movement phrase is going when an intention is added, simply return to executing your movement phrase without intention.

Keep playing until you feel a message revealing itself. And while this work can ultimately be "movement for the sake of movement,"[3] it helps to try on these infinitives in order to inspire conflict (and ultimately resolution).

After fluctuating the energy with which you execute the movement, ask yourself:

> How did it feel to execute the movement phrase with a caressing quality? Was it jarring to switch from a caressing to a stabbing energy? Maybe so, but could you feel how the shift in energy could help to unearth a conflict?

2: ***The second goal is to develop intention in the movement phrase.***

Next, perform the movement phrase in relation to or in response to another force (which can be real or imagined). It helps to unlock ideas if you begin to interact with another performer or focus on an imagined entity outside yourself. So, try performing the movement phrase, imagining your partner as some or all of the following:

> your best friend; your lover; a family member; your favorite film/TV/ music star; a saint or god or heavenly creature; a devil or evil person; your greatest fear; your biggest dream; a haven or safe place; your unborn child.

The more clearly you can envision that person, place, or thing, the more focused the energy.

3: ***The third goal is to help inspire a relationship between you and another force, thereby adding motivation and focus to the movement phrase.***

Next, try speaking aloud literally whatever comes to mind after repeating the movement sequence several times with a chosen infinitive and relationship to another being. So, for example, you may have chosen to perform your movement sequence using the energy that the infinitive "to caress" creates, and you may have chosen your imagined scene partner to be a devil. While performing the movement phrase, you might say, "I can't resist you."

Can't find anything to say? Not to worry! Try one or more of the following:

"I can't love you anymore"; "Why is everything so difficult with you?"; "You owe me"; "I know what you did"; "That hurt"; "You couldn't have known"; "Not me"; "Whoops!"; "I'm not crying, you're crying"; "That's ridiculous"; "How dare you?!"; "Bring it on"; "There must be some mistake."

4: *The fourth goal is to further conflict through voice and sound, thereby using the performer's entire instrument to communicate.*

Finally, repeat the movement sequence using a different infinitive that opposes the first, while keeping the same scene partner relationship. So, for example, your scene partner remains a devil, but the infinitive changes to "to push." Again, see what words come to mind and say them. In this example, I could say, "But I must resist you." Here are some other lines you might wish to try:

"I love you more and more"; "Difficult is never dull"; "But I owe you"; "I can't thank you enough"; "Do it again"; "You knew all along"; "Was it you?"; "That was no accident"; "Now she's crying"; "I think I like it"; "I dare you"; "I'm scared"; "There's no mistake."

5: *The fifth and final goal is to find a resolution to the piece.*

You've now created a work with a *beginning, middle,* and *end.* You created *action,* a *relationship, conflict,* and *resolution,* and you used your *entire instrument* to do it. While your work may not have been a minute long, it's a start! Take some time now to free write any ideas that came to your mind while working through this exercise. Maybe you found some movement that you might like to explore further. Maybe a new character started to surface. Maybe it unlocked an entire story. While it's just an exercise, it can ignite ideas!

Figure 7.4 Danielle Mumpower and I finding our balance in *Memoir of a Mytho-maniac: The True Story of a Compulsive Liar (or Tallulah Dies)*. I wrote, directed, choreographed, and performed in it as part of the Cincinnati Fringe Festival, produced by Know Theatre. The production took home the Dr. Robert J. Thierauf Producer's Pick of the Fringe Award.
Photo credit: Jeff Burkle

Now that you have created a new work of your own, let's explore ways of navigating established theatrical works.

Established Works

At ETSU, I am charged with directing and choreographing dance concerts, musicals, and any movement sequences needed in plays. This makes for diverse creative experiences, but most often I direct and choreograph established works, and I imagine that you too will find yourself regularly working on productions that have already premiered. How can you as a performer and theatre maker offer a fresh perspective on what's been done many times before?

Take *Oklahoma!* as an example. As director/choreographer of *Oklahoma!*, I'm bound by the confines of the time period of the musical and therefore the style of dance required of this particular musical. I also feel bound by the legacy of the original choreographer, Agnes de Mille. I don't want stray too far from de Mille's pioneering vision – I feel the need to honor aspects of her work, particularly during the *dream ballet* at the end of the first act. After all, her work on *Oklahoma!* transformed the role of dance in musical theatre; her dances were able to further the storyline in ways spoken word and song could not. So, I wouldn't dare argue against the enormous influence de

Mille's choreography of *Oklahoma!* had on the development of musical theatre dance, and I feel the weight of her presence, her mark on this show.

But I also feel the need to make *Oklahoma!* palatable for a contemporary audience, which consists primarily of college students, faculty and staff at ETSU, and the general public from Johnson City, Tennessee. The original production of *Oklahoma!* was well over three hours long and featured lengthy dance breaks filled with mimetic dance gesture; you could see the clear influence of Martha Graham in de Mille's work (de Mille and Graham were contemporaries and friends). However, I think today's audience might find the repetition of movement fatiguing and some of the Graham-esque hard lines and sharp angular actions a bit out of place within the context of some scenes, and so lots of reworking and re-imagining takes place.

In the case of *Oklahoma!*, Agnes de Mille loomed large. But by researching the production's vast history, taking note of how other directors and choreographers contributed to their productions of the musical (in particular Tony award winner Susan Stroman's innovative work on the Royal National Theatre's 1999 production of *Oklahoma!*, which breathed new life into the musical), and then embracing the unique circumstances of our own production, the rather large shadow cast by the incomparable Agnes de Mille was managed.

When directing, choreographing, or performing musical theatre, you are often working within strongly built parameters (often established by the playwright's estate and monitored by their publishing company). If the musical is highly structured (like *Oklahoma!*), creating something fresh and exciting can be a challenge. You rise to the challenge by acknowledging and building upon previous interpretations.

Figure 7.5 Oklahoma!
Photo credit: ETSU Photographic Services

Directing, choreographing, or performing an established work is not always filled with constraints. Choreographing *RENT*, for example, felt completely different from many other musical theatre experiences because the show is more open to interpretation when it comes to movement and dance. With the exception of a tango, pretty much anything goes in terms of choreography. Just like the performer devising new theatre, a performer must enter the rehearsal of an established theatrical work prepared to demonstrate a variety of interpretations. When opportunities for unique interpretations arise in a performance, it is the performer's chance to show the director and choreographer their ideas.

Sometimes a theatre maker feels so strongly about brandishing their mark on an established work that their concept can feel a bit heavy handed. There are countless wonderful examples of a new concept bringing renewed vitality to a revival. However, reimagining established works to the point of being

Figure 7.6 In *RENT*, I decided to embrace the lack of restrictions. I used aerial fabric, dance body bags, and aerial pole dance in this production (kudos to Reagan James for singing while upside down!). *RENT* became a kind of rite of passage for many of us on the production; it is a draining show both emotionally and physically, and while the production was somewhat plagued with issues, the process truly united the cast and crew. I am eternally grateful for the experience; seeing how theatre makers come together for a common goal, despite obstacles, invigorated my commitment to the art form. I can also remember having a similar feeling when choreographing *Godspell*, like I had complete artistic freedom. The absence of strict parameters is both liberating and terrifying. Arming yourself with a knowledge of previous productions of the work, presenting a variety of interpretations in rehearsal, and trusting your instincts on how you can provide a unique perspective to the work are key components in developing your portrayal.

Photo credit: ETSU Photographic Services

virtually unrecognizable may not prove the best way to serve the story. While it is important to bring an interesting perspective to a production, remember to question your intentions. This is not to say you can't stage *Hamlet* in outer space; you just need a good reason for doing it.

Quite often, the work is there for you in the script, and as a director, choreographer, designer, or performer, you really just need to orchestrate the vision that's on the page. From the precise execution of a scene change, to a lover's embrace, to a heated duel, every action is an opportunity to communicate the story. There have been times when I've felt like the dances choreographed themselves and my role as a choreographer was to simply facilitate the action of the song because the musical was so incredibly well written. If the performance comes easily, get out of your own way and enjoy the ride.

Divine Dissatisfaction

All too often we as performers and theatre makers make the work harder than it has to be. That said, it's a foregone conclusion that you will face a myriad of issues throughout the creative process. You might not connect particularly with the character in the script, or the space is ridiculously cramped, or the theatre can't accommodate your amazing multimedia ideas, or you're having a hard time getting on the same page with the costume designer or lighting designer, and so on and so on. But sometimes the biggest obstacle that stands in your way is... *you*. You know that voice that says, "This isn't good enough; you are the least original person in the world; stop pretending you know what you're doing."

Agnes de Mille described a conversation she had with Martha Graham discussing her turmoil over why she found success in choreographing *Oklahoma!*, which she felt was only "fairly good" after many years of producing other works that did not get anywhere near the same level of attention. She explained to Graham:

> I was bewildered and worried that my entire scale of values was untrustworthy... I confessed that I had a burning desire to be excellent, but no faith that I could be. Graham responded, very quietly: There is a vitality, a life force, an energy, a quickening that is translated through you into action, and because there is only one of you in all of time, this expression is unique. And if you block it, it will never exist through any other medium and it will be lost. The world will not have it. It is not your business to determine how good it is nor how valuable nor how it compares with other expressions. It is your business to keep it yours clearly and directly, to keep the channel open. You do not even have to believe in yourself or your work. You have to keep yourself open and aware to the urges that motivate you. Keep the channel open... No artist is pleased... [There is] no satisfaction whatever at any time.

There is only a queer divine dissatisfaction, a blessed unrest that keeps us marching and makes us more alive than the others.

(de Mille, 1992, p.264)

It would be great if conquering the incessant naggings of insecurities was easy, but alas, it is not. What can be helpful, when the bad days seem overwhelming, is to simply take a moment to acknowledge the fact that you are doing the best you can and strive for a sense of balance. Take solace in the "blessed unrest" that is theatre making!

Performer + Theatre Maker = Problem Solver

Restrictions have helped to shape my ongoing journey as a maker of theatre. There are always going to be obstacles during the creative process. Not only do I encourage you to embrace practical obstacles, I invite you to create self-imposed constraints. Why? Because solving problems unleashes creativity. Now all this to say, if a self-imposed constraint is leading you to a dead end, get rid of it. If it's not doing its intended purpose, which is to help bring about creativity, then let it go (though give it a minute before you give up on it). But seriously, if you can shift your perspective seeing "problems" as "opportunities," you will become a valuable asset in the world of performance.

Writing Prompt: What's in Your Toolbox?

What creative and analytical qualities do you possess that give you an eye for detailing composition and the artistry to visualize overall design? You'd be surprised at what you already have in your toolbox. Let's say you love organizing your clothes by color or fabric or your bookshelf or vinyl collection is arranged in some order only you can understand. Perhaps you not only hear music, but it also takes on a visual quality for you as though you can *see* images to the music (a musician friend of mine says he sees color in music and that each musical note he hears has its own specific hue, a phenomenon known as synesthesia). Perhaps you're the person in your friend group who can predict the ending of films. Or maybe you play a sport or enjoy chess and can envision multiple moves ahead (I always enjoy watching a good game of soccer where players can position themselves beautifully to receive a pass). These qualities are not just personality traits and can inform how you develop your personal aesthetic as a performer and theatre maker. Think on the many ways in which you are creative and free write about this in your journal.

Imitation vs. Inspiration

It's time to address the elephant in the room, and that is the goal of creating something *new* (I have already used the word "new" on a number of occasions when describing the creative process). The idea of constructing something wholly original can be paralyzing. Perhaps realizing the fact that *it's all been done before* is just the liberating thought needed to move past any concerns of creating a cutting-edge theatrical performance and to forge ahead regardless of any impact the performance may or may not have. Kleon says, "Nothing is original... If we're free from the burden of trying to be completely original, we can stop trying to make something out of nothing, and we can embrace influence instead of running away from it" (2012, pp.7–8).

As a performing artist, you spend a lot of time trying to be innovative. Simultaneously, you also know that you are constantly influenced by your environment, the people in your life, and the media. Ask yourself:

- What does it mean to be inspired by another work?;
- What does the quote, "every artist is a thief" mean to you?;
- What is appropriation? How is it different from appreciation?;
- What does it mean to have ownership of art?;
- What does it mean to "borrow"?;
- Is there a hard and fast rule by which you can identify when a performance is inspired by another work or when it is merely a copy or imitation of another work?;
- What does it mean to pay tribute or homage to another's work?

I'd like to further explore these questions when it's "all been done before" and what it means to "be original" with two examples – one from personal experience as director/choreographer of *Mr. Burns, A Post-Electric Play* and one from a pop culture icon who has the world watching.

Mr. Burns, A Post-Electric Play

Before we can discuss themes of art and inspiration in *Mr. Burns, A Post-Electric Play*, some background information is needed. Let me begin by providing a synopsis of the play:

Mr. Burns, A Post-Electric Play by Anne Washburn is a play in three acts. The first act begins after an apocalyptic event, leaving survivors to fend for themselves without electricity or the comforts of everyday life. Surrounded by a campfire, a small group of strangers, thrown together by chance with nothing but time on their hands, decides to recount from memory the episode "Cape Feare" from *The Simpsons* as a diversion from the horrors they've recently experienced.

The second act takes place seven years later. These same characters have formed an amateur acting company who tour and perform *The Simpsons* episodes for other survivors around the country. No longer just an entertaining distraction, *The Simpsons* becomes the key to their survival – a good performance means they'll have earned enough to eat that night.

The third act takes place 75 years later. *The Simpsons* characters are elevated to mythic proportions and a grand performance of the episode "Cape Feare" is entirely sung with the bravado of an operatic tragedy performed by seasoned players.

In her notes on *Mr. Burns*, playwright Washburn discusses her desire to examine, "What would happen to a pop culture narrative pushed past the fall of civilization?" (Washburn, 2017, p. 119). With *The Simpsons* as her muse, Washburn illustrates the power of storytelling. She says, "Since all stories, no matter how fanciful, are in some way constructed from our experiences, real or imagined, all storytelling is a remaking of our past in order to create our future" (quoted in ACT SF, 2017). In the post-apocalyptic world of *Mr. Burns*, characters turn to storytelling for their salvation. And what better subject for them to explore than that of *The Simpsons* "Cape Feare" episode?!

The Simpsons has been around since 1989, long before today's college students were born, and its ability to embody both lowbrow and highbrow humor surely helps explain its longevity. There is something for everyone in the show, and we can all see a little of ourselves in the archetypal characters that populate Springfield. The characters in *Mr. Burns* not only find solace in trying to recapture the essence of "Cape Feare," but their very life depends upon it. In an interview with Washburn, journalist Nirmala Nataraj commented, "Mr. Burns has accordingly been lauded as a celebration of the human instinct to tell stories – and a reminder of how deeply this instinct is tied to our endurance as a species" (ACT SF, 2017).

The "Cape Feare" episode was the catalyst to examine the necessity of storytelling to great effect *and* served as the perfect foil for Washburn to explore the grey area of artistic ownership. *The Simpsons* is a show that's been around for so long that most have at least heard of it and with pop culture references littered throughout the "Cape Feare" episode, there is much on offer to appeal to our mainstream consciousness. And Washburn ironically borrows Matt Groening's iconic characters to explore plagiarism, copyright infringement, and poetic license, all themes in the play.

Working on this show was a major "life imitating art" experience. While the characters in Act II discuss buying bits of dialogue from other survivors who remember *The Simpsons* episodes, the producer and I were working with copyright lawyers to see if we could purchase the rights to Britney Spears' *Toxic* for the actors to perform in the show. While Ms. Washburn requests the use of that song in Act II, and the melody of *Toxic* is used in

Act III with different lyrics, we did not automatically acquire the rights to the song when we purchased the rights to perform *Mr. Burns*.

We also had to get approval for our scenic design from Universal Studios to be sure that our design did not resemble the setting or drawing style of *The Simpsons*. And there could be no visual reference to any *The Simpsons* character on the programs or marketing materials. These are just a few instances where I as director had to work with the producer to make sure that we had the artistic rights to perform all that Ms. Washburn intended for her play.

Meanwhile the characters on stage speak about how competing acting troupes performing *The Simpsons* episodes are "stealing" lines from them. It felt like a cruel joke at the time, but I now realize how Washburn was illustrating the difficulties in pinpointing artistic ownership and how so much is borrowed, stolen, and imitated. While it is clear that Washburn uses *The Simpsons* as a backdrop to create a common ground for her audience and is in no way copying or imitating that work, she demonstrates just how difficult it can be to build on other artists' work to create something new with your own art.

Figure 7.7 I asked *Mr. Burns'* costumes designer, Beth Skinner, to incorporate the classical stylings of the Greek chorus, to seek inspiration from Martha Graham's *Lamentation* costume, and to use the golden hue of *The Simpsons* family in her color palette. Layering these ideas led to her innovative costume design and the creation of a captivating and specific visual. With Francois Delsarte's gestures as inspiration, I created this tableau, hoping to embody the grandeur of the heightened theatrical moment.

Photo credit: ETSU Photographic Services

Copyright: When is Imitation Stealing?

It is important for theatre makers to investigate the complexities involved in building upon another artist's work; for example, you may be infringing copyright when you use music in your production without express permission. And the complications that surround building on another artist's work confound even the seemingly "untouchable" icons in the industry... even Beyoncé.

The Beyoncé and de Keersmaeker Controversy

I was first made aware of the debate over the originality of some of Beyoncé's work when I attended a lecture and discussion led by Dr. Heather Young Reed with her students at University of Lincoln, UK. I have always been a fan of Beyoncé, and I was surprised to learn of plagiarism accusations made against her for her work in the music video "Countdown." In it, Beyoncé mines and combines choreography and other design elements from several sources, such as the costuming and dance first seen in the film *Funny Face*. But it was her borrowing from the Belgian choreographer Anne Teresa de Keersmaeker that caused a strong reaction from critics, fans, and a response from de Keersmaeker herself. Like all artists, Beyoncé draws inspiration from a variety of sources. But had she gone too far in "Countdown"? Erika Ramirez in an op-ed for *Billboard* gave her view on the issue, saying,

> As the video continues, we see Bey' using the same choreography, cinematography and costumes that Belgian choreographer and dancer, Anne Teresa de Keersmaeker, used in "Rosas Danst Rosas." It's one thing to be inspired by someone else's work and revamp with one's personal style, but it's another to duplicate exact movements, which is ultimately violating the artist's intellectual property. Context matters.
>
> (Ramirez, 2013)

Sarah Kaufman provides another view in *The Washington Post*:

> the pop star has done nothing radical or unusual. But by virtue of her enormous celebrity, Beyoncé has attracted wide attention to one of the world's most common creative strategies: the art of stealing. Beyoncé's appropriation of moves and staging from Belgian choreographer Anne Teresa de Keersmaeker in her new music video "Countdown," released last month, has sparked an internet uproar... But though the scoldings throughout the blogosphere are compelling – Beyoncé has been bawled out for being a copycat and for lacking imagination and respect and so on – much of art history says that the recording artist and dancer has done nothing out of the ordinary. Existing material has formed the core of countless artworks,

including those now enshrined as masterstrokes… The openness of the copying (or tribute?) in Beyoncé's "Countdown" is striking, and that's precisely how the word got out that it's de Keersmaeker's work, not bad publicity for an artist on the fringes. The scenes in question account for just a few seconds of the video's 3 ½ minutes of dizzying cuts from one cultural reference to another, but the gray T-shirts, raw warehouse set and even the cold, flat lighting are accurately – if playfully – reproduced from the Belgian clips.

(Kaufman, 2011)

Beyoncé responded to the backlash with:

Clearly, the ballet "Rosas danst Rosas" was one of many references for my video "Countdown." It was one of the inspirations used to bring the feel and look of the song to life… I was also paying tribute to the film *Funny Face* with the legendary Audrey Hepburn. My biggest inspirations were the '60s, the '70s, Brigitte Bardot, Andy Warhol, Twiggy and Diana Ross… I've always been fascinated by the way contemporary art uses different elements and references to produce something unique.

(quoted in Higgins, 2011)

de Keersmaeker also responded, saying:

People asked me if I'm angry or honored.

Neither, on the one hand, I am glad that "Rosas danst Rosas" can perhaps reach a mass audience which such a dance performance could never achieve, despite its popularity in the dance world since 1980s. And, Beyoncé is not the worst copycat, she sings and dances very well, and she has good taste!

On the other hand, there are protocols and consequences to such actions, and I can't imagine she and her team are not aware of it.

(The Performance Club, 2019)

Assignment: You Be the Judge

Watch the Beyoncé video, "Countdown," and de Keersmaeker's "Rosas Danst Rosas," and "Achterland." (all available on YouTube; see Bibliography for links). Now that you have seen the works yourself, give your opinion as to whether this was a case of plagiarism or inspiration. Do you feel Beyoncé's video used de Keersmaeker's work as inspiration to create something new? Should Beyoncé have sought permission from de Keersmaeker before making the video and/or do you think she should have credited de Keersmaeker at the end of the video?

In Summary

Producing a performance involves a team of people working together for a common goal. As a performer, you are a member of a team. You make many contributions to the development of a production. It's necessary and important to understand the responsibilities of the performer and also appreciate the many contributions of your colleagues in production and design. As a performer, you encounter every facet of a production, and the more you seek to understand all the moving parts in a production, the better a performer and colleague you will be.

Your path as a theatre maker may evolve with you taking on other positions within a production (as writer, director, producer, choreographer, and more). Given the competitiveness of the industry, you may want to consider creating performance opportunities for yourself by working with your peers in performance and design to produce a new or established theatrical work. It is something worth considering and may to lead to more opportunities.

A lot of performers and theatre makers feel the pressure to be innovative. When that pressure becomes overwhelming, remember that there is only one of you in the world. You are unique. Embrace that which excites and inspires you. Acknowledge what influences you, and let it inform your work. But know that your experiences are singular, and audiences want to see *your* interpretation.

Now that we've reflected on some of the complexities of producing theatrical works, let's change gears and move into the realm of nurturing your instrument (that's you!).

Notes

1 In her book, *Dance Composition Basics: Capturing the Choreographer's Craft*, Pamela Anderson Sofras states, "In dance, gestures are abstracted. The quality of the gesture rather than the literal gesture becomes important," (2006, p.13). Her exercise on dance gesture provided the springboard for my exploratory movement work in the early stages of choreographing *The Physics of a Teardrop*.

2 In *Dance Composition Basics: Capturing the Choreographer's Craft*, Pamela Anderson Sofras describes an exercise that utilizes "gestures first identified by their literal usage and then combined with dance concepts of time, space, and energy to become dance movements," (2006, p.13). While I adjusted the exercise to suit my needs when choreographing *The Physics of a Teardrop* to include mimetic acts (e.g., putting the hand to the eye) rather than solely "natural body operations" or "gestures" as she refers to it (e.g., sneezing), the crux of the exercise is the same.

3 "Movement for the sake of movement" describes modern dance pioneer Merce Cunningham's philosophy of choreography and dance.

Bibliography

ACT SF. (2017). *Survival of the Fittest Stories: An Interview with Playwright Anne Washburn*, 16 March. blog.act-sf.org/2015/02/survival-of-fittest-stories-interview. html

Beyoncé. (2011). "Beyoncé – Countdown (Official Video)" [Video]. *YouTube*, uploaded by Beyoncé, 7 October. www.youtube.com/watch?v=2XY3AvVgDns

"Beyoncé / Keersmaeker (Montage E. Verlinden)." (2011). [Video]. *YouTube*, uploaded by Elodie Verlinden, 10 October. www.youtube.com/watch?v=lXE6rM0d3jg

"Danza Contemporanea / 'Achterland' – Anne Teresa De Keersmaeker." (2011). [Video]. *YouTube*, uploaded by Ana Moyano, 20 November. www.youtube.com/watch?v=mTCIVAXDstk.

de Mille, A. (1992). *Martha: The Life and Work of Martha Graham*. Random Century.

Higgins, C. (2011). "Beyoncé pleasant but consumerist, says plagiarism row choreographer." *The Guardian*, 11 October. www.theguardian.com/music/2011/oct/11/beyonce-pleasant-consumerist-plagiarism-row

Kaufman, S. (2011). "Beyonce: 'Countdown' video and the art of stealing." *The Washington Post*, 18 November. www.washingtonpost.com/lifestyle/style/beyonce-countdown-video-and-the-art-of-stealing/2011/11/15/gIQAj0WbYN_story.html

Kleon, A. (2012). *Steal Like an Artist: 10 Things Nobody Told You about Being Creative*. Workman.

Macaulay, A. (2011). "In Dance, Borrowing Is a Tradition." *New York Times*, 21 November. www.nytimes.com/2011/11/22/arts/dance/is-beyonce-a-choreography-thief-in-countdown.html

McKinley, J.C. (2011). "Beyoncé accused of plagiarism over video." *New York Times*, 10 October. https://artsbeat.blogs.nytimes.com/2011/10/10/beyonce-accused-of-plagiarism-over-video/?searchResultPosition=1

The Performance Club. (2019). "Anne Teresa De Keersmaeker responds to Beyoncé video." 29 June. https://theperformanceclub.org/anne-teresa-de-keersmaeker-responds-to-beyonce-video/

Ramirez, E. (2013). "Op-ed: When Beyonce's inspiration turns into imitation." *Billboard*, 1 May. www.billboard.com/articles/columns/the-juice/1560092/op-ed-when-beyonces-inspiration-turns-into-imitation

"Rosas | Rosas Danst Rosas." (2011). [Video]. *YouTube*, uploaded by Kaaitheater, 10 October. www.youtube.com/watch?v=oQCTbCcSxis

Sofras, P. (2006). *Dance Composition Basics: Capturing the Choreographer's Craft*. Human Kinetics.

Sternbergh, A. (2011). "When is a homage more than a homage?" *New York Times*, 3 November. https://6thfloor.blogs.nytimes.com/2011/11/03/when-is-an-homage-more-than-an-homage/?searchResultPosition=3

Tharp, T., & Reiter, M. (2006). *The Creative Habit: Learn It and Use It for Life*. Simon & Schuster.

Washburn, A. (2017). *Mr. Burns and Other Plays*. Theatre Communications Group.

8 On Health & Wellness

Self-Care for Longevity as a Performer

As a performing artist, your *body* is the *instrument* that creates your art. When I refer to your *body*, I mean all of it – your physical body, your mind, your soul or spirit or energy (or whatever you like to call it). Caring for and developing your body is part of the job, and by caring for your body, you get the added benefit of a better quality of life. Getting to know your body and how you like to move it, learning what your body needs for energy (physically, mentally, spiritually), and appreciating what is unique about your body must be core values in your performance training.

Imagine the self-care needs of a professional musician – a violinist, for example. They spend a great deal of time and money caring for their violin; they clean it, tune it, replace damaged parts, and place it in a case lined with a velvety soft material after each use. They must also care for themselves, following a rehearsal regimen that consists of methodic repetition, tirelessly practicing fundamentals to warm-up before diving into advanced melodies. Like the violinist, every theatre and dance performer must nurture and protect their instrument and diligently work to safely achieve set goals using proper technique.

Diet, Physical Activity, & Sleep Patterns

Ensuring successful and lasting progress as a performer includes maintaining health and wellness and increasing strength, flexibility, and endurance both physically and mentally. First, we need to observe your current state of fitness and assess areas you might wish to adjust, so you can create an action plan that helps to make your vision of the performer you want to be a reality.

Assignment: Recordkeeping

Observe your current routine by keeping a detailed report in your journal for one week of the following:

1. Daily food and beverage intake.

DOI: 10.4324/9781003149699-9

2. Physical activity per day.
3. Hours slept each night.

Please note this assignment is in no way intended to judge or pressure you into feeling the need to be a certain size or shape. Rather, it is intended to gauge health, wellness, and preparedness for the physical and mental demands of performance. Think of this as simply gathering data. The information collected in the journal is for your eyes only, and honestly recording the information is necessary for successful personal reflection at the conclusion of the week.

Assignment: Assessing Food & Beverage Intake

Upon completion of your weeklong recordkeeping, answer the following questions:

On average, how much water did you drink per day? Did you ever feel dehydrated? If so, do you think this is something you should continue to monitor? If water is a drink you tend to avoid, list ideas on how you might increase your water intake. Then, consider trying one of those ideas for the next week. Be specific. For example: "Every night before going to bed, I will fill a bottle of water and place it on my nightstand. As soon as I wake in the morning, I will drink it while getting ready for my day. I will do this for the next seven days."

On average, how many caffeinated drinks did you consume per day? How many of those drinks were soda (diet and/or regular)? How many were coffee/tea drinks? Given the generally recognized amount of caffeine deemed safe for most fit adults is up to 400 milligrams (mg) per day (Office of the Commissioner of the FDA, 2018), do you consider your caffeine intake at a healthy level? Here's some information to give perspective:

- 16 oz. Starbucks® Grande Pike Place Roast contains 310 mg of caffeine;[1]
- 12 oz. Coke® contains 34 mg of caffeine;[2]
- 12 oz. Diet Coke® contains 46 mg of caffeine.[3]

Also, bear in mind that caffeine is present in some foods, such as certain chocolate and chewing gums. If caffeine intake is causing concern, list some ideas to slowly decrease your caffeine consumption. Consider trying one of your ideas for the next week. Perhaps replacing one caffeinated drink with a glass of water per day would be something to consider. You'd be killing two birds with one stone that way.

(If you do not consume alcohol, you can skip to the next section.)

On average, how many alcoholic drinks did you consume per day/ week? Did you find the amount of alcohol consumed on a given day affected your ability to function at full capacity on the following day? (e.g., Did you wake with a headache? Did you feel a bit depressed or sluggish throughout the morning or day?). Did you feel pressured by internal or external forces (i.e., peers or stressful situations) to consume more alcohol than you originally intended?

The *Dietary Guidelines for Americans 2015–2020* state:

> If alcohol is consumed, it should be in moderation – up to one drink per day for women and up to two drinks per day for men – and only by adults of legal drinking age. For those who choose to drink, moderate alcohol consumption can be incorporated into the calorie limits of most healthy eating patterns.
>
> (US Department of Health and Human Services, 2015b)

The Centers for Disease Control and Prevention states:

> Excessive alcohol use includes binge drinking, heavy drinking, any alcohol use by people under the age 21 minimum legal drinking age, and any alcohol used by pregnant women… For men, heavy drinking is typically defined as consuming 15 drinks or more per week. For women, heavy drinking is typically defined as consuming 8 drinks or more per week.
>
> (CDC, 2020)

Given this information, how would you describe your alcohol consumption? Do you think your alcohol intake is something you should monitor and/or attempt to decrease? If so, list ideas on how you might attempt to decrease it.

Questions for reflection:

On the whole, did you feel that the food and drink you consumed provided the fuel needed to successfully navigate your way through the demands of the day? Did you find that your food intake indicates balanced eating patterns? Were you able to eat a wide variety of foods reasonably portioned? Generally speaking, how important is food to you? Do you consider food preparation and consumption an enjoyable ritual and communal activity or a guilt-inducing test of will? Do you ever eat to calm nervousness or relieve stress? Would you say you "live to eat" or "eat to live"? Is there anything you would like to change about your eating/drinking habits? If so, describe ways in which you might safely make the desired changes over time.

Analysis: Food for Thought

Feeling a bit confused about what it really means to eat and drink healthily? It seems like a new report on nutrition comes out every week. While it is impossible to find a diet that satisfies the needs of every person (there are many factors to consider, such as health issues like diabetes, thyroid inflammation, irritable bowel syndrome, etc., whether the individual is vegetarian or vegan, whether the individual has a vested interest in health and wellness in relation to diet, and so on), there seems to be a general consensus about *added sugar*. I'm not talking about the sugar found in whole fruits, which is offset by the amount of fiber also present. I'm talking about foods with high amounts of *added* sugar, found in such favorites as soda, candy, and white bread, which are best to be avoided or consumed in moderation to consist of less than 10% of your daily caloric intake (CDC, 2019).

The *Dietary Guidelines for Americans 2015–2020* states that a healthy eating pattern consists of:

> a variety of vegetables from all of the subgroups – dark green, red and orange, legumes (beans and peas), starchy, and other; fruits, especially whole fruits; grains, at least half of which are whole grains; fat-free or low-fat dairy, including milk, yogurt, cheese, and/or fortified soy beverages; a variety of protein foods, including seafood, lean meats and poultry, eggs, legumes (beans and peas), and nuts, seeds, and soy products; oils.
>
> (US Department of Health and Human Services, 2015c)

It also states that healthy eating limits saturated fats, trans fats, sodium, and alcohol. If this sounds like your diet, then you are actively pursuing the strong physical environment needed for the conditioning work of performance.

That said, we all know too well that there are many opportunities to splurge. Literally every month of the year in the US offers a day to take a break from healthy eating and enjoy a sugar-induced food coma. Just take a look:

Table 8.A An incomplete list of holidays that many in the US celebrate

January	New Year's Day
February	Valentine's Day
March	St. Patrick's Day
April	Easter
May	Mother's Day
June	Father's Day
July	Independence Day

Table 8.A (Continued)

August	My Birthday
September	Labor Day
October	Halloween
November	Thanksgiving
December	THE HOLIDAYS

Ok, so maybe my birthday isn't a holiday per se, but you get the picture. And if we include not only our own birthday, but that of our friends and family and children's friends, and co-workers and so on, opportunities to chuck the healthy lifestyle abound.

Many also tend to overlook just how frequently we make food choices. A study comprised of 139 staff members and students at Cornell University found that people grossly underestimate the amount of food decisions they make each day. In the study, people felt that on average, they make about 15 food- and beverage-related decisions each day. But in reality, they make more than 200 such decisions (Wansink & Sobal, 2007). With so many decisions to be made about food and drink each day, it's easy to fall off course (just think about how many choices you make when you are out grocery shopping). The unhealthy option is often cheaper and quicker to prepare. Those who are under financial and time pressure struggle more. When you combine the pressure almost everyone feels at one time or another to look a certain way with the often financial and time-saving benefits of eating unhealthily, you're left living in a paradox. A life of health and wellness is the harder choice and one that needs to be made at least 200 times in a single day!

No wonder weight management is difficult for so many. While some believe willpower is the primary determinant to achieve the "ideal body," the reality is that a variety of factors leads many to continuously struggle with their weight no matter how hard they try. Preexisting issues are often overlooked, leaving a person confused and downtrodden when they do not fit the mold of society's manufactured image of a healthy individual. Aiming for a balanced diet while recognizing that most of us do not have an endless reserve of discipline is really the best any of us can do.

Looking to Make Healthier Dietary Decisions?

I'd like to share a theory that a CrossFit trainer once told me and that I later learned was an established general rule of thumb in the health and fitness community. He said that a person should focus about 80% on maintaining a healthy diet and about 20% on exercise. It's easy to conveniently rationalize that exercise can erase unhealthy eating, so it may be surprising to learn how much emphasis is placed on a healthy diet. If you've ever said to yourself, "Oh I can eat this doughnut because I'm going to the gym later today and I'll burn it off," then you've been caught in a counterproductive mindset; to burn substantial calories through exercise takes time and energy, so to burn off the doughnut would take about a four-mile run (Wexler, 2017). You've burned off the 500-calorie doughnut, but that's it. And the more you exercise, the hungrier you get.

For those seeking weight loss as a means of increasing health, it is important to note that in order to shed a single pound of fat, you need to achieve a 3,500-calorie deficit. Without making any changes in diet, that would mean a WHOLE lot of time at the gym. So, the theory of exercising away a bad diet is not practical. It stands to reason that changes in diet must be made in order to take in fewer calories than you burn. Dietician Albert Matheny says, "If you're following the 80/20 ratio, you'd want to burn approximately 750 calories through exercise and an additional 3,000 calories through dieting. That's a total deficit of 3,750 calories for the week" (quoted in Gomez, 2019). Slow and steady is the way to go in order to make a lasting change and when you think of it, the 80/20 ratio feels doable.

If weight loss is not a goal for you, but you want to make healthier choices in your diet, ask yourself, "Do I prioritize cooking? Do I feel I can afford healthier foods? Do I think about what I am going to eat before I am hungry? Do I make a grocery list before heading off to the store? How much time do I spend along the periphery of a grocery store (where produce is located) vs. the center aisles (where processed foods monopolize the space)? Does my energy level dip after eating or do I feel rejuvenated? What small change can I make in order to kick start a healthier lifestyle?" Remember, experts agree that starting with a small modification and then slowly working up to bigger adjustments is the best way to achieve *lasting* change. For example, if you are a meat lover, try treating meat as part of a meal with lots of other foods mixed in, rather than the main food source for every meal. After a while, try to eat one vegetarian dinner per week. Not only will your meat intake reach a healthier range, but you will also be reducing your carbon footprint (hoorah, you're helping the environment!).

While a healthy diet is an important component of performance training, it is a topic that is often shied away from in acting and dance classes. There's a sense that most performers and especially dancers should be *thin*, but the ways in which one maintains that figure are not prioritized; the subject may not even be addressed, but it is felt by many performers as an "unspoken rule." I remember having weekly weigh-ins as a young dancer. The first night I broke 100 lbs. was traumatic. I thought that was the end for me. I was 12 years old and weighed 100 lbs. Surely, my dream of a career as a ballerina was over. Whether real or imagined, I felt my instructor's disgust when she said to me, "You've gained two pounds this week. Better watch it." Well, of course I had gained two pounds – I was having my very first period. But then the curves arrived. Everything on me was growing, except what I wanted, what I thought I needed was just to grow a little taller. But there was no chance of that happening. All the while, nothing was said about *how* I should stay thin.

With no guidance, it's easy for many to gravitate towards unhealthy methods of maintaining perceived weight ideals, like smoking cigarettes to suppress appetite or using drugs to boost energy. These may sound like harsh or overly dramatic examples of preserving the performer's physique, but these and other debilitating patterns exemplify the dark cloud hovering over many performers, which is compounded in the dance world. A study of Croatian ballet professionals (16 female and 9 male) found:

> More than one third of the male dancers reported binge drinking, while 20% of the females smoked more than a box of cigarettes per day. Almost 25% of these dancers will use "doping" if it will ensure successful ballet performance, regardless of negative health consequences. In males, the risk of potential "doping" behavior increased with age… Results suggest that there is evident need for more specific medical and/or psychological services in professional ballet.
>
> (Sekulic et al., 2010, abstract)

Eating disorders and substance abuse are not altogether surprising in a field where a certain body type reigns supreme. And while you may be thinking drug use, binge drinking, and the like only affect a small number in the high-stakes professional world of performance, it can occur in any setting. I once found myself at a rehearsal screaming out for someone to dial 911, when a dancer collapsed following a run through of a vigorous dance. Other dancers at the rehearsal intimated that she had been self-medicating with an illegal substance to cope with stress. I was shocked and saddened to see this dancer suffering and felt ill-equipped to help. With the clarity that conveniently comes with hindsight, I remembered that she had been looking fatigued, malnourished, and underweight, but I didn't really see the signs until after the incident. While you personally may not have experience with these issues, it permeates our society and enters the studio more often than we'd care to admit.

Fortunately, there is movement toward health and wellness in the theatre and dance world, the desire for strong and sinewy musculature outweighing waifish child-like thinness and the awareness that healthy individuals come in different shapes and sizes. But society's obsession with thinness and the body shaming culture that surrounds anyone who doesn't "fit the mold" is everywhere we look. And feeling the need to be thin at any cost is particularly evident amongst women. I fear we are brainwashed by the airbrushed, photoshopped, digitally enhanced images of women in their stereotypical archetypes as "sexy vixen," "innocent damsel in distress," "perfect mother who can do it all," "superhero ninja warrior," "girl next door," "bad girl with a heart of gold," "gigantic bottomed, tiny waist-lined, lip-injected, high cheek boned" seemingly everywhere and literally nowhere paradigms of women. These images permeate our life, and I am anxious about passing on these beauty standards to yet another generation of women, leading to more insecurity and low self-esteem.

When considering the media and society's stronghold in shaping our evaluation of our own self-worth, I want to beg for help. Somebody, anybody, *everybody*, please stop this cycle of women being judged and judging themselves by their body instead of their brain. *How* can it be stopped in this society, where sex sells; where our female role-models are reduced to objects? And female objectification isn't limited to dance or the arts and entertainment industry. Just ask any woman you've ever met in your entire life. While I have spent a lot of time speaking about the female experience (because that is my point of view), I want to strongly emphasize that our male counterparts are certainly not exempt from the pressures and insecurities that stem from feeling the need to look a certain way. And if binary stereotypes are difficult for cisgender people to overcome, the obstacles placed by society on non-binary people are prodigious and could feel insurmountable for many in the non-binary community. Attractiveness, an inherently subjective thing, is universally sought after and valued as an important component of the successful individual.

The solution to body image issues is acceptance; if we try to be less judgmental of ourselves and others, engage in a more sympathetic relationship with our bodies, and acknowledge the complex nature of self-perception, we will have a stronger connection with our instrument. While the solution is acceptance, the journey to self-acceptance is enormously difficult. Your body changes through aging, life events, new circumstances in health, etc., and you have to accept these changes as and when they occur.

Acceptance is also hard because those societal pressures never go away. It's like trying to protect a sandcastle from the tide. It takes constant management. Standards of beauty are so engrained and fundamental to our society, but more and more people are embracing their uniqueness, and that is no small thing. *Body acceptance and positivity* is a movement that is gaining momentum, and lasting change happens when people join forces.

This discussion of body image and societal pressures may feel like a digression, but it is so very important to understand the reasons *why* we choose to seek a life of health and wellness. If the answer is only to look a certain way on the outside in order to fit into social norms, more work may need to be done on the inside in order to sustain any kind of lasting changes. Part of my desire to live healthily is for reasons I feel very proud to share – I want to live a long life for myself, my husband, and children; I have more energy to care for myself, my family, and my work when in good health; I want to act and dance my whole life long.

Ever the walking contradiction, I must confess that another component of my desire to pursue healthy living is out of sheer vanity. And because I worry that these desires are the result of years of indoctrination by society, I carry guilt for having what feel like superficial physical goals. Is it inherently delusional and shallow to want to look a certain way? Life coach Jessi Kneeland says:

> With so much talk about the high moral character of any woman who rocks her body –flaws and all – one might easily start to think that striving to change any of those "imperfections" is some kind of sin... There's no real reason for any kind of moralizing or divide here. Each person is entitled to do whatever she likes with her own damn body. And there is zero reason for anyone to judge another person's body – or her motivation for training it.
>
> (Kneeland, 2019)

We can accept who we are in this moment and also desire transformation; acceptance and ambition can go hand in hand. After all, we are a work in progress. Striving for health and wellness is a good thing. Self-love and self-care are paramount.

When confronted with self-doubt and negativity, consider the wise words of Misty Copeland from *Ballerina Body*:

> Your body is perfect for you. My body was and is perfect for me, just like the body you're in is perfect for you. Didn't it pop out of bed when it was still dark outside and hold you up through homeroom, algebra, and band rehearsal after school? Didn't it carry you across the campus quad, through your procession of classes, and then forward, until you headed home from your part-time job? Didn't it carry your twins for nine long months and then usher them into the world? Hasn't your body held you in good stead throughout the decades and isn't it sustaining you now in middle age?
>
> Like I said. You are perfect.
>
> You may have to start fueling your body differently so that you can climb the stairs without losing your breath. You may have to strengthen your core so your bearing is as regal as you are. You may need to incorporate some physical rituals that can help you feel more alert when you hit that midway point in the afternoon, or reframe your thinking so you can enter that marathon and run it to the end.
>
> But that doesn't mean there's anything wrong with the body you're in, that your physique should be the replica of your favorite singer's, athlete's, or movie star's. It just means fine-tuning, tweaking, honing, what you've already got, taking control of and subtly re-etching the outer self that is divinely you.
>
> (Copeland & Jones, 2017, p.7)

The facts are these… all shapes and sizes and ages could and should enter the world of performance. Taking the best possible care of your body and mind will lead to progress in the art form. The effort that is required in performance is truly demanding and the needed mental and physical strength can partially be developed through a healthy diet. A poor diet may be an obstacle in your progress and a cause of frustration due to low energy reserves. If improving diet and increasing physical activity will lead to a healthier you, the first step is to contact a medical professional to be sure there aren't underlying health issues that may inhibit your progress. Once you have received a clean bill of health and discussed your plans with a doctor, you can move forward safe in the knowledge that all is well with you.

More on Physical Activity

We've talked a lot about diet and only briefly touched on exercise. Let's dig a bit deeper into the subject by assessing your report on one week of physical activity.

Assignment: Assessing Physical Activity

Answer the following questions regarding your physical activity:

On average, how much time did you spend over the course of the week being physically active? The US Department of Health and Human Services describes physical activity as:

- *Moderate-intensity* (brisk walking, dancing, swimming, cycling on a level terrain);
- *Vigorous-intensity* (jogging, singles tennis, swimming continuous laps, cycling uphill).

It lists 300 minutes per week of moderate-intensity or 150 minutes per week of vigorous-intensity (or an equivalent combination of moderate- and vigorous-intensity activity) as the recommended amount for extensive health benefits. In addition, they recommend muscle-strengthening activities on two or more days a week and state that additional health benefits are gained by engaging in physical activity beyond this amount (US Department of Health and Human Services, 2015a).

To see this information practically applied, take a look at the chart below, which provides just one example of a schedule that achieves the US Department of Health and Human Services' weekly recommended amount of physical activity:

Table 8.B Example of recommended weekly physical activity

Day1	Day 2	Day 3	Day 4	Day 5	Day 6	Day 7
1 h 15 m bicycle	strength training	1 h 15 m brisk walk	1 h 15 m bicycle	strength training	1 h 15 m brisk walk	REST

Given this information, do you consider your physical activity per week at an optimum level? If you answered "no," do you think this is something you should continue to monitor and attempt to increase? If so, how will you attempt to increase it? Create a chart like the one above with your schedule of planned physical activity for next week.

Analysis: Exercise These Thoughts

At this point, you might be asking yourself, "How do performance classes factor into my week of physical activity?" Ballroom, modern, yoga, and ballet dance are generally considered moderate-intensity activities, while aerobic dancing, like Zumba, clogging, and tap can fall into the category of vigorous-intensity activities. The general gauge is that if your heart rate is up, but you can still carry on a conversation with relative ease, then you are at a moderate-intensity level of physical activity. If your heart rate is up and you can only really say a sentence or two, then you are at a vigorous-intensity level of activity. An hour-long aerial dance class would likely fulfill one strength training session for the week.

There have been many times that I have walked out of an hour-long dance class knowing that I did not reach a moderate- or vigorous-intensity level of activity for any meaningful length of time, due to the complexity of the combination on that day, which required more discussion and breaking down of movements. I have also left many a yoga class really appreciating the time I gave my body to recover from physical and emotional stress, while also realizing that day's practice fell more into the category of meditation and did not qualify as even a moderate-intensity level of activity for any meaningful length of time. While both examples led to very productive outcomes, I mention them because dance and stretch and flexibility-based classes may not reach a high level of intensity for extended periods. If that is the case, there remains the need to add in endurance work to build the stamina required for performance.

Choreographer Twyla Tharp in her book *Push Comes to Shove* (1993) discussed the importance of stamina in reference to ballet great, Mikhail Baryshnikov:

> But his [Baryshnikov's] wandering was also due to fatigue. In Russia, he performed rarely; one performance a month was not uncommon in the large

Kirov company. This problem was compounded by the structure of ballet classes, the morning exercises made into combinations that don't develop aerobic or muscular endurance beyond what is required for the short variations in the ballet repertoire.

(Tharp, 1993, p.15)

For all ballet lovers, it feels almost blasphemous reading those lines, doesn't it? There's no debating Baryshnikov's talent, discipline, artistry, and strength, but Tharp's comments really hit home how even the very best dancer constantly needs to develop strength, flexibility, *and* endurance, and that kind of training may not be consistently found in some dance classes (it's still hard to imagine Baryshnikov being tired or out of breath; he makes it all look so easy).

You may experience a plateau with regard to strength, flexibility, and endurance if you are dancing, but not engaging in other physical activities with enough regularity. While the "dance only" formula may work for many, you may find that relying on dance alone for physical activity is simply not enough and that cross-training is an absolute necessity for continued growth. Once, I had a conversation with one of my students, who was also a professional body builder and fitness model. She had asked what I did over the Thanksgiving holiday, and I told her about my running a 10k race and enjoying a wonderful turkey dinner with my extended family after. She responded that she could not even run a city block, let alone a 10k. I remember feeling shocked by her response. Here was a woman whose every muscle was clearly defined. She looked the picture of complete fitness (absolutely no photoshop needed!). I'd seen her on numerous occasions at the gym, me on the treadmill and her at the weights and thought how I could never in a million years reach her level of fitness. How could it be possible that someone with such strength lacked aerobic endurance? And how could I run for miles, but not complete a single pull up?

I wasn't training the way I knew deep down I should; I was satisfied with my level of endurance, but was severely lacking in the strength department. I needed to expand my physical activity to include resistance training. Intimidated though I was at the thought of strength training, I approached another dance student who was working as a physical trainer. With his help, I conquered my fear of bulking up and quickly felt the benefits of weightlifting. It was the combination of strength training, cardiovascular exercise, and dance technique classes that lifted me out of an ages-long plateau. I had more energy for floor work in modern; dancing an allegro no longer made me feel near hyperventilation once off stage; and the *pièce de résistance* was successfully completing an inversion while in the air on the aerial fabric.

You might find yourself asking, "What does it mean to be *fit* anyway?" Fitness is a relative term in many ways, so it is up to *you* to define what it means to be fit by clearly outlining *your* goals. You can define and refine your fitness program to meet those goals. Ask yourself, "What do I want?" Envision your future self. Do you imagine yourself as a professional performer? If so, think of the energy that is required to perform eight shows a week or tour the country for six months at a time. Your fitness program should be one that helps you to keep up with that fast pace and will be an immeasurable aid to your success. And again, this isn't about getting you to look a certain way. One of the many things so wonderful about you is that there's no one quite like you! Considering how you're going to handle the demands of performance for the long term so that you can be *exceptional* is simply a practicality that must be addressed.

The next step is to find a partner (or partners) in crime; people you can trust with similar health and fitness goals. For some, being a lone wolf who trains on their own works. For most, it takes a village. Accountability can be a major motivator, and the best way to achieve goals is by having someone there as a sounding board, a friend, coach, and confidant. I don't really think of myself as naturally competitive, but time and again I find that I push myself harder when I set goals with others. And I am helping them just as they are helping me. You'd be surprised at how many around you want to pursue fitness and reaching out to them could be the start of something really special. I have a completely non-judgmental support system whose encouragement I value more than I can say. I sincerely wish that for you.

You may also wish to work with a personal trainer, life coach, or mentor. My university offers two free personal training sessions to any interested faculty, staff, and student with the option to purchase more sessions. If you have the means to work with a certified trainer, take advantage of the opportunity. Certified personal trainers are a wealth of information and in my experience they seem glad to answer any and all questions about training programs. And yet, I've had students tell me they don't go to the campus gym, a state-of-the art facility, because they feel awkward working out around their peers. To that I say apply the adage *dance like no one is watching* to working out. Workout like no one is watching! There is no shame in wanting to increase fitness. Change the narrative – be proud of your super sweaty workout self and embrace the awkwardness that inevitably comes with trying an exercise you've never done before.

Ask yourself, "What is my biggest priority?" When asking open-ended questions, I always say to my students that there is no right or wrong answer; but in this case I do hope that your answer is, "Me." It is in everyone's best interest to give themselves permission to place health as their number one priority. You might be thinking that it's selfish to put yourself first. But when so many around you are depending upon you, how can you *not* put yourself first? Sounds simple enough, but believe me, I am well aware of what I am suggesting. Being a "yes" person too (the word "no" can be tough to say),

I understand the difficulty of finding the discipline, not to mention time, for physical activity before tackling all of the other demands on your time, which I can imagine are too many to count. But we can try, can't we? I am reminded of the ancient Hebrew teaching, "If I am not for myself, who will be for me? If I am not for others, what am I? And if not now, when?".[4]

Assuming you are ready to make developing your instrument a real priority, the next step is to create a plan of action. Many students find they have the desire to improve their skills but lack follow-through because the task can seem too monumental. It's hard to know where to begin, and most want to make serious headway *now*, when the reality is that progress takes *time*. It's an overwhelming feeling, like there is so much to do and not enough time to do it. Before we know it, we've sabotaged ourselves before we really even got started. While setting an intention and having the desire is beneficial, it is absolutely essential that intention is followed by *action*. To avoid the vicious cycle of starting and stalling, try the following strategies:

1: **Embrace the frustration inherent in fitness and performance training.**
If you never experience frustration when training, you are likely not challenging yourself enough mentally and physically. So, think of frustration as a good sign. By changing your reaction to frustration from that of despair to excitement, you can alter your body's response entirely. Remember, your performance goals cannot be mastered in a day, just as a golfer cannot master their swing in a day. The rule of thumb is if you are consistently the best in the class, you are in the wrong class. You need to be challenging yourself more! What better sign that you are challenging yourself than feeling frustrated? Embrace it, own it, and seek it out.

2: **Set mini-goals.**
Studies have shown that setting concrete mini-goals will help you along the way towards achieving your long-term objectives (Moore, 2020). Dedication to clear, practical, and specific tasks is the essential key to progress.

Take some time every Sunday evening to check on whether a mini-goal is working for you and make any necessary adjustments for the week ahead. It will give you that sense of readiness you need and relieve any anxieties you may be feeling about the goals you are seeking to achieve. Having your "ducks in a row" can really help you to face the week head on. Once you've completed a three-week cycle, create another action plan for Weeks 4–6, with weekly check-ins, tweaking as needed.

Trial and error may be necessary, but here's what's really hard. You also have to stick with a program for a while to yield results. All too often, we try something for a short period of time and then give up because a noticeable change hasn't occurred as quickly as we wish. What's especially demoralizing is that it may appear that improvements are occurring more rapidly for others. First, we don't typically have the perspective to observe internal and external changes as and when they are happening, and second, *lasting change takes time*. We've got to learn to be patient with the process and less concerned with the product. If there is no joy in the process, we will quit. All too often I have seen performers with real talent give up because they lacked the patience to persevere.

That said, if your program is making you feel overly depleted or is causing physical or emotional pain (more than just soreness or moments of frustration), then it's time to reassess. There are also life occurrences that will inevitably require you to alter your path. Traumas, such as the loss of a loved one, will require you to reexamine what you need as a performer moving forward in your training and career. Reworking how you train throughout various stages in your life is important and necessary. There is, after all, the simple fact that the body changes as it ages, and we all have to deal with those changes throughout our lives. If we can flip the script on our perspective of our aging minds and bodies, we can look at the necessary adjustments we need to make to accommodate these changes through a lens that is positive. Legendary musician Tom Petty once said, "If you're not getting older, you're dead" (Petty, 2017). When you consider the alternative to aging, getting older really does seem like a great thing! Embracing the wisdom and beauty that comes with age and the different opportunities that will arise for you as a performer simply because you're older is wonderful. I'm willing to bet that many of the characters you'll get to play will be even more challenging than the characters you play in your youth.

Assignment: Create an Action Plan

With the above strategies in mind, create an action plan. This appeals to the practical side of the brain and encourages you to aim for goals within a given timeframe. So, for example, let's say your goal is to significantly increase flexibility. Here's a look at a sample action plan, which is specific to that goal:

Table 8.C Sample action plan for increasing flexibility

Week 1 – Week 3
"The harder you work for something, the greater you'll feel when you achieve it."

Day 1	Day 2	Day 3	Day 4	Day 5	Day 6	Day 7
yoga	30 m cardio 15 m leg & core stretch	yoga	rest	30 m cardio 15 m upper body stretch	30 m cardio 15 m hip flexor & back stretch	gentle yoga (or rest)

Set a goal. Create an action plan. Then go for it.

Journal Writing Prompt: Enrich Your Training

What can you do for yourself before, during, and after a performance training session to enrich and enliven the experience? What new rewarding ritual could you try out? With specific examples, discuss how to break the monotony in your training.

Journal Writing Prompt: Outside In, Inside Out

Consider what you wear to your performance training sessions. Are you comfortable in what you wear? Does your performance training kit make you feel good? Try to think in terms of working from the outside in (liking what you wear, which leads you to feeling good, which leads you to thinking good thoughts). And then think in terms of working from the inside out (visualizing yourself succeeding, speaking positively, doing good things). Describe your visualization.

Sleep

Diet and exercise are important, but without adequate sleep, every decision is that much harder to make. Let's take a look at your sleep habits and assess your report on hours slept per night.

Assignment: Assessing Sleep Patterns

Answer the following questions regarding your sleep patterns for the week:

On average, how much sleep did you get per night? Given the generally recognized recommended amount of sleep for an adult to function fully is 7–9 hours (Sleep Foundation, 2019), would you say that you got enough sleep? If you answered "no," do you think this is something you should continue to monitor and attempt to increase? If so, how will you attempt to increase it? Generally speaking, do you feel well rested when you wake and alert throughout your entire day? Do you have difficulties falling and staying asleep? Do you feel that you have a strong quality of sleep or would you describe yourself as a restless or light sleeper?

Analysis: Sleep, the Best Gift You Can Give Yourself

I genuinely wonder if the biggest issue my students face is lack of sleep. Most of my students have a full-time class load, work nearly every day, *and* regularly rehearse in the evenings for theatre and dance productions; it's really no wonder they have little time for sleep. The level of stress they face on a daily basis must feel overwhelming without adequate sleep. Research shows that quality of sleep "directly affects your mental and physical health and the quality of your waking life, including your productivity, emotional balance, brain and heart health, immune system, creativity, vitality, and even your weight. No other activity delivers so many benefits with so little effort!" (Smith & Segal, 2019).

Sleep, the best gift we can give ourselves, can be elusive. You might find yourself in a vicious cycle of trying to play catch-up by sleeping in on the weekend, only to find yourself unable to get to sleep on Sunday night. Then, Monday rolls around and you feel awful. So, you drink caffeine during the day to stay alert, but then not surprisingly you can't sleep at night. And even when your bed is calling, it still feels like there are other pressing matters to address before turning out the lights. Then, you feel like you do not have the time to reset your sleep habits. On and on it goes, until you get knocked out completely with a cold or flu. This may not be your story exactly, but many of us do not value sleep as we should, nor do we get the quality of sleep we should. If you feel an afternoon slump nearly every day, feel drowsy or fall asleep during lectures, or need a nap to make it through the day, it may be time to reassess priorities, moving sleep higher on your list.

When I was a student, I nearly always got sick either during tech week or immediately after the show closed. Why? I wasn't sleeping enough, I wasn't eating and drinking healthily, I hardly ever made time for exercise, and I was stressed out. Does any of that sound familiar to you? If so, what is one small change you could make to your sleep routine to encourage a healthy physical and mental environment for yourself?

Mental Health & Performance

We've talked at length about physical health and fitness, and I'd like to change gears now to discuss mental health and wellness. Mental health is absolutely vital to sustaining a career in performance, and your *quality of life* depends on it. The *National Institute of Mental Health* says, "Research shows that mental illnesses are common in the United States, affecting tens of millions of people each year. Estimates suggest that only half of people with mental illnesses receive treatment" (National Institute of Mental Health, n.d.). A recent study published in the *Journal of Abnormal Psychology* shows that a person is *more* likely to experience mental illness than develop heart disease, diabetes, or any kind of cancer (Schaefer et al., 2017). These findings illustrate the prevalence of mental illness, and the hope is that this knowledge can help people overcome any shame they might feel about treatment and realize the vital importance of seeking help from a medical professional. However, many still misunderstand mental illness and feel it is something a person should just "get over." This lack of understanding causes the cycle of shame to continue.

As a performer, you are tapping into strong emotions on a regular basis. You are manipulating your emotional state to seek truth in performance. When you fully commit to a character, your body and mind recreates the experiences of your character. And while yes, technically you are "acting," you feel real emotion. If you are tuned into the emotion of a scene and your character is in conflict with another character, you may sense the adrenaline surging through your body and could even find yourself shaking afterwards. A study of 20 professional Australian actors found that the actors are highly vulnerable to mental health problems. The study found, "Actors also report experiencing vicarious trauma through their acting experiences – they are so emotionally, intellectually, and physically engaged in their roles that it can be difficult to switch off. Some report having nightmares and intrusive thoughts related to their roles" (Ellis, 2016). I remember once my husband picked me up from a rehearsal and I was still feeling the intensity of a scene I had been working on minutes earlier. Throughout the drive home, my voice sounded different to him, my mannerisms were different, and he finally said, "Where are you? I'd like my wife back, please." It was alarming that I hadn't fully released the emotion or returned to the present real-life moment.

I've also tried emotional memory, but found the idea of conjuring real life memories too painful. Imagine if you tried to perform eight times a week for six months using emotional memory. It's not a viable method for anything long term. It's really no wonder that performers often turn to outside substances to help them recover from jarring and emotional experiences they have on stage. Rather than seeking therapy or group support, they might opt for a drink or drugs or emotionally eat. It is not at all surprising to hear of addiction and mental illness in the performance industry. While so much press focuses on the glamour, the reality is that performance is incredibly taxing on the body and mind. By acknowledging the dangers, you are more prepared to identify these issues if they should arise in your own work. And if you identify a mental health issue, please know that you are not alone, and there is absolutely nothing to feel ashamed of. It is difficult to take the first step of reaching out for help, but *you can do it*.

In Summary

We've discussed the necessity of valuing self-care and prioritizing health to encourage longevity in performance. After all, the *body* is the instrument that produces the performance. And remember, that includes the *mind*. In addition to the practicalities of diet and fitness, a performer should dedicate themselves to pursuing mental health and wellness.

Developing your instrument does not mean immediately rearranging your entire life; when you completely uproot everything all at once, it's a bit too overwhelming to your system, and you are at a high risk for backsliding into old habits before you've even begun to establish a new one. But part of making progress involves identifying unhealthy habits and considering how you might take a proactive approach for growth. It's difficult to find perspective in the midst of all that you need to do to make it through a single day, and there are a million reasons (and excuses) as to why you make the choices you make. That said, self-reflection followed by action is absolutely essential if you are to begin taking your development as an artist seriously.

Notes

1 www.starbucks.com/menu/product/480/hot?parent=%2Fdrinks%2Fhot-coffees%2Fbrewed-coffees
2 https://us.coca-cola.com/products/coca-cola/original/
3 www.dietcoke.com/products/diet-coke
4 "Pirkei Avot 1:14." www.sefaria.org/Pirkei_Avot.1.14?lang=bi

Bibliography

CDC. (2019). "Know your limit for added sugars." Centers for Disease Control and Prevention, 3 April. www.cdc.gov/nutrition/data-statistics/know-your-limit-for-added-sugars.html

CDC. (2020). "Alcohol questions and answers." Centers for Disease Control and Prevention, 15 January. www.cdc.gov/alcohol/faqs.htm

Copeland, M., & Jones, C. (2017). *Ballerina Body: Dancing and Eating Your Way to a Lighter, Stronger, and More Graceful You.* Sphere.

Ellis, D. (2016). "Actors highly vulnerable to mental health problems." *Medical Xpress*, 19 July. https://m.medicalxpress.com/news/2016-07-actors-highlyvulnerable-mental-health.html

Gomez, A. (2019). "Is weight loss really 80 percent diet and 20 percent exercise?" *Women's Health*, 11 June. www.womenshealthmag.com/weight-loss/weight-loss-80-percent-diet-20-percent-exercise

Sleep Foundation. (2019). "How much sleep do we really need?" 1 September. www.sleepfoundation.org/articles/how-much-sleep-do-we-really-need

Kneeland, J. (2019). "What no one is saying about the body-positivity movement." *Greatist*, 16 May. https://greatist.com/live/no-one-saying-body-positivity

Lang, S.S. (2006). "'Mindless autopilot' drives people to dramatically underestimate how many daily food decisions they make, Cornell study finds." *Cornell Chronicle*, 22 December. https://news.cornell.edu/stories/2006/12/mindless-autopilot-drives-people-underestimate-food-decisions

Moore, C. (2020). "How to set and achieve life goals the right way." *PositivePsychology. com*, 29 April. https://positivepsychology.com/life-worth-living-setting-life-goals/

National Institute of Mental Health. (n.d.). "Mental Health Information: Statistics." www.nimh.nih.gov/health/statistics/index.shtml

Office of the Commissioner of the FDA. (2018). "Spilling the beans: How much caffeine is too much?" FDA, 12 December. www.fda.gov/consumers/consumer-updates/spilling-beans-how-much-caffeine-too-much

Petty, T. (2017). "Tom Petty 2009.11.29 Career Profile CBS Sunday Morning" [Video]. *YouTube*, uploaded by Frank Musillami, 25 January, www.youtube.com/watch?v=0mFQAoQUxSo

Reuben, A., & Schaefer, J. (2017). "Mental illness is far more common than we knew." Scientific American Blog Network, 14 July. https://blogs.scientificamerican.com/observations/mental-illness-is-far-more-common-than-we-knew/

Schaefer, J.D., Caspi, A., Belsky, D., Harrington, H., Houts, R., Horwood, L., Hussong, A., Ramrakha, S., Poulton, R., Moffitt, T. (2017). "Enduring mental health: Prevalence and prediction." *Journal of Abnormal Psychology*, 126(2), 212–224. DOI: 10.1037/abn0000232.

Sekulic, D., Peric, M., & Rodek, J. (2010). "Substance use and misuse among professional ballet dancers." *Substance Use & Misuse*, 45(9), 1420–1430. DOI: 10.3109/10826081003682198.

Smith, M., & Segal, R. (2019). *Sleep Needs*. www.helpguide.org/articles/sleep/sleep-needs-get-the-sleep-you-need.htm

Tharp, T. (1993). *Push Comes to Shove: An Autobiography*. Bantam Books.

US Department of Health and Human Services. (2015a). *Appendix 1: Physical Activity Guidelines for Americans – 2015–2020 Dietary Guidelines*. https://health.gov/dietaryguidelines/2015/guidelines/appendix-1/

US Department of Health and Human Services. (2015b). *Appendix 9: Alcohol – 2015–2020 Dietary Guidelines*. https://health.gov/dietaryguidelines/2015/guidelines/appendix-9/

US Department of Health and Human Services. (2015c). *Key Recommendations: Components of Healthy Eating Patterns – 2015–2020 Dietary Guidelines*. https://health.gov/our-work/food-nutrition/2015-2020-dietary-guidelines/guidelines/chapter-1/key-recommendations/

Wansink, B., & Sobal, J. (2007). "Mindless eating: The 200 daily food decisions we overlook." *Environment and Behavior*, 39(1), 106–123. DOI: 10.1177/0013916506295573.

Wexler, S.Z. (2017). "Is exercise or diet more important for weight loss? Here's the truth." *The Huffington Post*, 6 December. www.huffingtonpost.com/2014/04/30/exrcise-vs-diet-for-weight-loss_n_5207271.html

Wisner, W. (2019). "32 Surprising Mental Health Statistics." *Talkspace*, 30 April. www.talkspace.com/blog/mental-health-statistics/

Final Thoughts

Everybody has a reason for choosing performance. Maybe you'd been dancing for years and felt ready to take your training to the next level. Maybe you'd never taken a dance class, but you love acting and have always yearned to stretch the boundaries of what your body can do. For some, the desire to perform is born out of an eagerness to express themselves. For others, it might be the desire to break out of their comfort zone. For most it's a calling, a sense that you were meant to perform; it's as though *performance chooses you.*

Take a moment and ask yourself, "Why performance?" Be willing to dig deep and reflect on why you chose to dedicate your time and energy to the study of performance. Our time together is drawing to end, and you may hit roadblocks on your performance training journey in the future. If ever you find yourself at a crossroads in your training, revisit your journal notes and ask yourself again, "Why performance?" to reaffirm your commitment and discover new reasons to pursue performance training. The goals and ideals you construct and reconstruct will motivate you as you continue to develop your craft.

***

Theatre and dance moves people. When you watch a performance, you can feel the energy and emotions from the performers. When you perform, you are empowered. You can be anything, and when you perform as the best version of yourself, the fullest most alive and expressive version of yourself, it is an inspiration to all who see it.

It's a privilege to work as a performer, and uniting with others to bring a performance to audiences is enormously gratifying. Forging strong working relationships is integral to a performer's success. However, the business component of this art form can be difficult, and it can influence how you communicate with others. The industry can have an "every man for himself" feel to it and competing with others for limited opportunities is a reality. Simultaneously, ensemble work is imperative because none of this can be done alone.

Think about how you wish to be treated in this industry and how you treat others. How well do you give and respond to feedback? What approaches to

DOI: 10.4324/9781003149699-10

working with others do you find successful? Regularly reflect on how you would like to be treated and check in on your behavior during interactions with others. What do *you* do to build a positive experience for the ensemble working together in class, rehearsal, on set, and in performance?

Continually develop best practices for working in partnership with others and explore how to cultivate the kind of environment that encourages everyone to do their best work by finding common ground with your peers. The more supportive the environment, the more others want to rise to the challenges presented in the work; be honest and direct with deep affection and admiration.

If you treat others how you wish to be treated, then the lines of communication open and the work can flourish. As a performer, you cannot underestimate the value of communication, respect, and kindness because *performance is all about collaboration.*

A performer's respect and appreciation for all the moving parts in a production helps the process enormously. Great ways to foster that respect and appreciation are to work as a technical crew member on a production team and to take some classes in theatre and film production and design. It is not that a performer needs to reach a high level of expertise, but it is incredibly beneficial to gain some perspective on how designers and tech crew work, and it also helps the performer to better communicate with members of the production team.

Once, a lighting designer on a production I was directing appreciated when I said to a student light board operator-in-training, who was having a technical issue, "Try pressing the 'dimmer release' button." Although that statement reveals only a basic knowledge of how a lighting board works, the designer was working with another student at the time and was glad to have some help with expediting technical rehearsal that day. This knowledge was the result of spending months in a tech booth as a light board operator during my internship at Ensemble Theatre of Cincinnati (ETC); not only was I learning about being a member of a production team at a professional theatre, I had the best seat in the house to watch the performers on stage night after night. During that time as an intern, I learned as much about performing as I did about theatre production. I would never trade my time as an intern, and the experience broadened my horizons. It made me realize just how much work goes into a theatrical production and how much more I had to learn. And it was an important first step toward me gaining the confidence to lead productions of my own.

During that year-long internship, I co-wrote a play with Jodie Meyn, who was also interning at the theatre. Together, we submitted the play to the artistic director of ETC, D. Lynn Meyers. Lynn agreed to produce our show at the theatre with Jodie and I as the stars. I went from working in the tech booth to rehearsing and performing a fully mounted production of our very own play at an equity theatre. The award-winning lighting designer who earlier in the internship taught me how to run a lighting board, Brian c. Mehring, designed our show. It was a dream come true. The advice and opportunities from leaders like Lynn and Brian exemplify the generous spirit of collaboration I so hope to impart to you.

***

We've discussed many ways to handle the rigors of performance which takes a productive mindset. To consistently produce compelling work, embrace every aspect of the *process* of making a performance and be a proactive performer. A proactive performer actively engages in the creative process. They don't sit around and wait for things to happen to them; they *make* things happen. They generate opportunities and value action.

Becoming a proactive performer starts by taking a positive approach to your training. It's so easy to sit back and let your classmates do the heavy lifting; you can "phone it in" during class, and it would hardly be noticeable. But who does that benefit? Certainly not you. Remember to take the initiative. Face obstacles in your performance training head on and work to rephrase negative thoughts, like "I can't do this" to "I am doing the best I can." Practicing positivity and gratitude for your training should be part of your daily routine. If you radiate positivity from your thoughts to your actions, you will find that positive energy return to you in many forms; it's like a boomerang. A positive mindset is absolutely integral to your success.

However, asking yourself to be happy every minute of training is an unrealistic goal. We simply cannot be positive all the time. We have days where the work just does not go as planned. Try as we might, we cannot spin every negative into a positive. By acknowledging this truth, you take a lot of pressure off yourself. It is often discussed in yin yoga that the aim is to *find comfort in the discomfort.* There will no doubt be intense periods of discomfort and vulnerability in your performance training, and these feelings should be recognized not ignored. You need to feel what you feel. If you need to cry, then you should cry. Really feel what you feel, and then … LET IT GO!

I'd like to share a journal entry I wrote after an aerial dance training session. On this day, I was a proactive performer:

> This morning I woke up sore and really considered taking a day off. But because I am heading out of town tomorrow for Christmas, this was my last chance to train on an actual apparatus for the next five days. Countdown: 5, 4, 3, 2, 1. Now, get out of bed and get it done! Within 15 minutes of training, I felt the idea of continuing nearly pointless. Then I took a three-minute rest. And it was a complete rest. I didn't stretch or pace and change the music… I just lay there. I then got back up and completed an inversion in the air for the first time in three months. Then I rest again. Then I did another inversion. Then I rest again. Then I did ANOTHER inversion.

Three inversions in one session! That's a first for me, even when I was in my best shape. I didn't quit, I just took a rest. I had worked out hard for three days in a row prior, but pushing through the soreness and actually resting in between led to the biggest break through I'd ever had. Sometimes going to work when you don't want to leads to the best surprises!

After weeks and months of training, all the effort finally paid off in a tangible way. But there will be many days where progress is elusive. And on those days, committing to the work and trusting the process need to sustain you.

I take class from a yoga instructor who regularly reminds us of the benefits we receive from *attempting* a pose. There are many positions in the hot hatha yoga class he teaches that are just beyond reach for many (including myself) in the class. It's very easy to feel like we're failing when we are unable to reach the fullest embodiment of a posture or to capture the essence of an intended movement. But the value of *effort* should not be dismissed; it is essential that we not only keep trying, but also realize that the benefit of our effort, while not always seen or felt, is achieved every time we try.

I remember my thesis mentor telling me that I would only begin to gain perspective on my experiences in graduate school once I had distanced myself from the program. He said that about five years after graduating, I would truly see and feel the benefits of that intense learning period. And he was right. While I was in the MFA program, I worked and worked, but was really unsure if I was making any progress. Fast forward to today, and all that I had learned during that time, I continue to use every day. Thank goodness I stuck with it. Embracing the process and finding gratitude for your effort are the essential ingredients needed to sustain your regimen.

Performers that want to perform but dread training for the performance will be discontented for the vast majority of their time. Of course, there will always be good days and bad days, but the performance cannot be the only reward. Payoffs must be cultivated in little moments. I remember catching the "travel bug" when I was an undergraduate student. I had just returned from the most amazing five weeks of my life studying theatre in London. Within days of returning home, I was planning a semester-long trip to Ireland to study literature and theatre there. I could not wait to get back to travelling again. I remember very clearly my mother saying how proud she was of me for wanting to see more of the world and for striking out on my own. And then she said to me, "But you need to find happiness here in the meantime. You cannot only live for the next big trip." And while it took me years to fully grasp what she was asking of me, I realize now that piece of advice is the most important of my life. Yes, she wanted me to make plans and she encouraged me to make *big* plans. She wanted me to work towards those goals in every way I could. But in order to live fully, I needed to find the beauty, the joy, the contentment in the everyday-ness of life.

All this to say, emphasize the joy in the journey rather than narrowly focus on the destination. Try to imagine the performance as part of the process. It is an important component of the process, but it is not the *only* important component of the process. Strive to love being in the studio training as much as on the stage performing.

***

This whole performance thing is *hard*. And people have really narrow ideas of what makes a successful performer. How much have you thought about what success looks like to you? How do you define success? Do you want to work full time as a performing artist? If so, will you only feel successful if you are performing on Broadway or in major motion pictures? Are you more comfortable with the idea of being a big fish in a small pond (being well known in a small community), a small fish in a big pond (being relatively unknown in a very large community), or a big fish in a big pond (being very well known in a very large community)? In other words, is fame necessary for you to feel successful? Is moving to a different city or state or country a goal? Do you feel influenced or pressured by your parents, family, friends, or peers' versions of success? How important is lifestyle to you? What would need to occur in your life for you to feel successful? And would it be so terrible if it didn't happen?

My idea of success was to have theatre and dance as my primary source of income. I've always thought that if my passion for theatre and dance could lead to paying the bills, then I would be well on my way to a happy life. I never thought much about being rich and famous. I just wanted to be doing what I love and making enough money to be comfortable. My first full-time professional job in dance was as a ballroom dance instructor. I was hired to teach in a gorgeous studio with floor to ceiling windows overlooking Michigan Avenue in downtown Chicago. The setting was positively idyllic. When I got the job, I felt that all of my dreams had come true. I was going to be the happy version of Jennifer Lopez's character in *Shall We Dance*. But, guess what… I hated the job. And here's why. It was as much a sales job as it was a teaching job. Not only was I teaching private dance lessons, I was also extremely pressured to ensure that the clients signed up for more and more lessons. The owner wanted me to take the "hard sell" approach, and I found the sales component of the job made me feel very uncomfortable. Every lesson was meant to be an opportunity to sell the client more lessons. And after each lesson, the owner would ask if I had made another sale; if I answered "no," it felt awful. The prices of the lessons were far out of my price range, and lacking confidence, I had a hard time convincing myself that a lesson with me was worth the cost. Of course, the clients lived way above my tax bracket, so they did not get sticker shock. But if

I couldn't convince *myself* that ballroom dance classes with me were worth the cost, how could I convince the *client*? And even though I believed in the "product," I still found teaching with sales incentives and deadlines stressful. Working on commission had me constantly distracted wondering, "Are they enjoying this enough? Am I giving them their money's worth? Are they going to purchase more classes?" I quickly realized that no matter how much I loved ballroom dancing and teaching, combining the two in a studio setting where aggressive salesmanship was a necessity just wasn't a good fit. I found that I could close a sale if under the watchful eye of the owner, but I *really* did not want to do it.

Others have a penchant for both the arts and its relationship to business, but I did not want to wear both of those hats. So, my idea of perhaps one day owning a dance studio was no longer of interest to me without a full-time sales manager to shoulder the business aspects of running a studio. That was an important lesson for me to learn because I realized that while starting my own small studio sounded good in theory, the reality of the demands of keeping it afloat would diminish the joy and creativity of the dancing if I were to attempt it on my own. Owning a dance studio requires a whole lot more than teaching dance. I am grateful for the opportunity to have observed what the owner of that ballroom dance studio went through to keep it running. And I learned that it was not for me. All this to say your *dream job* may not meet your expectations.

I now find myself happily situated in academia, where creativity, continuing education, and professional development are nurtured and supported. But there are hurdles and thankless tasks in academia too. The demands of teaching, creative research, and service can be intense, and seeking tenure and promotion was daunting and overwhelming. However, these duties fill me with both trepidation *and* excitement, and I *want* to make progress in these areas. When you find a job that challenges you in ways you want to be challenged, then exciting opportunities for growth lie ahead.

Defining success isn't as easy as it sounds, and you will likely have contradictory thoughts on the subject. You might desire recognition while simultaneously long for privacy. Or you might yearn for your career to be the center of your focus while also hoping for a large family. A personal trainer once said to me that there are three main areas in a person's life: their career, their personal life, and their ambitions for self-improvement. He told me that he believes you can only truly excel in two out of those three areas at any given time. He noted time and again that once a person got really serious about their fitness goals, something slipped in either their career or personal life. And most often that slip came in one's personal life. He said he saw more and more couples break up as one became serious about training, while their partner did not share the same goals. I listened to his theory and appreciated his candor.

I asked myself, "Why can't a person be in a wonderful relationship *and* be a creative artist *and* value self-care all at the same time?" Upon further thought, I wondered if this trainer was saying that we *can* achieve all that we wish to achieve, but we do need to prioritize. We cannot be the best at everything at all times, and sometimes other areas of our life will be neglected if we focus too much on perfecting one area. There may be extended periods where you cannot do all that you want to do as a performer because of other demands. Once you come to terms with the ebb and flow of priorities, you are released from the pressure to be all things to all people all at once. It's about finding and maintaining a delicate balance. I hope this book has provided you with some of the tools needed to achieve that balance.

***

And one last thing… a performer must expand their worldview. The best ways I can imagine doing so is through liberal arts education, travel, and life experience. Studying history, philosophy, world religions, arts, and sciences will inform and enrich the characters you play. If I had my wish, every performing arts student would study abroad for a semester or academic year; immersing oneself in a foreign culture is a sure way to broaden respect and empathy for those who are different from you.

Without doubt, resourcefulness and an unquenchable thirst for knowledge will enliven your work as a performer. And your unique life experiences with love, heartbreak, hard work, reckless (but not *too* reckless!) abandon, sorrow, and forgiveness will breathe life into the characters you play. *Live out loud* and your performances will reflect the energy of your life on stage.

Figure C.1 The yin yang symbol, representing the forces of life in harmony, can be seen in this image of choreography by performers Jessica Vest and Michael Maughon. The Eastern philosophical approach of finding balance rather than a wealth of one emotional experience is an important step in becoming a proactive performer. Balance for you might be about work and play or eating healthily and allowing occasional indulgences, or highs and lows of emotions. A wide range of experiences and emotions improves the artist-in-training's ability to perform. There's a parable told in *The Alchemist* by Paulo Coehlo, and the moral is: the secret to life is to enjoy everything you can, to the extent that you can, without ever forgetting your responsibilities. I think we spend our lives figuring out this balance.

Photo credit: ETSU Photographic Services

Bibliography

Coelho, P. (2018). *The Alchemist*. HarperCollins Publishers.

Appendix

Sample Assignment Schedule

Week 1

Introduction	
Assignment	**Notes**
Create a Journal with Vision	Students create their vision journal independently and bring the journal to class to display and discuss.

Week 2

Chapter 1	
Assignment	**Notes**
Theatre That Made a Lasting Impression	Students can complete the journal writing prompt in-class as closure to a training session.
Dance as a Display of Power	Students can complete the assignment in-class (if the instructor has access to the audiovisual equipment needed to show the video clips) or independently. A discussion of the assignment could take place during class.
Pay It Forward	Students can complete the journal writing prompt in-class as closure to a training session.

Week 3

Chapter 2	
Assignment	**Notes**
Mindful Maven	Students can complete the journal writing prompt in-class. Instructor should consider using class time to lead students through all of the exercises listed in this chapter prior to the *Mindful Maven* writing prompt.

(Continued)

Chapter 2	
Assignment	**Notes**
Just Breathe	Students can complete the journal writing prompt in-class. Instructor should consider using class time to lead the students through all of the exercises listed between the *Mindful Maven* writing prompt and the *Just Breathe* writing prompt.
Create Your Pre Warm-Up, Warm-Up, & Cool Down Routine	All students can create their routines independently and then perform the assignment simultaneously at the start of class.

Week 4

Chapter 3*	
Assignment	**Notes**
Walk the Walk Part I & II	Students can complete the assignment independently. A discussion of the assignment could start class.
Mirror, Mirror on the Wall	Students can complete the assignment in-class and discuss their observations during class time.
Observations of Épaulement	Students can complete the assignment in-class and discuss their observations during class time.

*All ballet technique exercises described in this chapter could be explored during class time.

Week 5

Chapter 4	
Assignment	**Notes**
Classical Monologue	Students rehearse their monologue independently and perform them in class.
Character Creative Writing	Students can complete this assignment independently and share their writing assignment aloud to the class.

Week 6

Chapter 4	
Assignment	**Notes**
Spit-Take, Double-Take on Film	Students create their film independently; an excellent free educational resource for uploading and sharing videos so that all students may watch and comment is www.flipgrid.com. Videos can be made secure, so that only those in the class can view. Once the class has independently watched all film submissions, a discussion sharing their experiences, observations, and reactions can be had in-class.

Rule of Three	Students can partner and work this assignment in-class or independently.
Children's Theatre Storyteller	Students work on the assignment independently and perform for their peers in-class. Depending on class size, students may perform for the entire class or the class may be divided into smaller groups, with students performing for their smaller group of peers.

Week 7

Chapter 4	
Assignment	**Notes**
Master of Physical Comedy	Students complete the assignment independently. A discussion of their reflections could start the next class.
Movement Only	Students work on the assignment independently and all perform simultaneously in-class.
Physical Comedy Sketch	Students work on the assignment independently and perform for their peers in-class. Again, class size depends on how the performances are presented.
A Performance with Distinction	Students reflect and write independently. A discussion of their reflections could start a class.

Week 8

Chapter 5	
Assignment	**Notes**
Jazz Music Pioneers	Students complete the assignment independently. A discussion of the assignment could start the next class.
Early Dance Crazes & Jazz Dance Pioneers	Students complete the assignment independently. A discussion of the assignment could start the next class.
Jazz Dance Technique Class	Students complete the assignment independently. A discussion of the assignment could start the next class.
Imagining Jazz Dance	Students complete the assignment independently. A discussion of the assignment could start the next class.

Week 9

Chapter 5*	
Assignment	**Notes**
Reflections on Expression	Students complete the assignment independently. A discussion of the assignment could start the next class.
Making a Connection Part I & II	Students reflect and write Part I independently. A discussion of their reflections could start a class, perhaps trying out a few of the ideas shared. Students rehearse their scenes independently and perform them for their peers in-class. They should also film their scene and note variances in performing for the camera vs. performing for a live audience.

*All jazz dance technique exercises described in this chapter could be explored during class time.

Week 10

Chapter 5	
Assignment	**Notes**
Making a Connection II (continued)	Scene performances continue in-class.
Song Performance	Students rehearse their song independently and perform their song for their peers in-class (depending on class size, song performances may be limited to 16 bars; students should, however, learn the entire song).

Week 11

Chapter 6	
Assignment	**Notes**
You and Your Interests	Students reflect on their own and write independently. A discussion of their reflections could start the next class.
Object of My Affection	Students work on the assignment independently and then discuss with a partner in-class.
Sharing a Memory	Students work on the assignment independently and then discuss with a partner in-class.
Common Themes	Students can complete the assignment in-class.

Did Someone Say Movie Night?!	Students complete the assignment independently – partnering is strongly encouraged.
Enough Talk. It's Time to Audition!	Students complete the assignment independently and could discuss in-class.

Week 12

Chapter 7	
Assignment	**Notes**
Create a New Work... NOW!	Students complete the assignment in-class.
What's in Your Toolbox?	Students can complete the journal writing prompt in-class as closure to the training session.
You Be the Judge	Students complete the assignment independently. A discussion of the assignment could start a class.

Week 13

Chapter 8	
Assignment	**Notes**
Recordkeeping, Assessing Food & Beverage Intake, Assessing Physical Activity, and Assessing Sleep Patterns	Students complete the assignments independently (after one week of recordkeeping). A discussion of the assignment should occur during class.
Create an Action Plan	Students complete the assignment independently and discuss in small groups.
Enrich Your Training	Students complete the assignment independently. A discussion of the assignment could occur during class.
Outside In, Inside Out	Students complete the assignment independently. A discussion of the assignment could occur during class.

Week 14

Final Thoughts
Notes
Students meet individually or in small groups with the instructor to discuss their plans moving forward.

Index

Note: *Italic* page numbers refer to figures and page numbers followed by "n" denote endnotes.

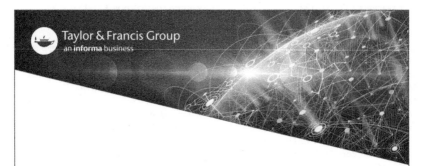